Trade Facilitation in the Multilateral Trading System

Negotiations on trade facilitation were concluded at the WTO 9th Ministerial Conference in 2013, and the Agreements on Trade Facilitation (TFA), therefore, became the first fully multilateral agreement in WTO history. Since then, trade facilitation has been in the limelight on the stage of the world trading system. During recent years, the TFA has been consistently on the agenda of the summits of G20, G7, and APEC. The Agreement has come into force and shall be implemented on a global scale. As a result, the WTO members shall be prepared to translate the Agreement into their domestic legislation, which will involve a series of reforms in trade laws and policies.

There are extensive voices demanding a comprehensive expatiation on trade facilitation and the TFA. It is essential to systematically delve into the genesis of trade facilitation, revisit the course where the TFA came into being, and analyze the well-turned legalese of the TFA. This book meets this demand.

This book is path-breaking in these aspects: it expounds on the rationales for trade facilitation and the significance of constituting an international accord on trade facilitation; it restores the one-century track of the international community's talks on trade facilitation, from the times of the League of Nations to the WTO era; it reveals how the WTO negotiating mechanisms enabled the TFA to be nailed down, which would be enlightening for trade diplomats engaged in other WTO negotiations; and it provides an in-depth commentary on the TFA articles, which will help stakeholders more accurately understand and implement the Agreement.

This book will be especially valuable for government officials and policy-makers, trade practitioners, lawyers, advisers, and scholars interested in international economic law, WTO law, international trade, international relations, and international development studies.

Hao Wu is currently working at the World Customs Organization (WCO), Belgium. Prior to joining the WCO, he served as a trade negotiator on the WTO Trade Facilitation Negotiations for a number of years.

Routledge Research in International Economic Law

Forthcoming:

A Chinese Perspective on International Investment Law
Guiguo Wang

Culture and International Economic Law
Valentina Vadi and Bruno de Witte

Defences in International Investment Law
Francis Botchway

WTO Trade Remedies in International Law
Roberto Soprano

Cohesion and Legitimacy in International Investment Law
Public International Law and Global Administrative Law Perspectives
Chisomo Kapulula

International Challenges in Investment Law and Arbitration
Mesut Akbaba and Giancarlo Capurro

State Interest and the Sources of International Law
Doctrine, Morality, and Non-Treaty Law
Markus P. Beham

Trade Facilitation in the Multilateral Trading System
Genesis, Course and Accord
Hao Wu

Trade Facilitation in the Multilateral Trading System

Genesis, Course and Accord

Hao Wu

Routledge
Taylor & Francis Group

LONDON AND NEW YORK

First published 2019
by Routledge
2 Park Square, Milton Park, Abingdon, Oxon OX14 4RN

and by Routledge
52 Vanderbilt Avenue, New York, NY 10017, USA

First issued in paperback 2020

Routledge is an imprint of the Taylor & Francis Group, an informa business

© 2019 Hao Wu

British Library Cataloguing-in-Publication Data
A catalogue record for this book is available from the British Library

Library of Congress Cataloging-in-Publication Data
Names: Wu, Hao (Lawyer)
Title: Trade facilitation in the multilateral trading system : genesis,
    course and accord / Hao Wu.
Description: Abingdon, Oxon ; New York, NY : Routledge, 2018. |
    Series: Routledge research in international economic law | Includes
    index.
Identifiers: LCCN 2018016873 | ISBN 9781138605411 (hbk)
Subjects: LCSH: Trade Facilitation Agreement (2013 December 7) |
    Foreign trade regulation. | Free trade.
Classification: LCC K4610.A32013 W8 2018 | DDC 382/.92—dc23
LC record available at https://lccn.loc.gov/2018016873

ISBN 13: 978-0-367-58859-5 (pbk)
ISBN 13: 978-1-138-60541-1 (hbk)

Typeset in Galliard
by Apex CoVantage, LLC

Disclaimer
The views and arguments in this book are only those of the author
and do not necessarily reflect positions of any organization or
administration.

Contents

Preface

I consider myself fortunate enough to have the chance of taking on the significant job of trade facilitation. Completion of the manuscript calls up my recollection of those frequent flights to Geneva several years ago. The days working with my colleagues in Beijing on the WTO affairs were memorable. From them, I learned gracefulness, exactitude, erudition and other qualities essential for serving as a trade negotiator. Participating in the negotiations on behalf of my country was a treasured period during my career. It was also my honor to be part of the WTO Negotiating Group on Trade Facilitation (NGTF), who eventually enabled the Agreement on Trade Facilitation (TFA) to come true.

When I was determined to write a book on trade facilitation, I was deeply aware that there ought to be a long and winding road ahead of me. However, I was not alone. I went along the way – formerly in Beijing and later in Brussels – with a number of brilliant minds, including trade diplomats, officials from international organizations, scholars and representatives from the private sector. I am indebted to a number of colleagues and friends who generously provided their support, guidance and knowledge to me. Without all these, publication of the book would not be possible.

In particular, I thank Mr. Yi Xiaozhun, Deputy Director-General of the WTO, for his support and encouragement. I profited sublimely from the expert advice, comments and editing by Robert Ireland (WCO), Nora Neufeld (WTO), Jan Hoffmann (UNCTAD), Poul Hansen (UNCTAD) on relevant parts of my manuscript. I would like to express my sincere gratitude to them for looking after my research in spite of their own tight schedules. Some contents of the book were published in journals, or presented at conferences in Brussels, Kiel, Oxford, St Petersburg and places elsewhere. I take the opportunity to give credit for facilitating discussions and exchanging views, which were enlightening for my research, to Edwin Vermulst, Jeffrey Snyder, Rolf Langhammer, Christian Volpe Martincus, Federico Weinschelbaum, Denis Galligan, Wieslaw Czyzowicz, as well as those who I apologetically might omit.

Additionally, I am grateful to the two anonymous reviewers for their evaluation of my manuscript. My appreciations are also due to Brianna Ascher, Nicola Sharpe, Siobhán Poole, Mary Del Plato and others at Routledge (Taylor &

Francis Group), for their patience and hard work that ensured a high-standard publishing process.

Finally, I dedicate the book to my family, whose love and devotion to me sustained my persistence in writing down my thoughts over the years. We make a gift of the book to our lovely little angel, who herself is a gift to our life.

Hao Wu

March 2018, Brussels

Introduction

Time to delve into the genesis, course and accord of trade facilitation

The world trading system has truly delivered[1] when the 'Bali package' (in particular the Agreement on Trade Facilitation (TFA) therein) was concluded at the ninth Ministerial Conference of the World Trade Organization (WTO) in 2013.[2]

The 'Bali package' comes at a time when global trade politics is not what it used to be.[3] Today's global trade politics speaks more about dealing with the 'behind-the-border' issues than liberalizing tariffs and quotas traditionally 'at the border', and in part drives countries to initiate trade talks among 'preferred' partners rather than within the whole WTO membership.[4] Given that there have been almost 350 preferential trade agreements (PTAs) in force,[5] the wave of regionalism, particularly the mega-regional trade initiatives around the Pacific (e.g., Trans-Pacific Partnership (TPP), Regional Comprehensive Economic Partnership (RCEP)) and the Atlantic (e.g., Transatlantic Trade and Investment Partnership (TTIP)), is hogging the limelight. In contrast, prior to Bali, the stagnation of the Doha Round had tarnished the WTO's fame of being the prime setting for negotiating trade rules. Indeed, many had despaired of the consensus-seeking global negotiations now and then mired in limbo; some even pessimistically conceived of the 'slow but certain demise'[6] of this 'out of date'[7] multilateral regime.

After dragging on for more than a slumberous decade, the current round of multilateral trade negotiations, embracing the largest number of participants ever, eventually turned the corner at Bali. Though the 'Bali package' is often regarded as a 'rather modest and partial' outcome,[8] it has, nonetheless, reinstated confidence in the WTO's negotiating abilities.[9] The Agreement on Trade Facilitation, as the centerpiece of the 'Bali package', thereby becomes the first fully multilateral agreement in the WTO history. In this sense, the significance of the Agreement is far beyond being only an early harvested trade deal in the suspenseful Doha Round: it heralds that 'the WTO is back on track'; [10] and it 'represents rejuvenation of the multilateral trading system',[11] which ironically should have already fallen down in the General Agreement on Tariffs and Trade (GATT) period according to some bearish forecasts (for example, held by 'Memorial Drive' school in the late 1980s)[12] but is firmly giving life to the very ideal of multilateralism.[13] As part of the WTO rulebook, the Agreement is also epoch-making: it breaks new ground for developing country Members and least developed country (LDC) Members in the way they will implement the Agreement (viz. implementation of the agreement is directly linked to the capacity of the Member to implement it);[14] and it results from the Member-driven, transparent and inclusive negotiations, and, thus, proves the WTO 'conventional wisdom'[15] wrong.[16]

It is a brilliant feat that the talk on trade facilitation came to fruition in the orbit of the WTO. In fact, the international community has been exploring the subject of trade facilitation for approximately 100 years since the League of Nations. Now that 'we already walked too far, down to we had forgotten why embarked', as poet Kahlil Gibran composed, many of the memorable footprints of trade facilitation on the century-long road, however, have been consigned to oblivion. Therefore, it is essential to delve into where trade facilitation came from and how it has evolved. As the Agreement on Trade Facilitation has recently entered into force, it is also of significance to spell out what the hard-won global trade deal denotes and how it is going to take effect. These initiatives fueled the writing of this book with a view to unscrambling the genesis, course and accord of trade facilitation in the context of the multilateral trading system.

This book opens with invoking the calls for free trade, which has patterned the modern world trade history and serves as the matrix of trade facilitation. However, operating trade, in real life, is a taxing errand and by no means for free. Chapter 1 of this book analyzes trade costs that are inimical to free trade. This chapter contends that trade costs have the nature of *externality*. According to the Coase theorem, the externality of trade costs shall be solved by the governments through building healthy business environments (including cutting tariffs and non-tariff measures (NTMs)). Therefore, cutting tariffs and NTMs remained the mainstream of the rounds of GATT negotiations. This study contributes a new methodological approach (instead of econometric models) to rationalize trade facilitation from the perspective of *economic jurisprudence* (stemming from 'economics from a legal standpoint').[17]

Chapter 2 goes on questing for the genesis of trade facilitation. After cutting tariffs and NTMs, there are still *procedural obstacles* to be solved. Trade facilitation was conceptualized to encapsulate the diverse solutions to the procedural obstacles (in other words, 'red tape') that produce 'threshold' effects to the flow of goods throughout the supply chains. However, trade facilitation was not so named at birth. This chapter reveals how trade facilitation got its name. Meanwhile, defining trade facilitation is a baffling job. From the various definitions of trade facilitation, this chapter draws the be-all and end-all of this concept. Once the concept of trade facilitation rises, its benefits are found to be immense.

The multitudinous trade facilitation initiatives on the agenda of different countries' governments seem comparatively anarchical. An international accord on trade facilitation that empowers a globally universal governance would be desirable. Chapter 3 discourses on the necessity of constituting such an accord on trade facilitation. *Constructivism* is instrumental in arguing the point. This chapter evokes the call of the business community, as represented by the International Chamber of Commerce (ICC), for an international accord on trade facilitation. This chapter also dusts off several past conventions and recommendations pertaining to trade facilitation from the times of the League of Nations to the birth of GATT, which have been apathetically obliterated from history, in order to trace the course, where the international community had been dedicated to establishing the accords on trade facilitation early on. With regard to the place that appropriately hosts a contemporary accord on trade facilitation, it is demonstrated that the WTO is the optimum one.

It took 18 years (1996–2014) for trade facilitation to turn from an obscure component of the 'Singapore issues' tabled at the first Ministerial Conference into the most conspicuous achievement reached in the history of the WTO. Nevertheless, the journey of trade facilitation negotiations in the WTO was long and arduous, usually 'two steps forward, one step back'.[18] Chapter 4 revisits this journey and gives a chronological account of the status of the negotiations on trade facilitation at some of the important WTO moments (e.g., General Councils, Ministerial Conferences) that marked consecutive mileposts along the whole journey. It transpires that the entire negotiations (including putting the subject on the Doha Development Agenda, conducting analytical work, formulating the negotiation modalities, carrying out negotiations, nailing down the deal and ratifying the agreement) had been treading a fine line from beginning to end. From the journey of trade facilitation, it follows that other ensuing Doha talks are supposed to stride in a similar vein.

Negotiating the TFA was like hatching a duck-yard-born egg to a swan. The deal on trade facilitation was not concluded by accident, because there were a certain set of conditions that enabled the TFA to come true. Chapter 5 examines the enablers. First, it was the Negotiating Group on Trade Facilitation (NGTF) that served as the hatchery, where the multilateral negotiations on trade facilitation took place on a regular basis. Second, although the WTO membership was divided into groupings (e.g., the Core Group,[19] the Colorado Group)[20] that debated the deadlocked questions (e.g., launching negotiations on trade facilitation or not, having the rules be binding or not), it was the principles for organizing and managing the negotiations (including single undertaking, inclusiveness, transparency, member-driven) that allowed the groupings' compromise on their well-entrenched positions in pursuit of consensus. Additionally, post-clearance audit (PCA) is given as an example in this chapter to illustrate how a proposal from some Members grew up to a TFA article.

At present, the TFA has become constitutive of the WTO rulebook and public international law. Chapter 6 expatiates on the legalese of the TFA article by article. This chapter provides a commentary on Section I of the TFA, which is about the trade-facilitative measures that clarify and improve relevant aspects of GATT Articles V, VIII and X and cement customs cooperation. This chapter then interprets the TFA Section II, which is pertinent to the special and differential treatment (S&DT) for developing country Members and LDC Members. The preamble and Section III of the TFA are also analyzed. The commentary on the TFA articles from cover to cover is conducive to holistic insights into the agreement (including not only its delicacy but also its loopholes). With these insights, the WTO Members will be able to implement the TFA more appropriately.

According to the Annex D of the 2004 'July package',[21] several international organizations were mandated to 'undertake a collaborative effort' in order to 'make technical assistance and capacity building (TACB) more effective and operational and to ensure better coherence'.[22] Thenceforth, they were called the 'Annex D organizations'. Chapter 7 introduces the work that the 'Annex D organizations' (including IMF, OECD, UNCTAD, WCO and the World Bank) had respectively pioneered in trade facilitation.[23] Their work, however, is confined to recitals unless the organizations[24] play a trade facilitation symphony (e.g., the WTO Committee on Trade Facilitation, the Trade Facilitation Agreement Facility, the Global Alliance for Trade Facilitation) on the stage of 'an integrated, more viable and durable multilateral trading system'.[25]

As Miguel de Cervantes Saavedra wrote, 'there is no book so bad that it does not have something good in it'.[26] In sum, this book endeavors to depict a panorama of trade facilitation: a chronicle from the 1920s to the present in the vertical axis and a roll-call of major players in the horizontal axis. 'What's past is prologue'.[27] The genesis, course and accord of trade facilitation demonstrated by this book are, hopefully, the prologue for full implementation of the TFA.

Notes

1 Roberto Azevêdo, 'World Back in WTO', speech at the ninth WTO Ministerial Conference, December 7, 2013.
2 Agreement on Trade Facilitation was officially adopted by the WTO General Council on November 27, 2014.
3 Alasdair R. Young, 'Trade Politics Ain't What It Used to Be: The European Union in the Doha Round', (2007) 45 *Journal of Common Market Studies* 789, pp. 789–811.
4 See Gabriel Siles-Brügge, 'Global Trade Politics and the Transatlantic Trade and Investment Partnership', *E-International Relations*, May 5, 2014, www.e-ir.info/2014/05/05/global-trade-politics-and-the-transatlantic-trade-and-investment-partnership/.
5 See Global Preferential Trade Agreement Database of the World Bank, http://wits.worldbank.org/gptad/trade_database.html.
6 Rorden Wilkinson, *What's Wrong with the WTO and How to Fix It* (Polity Press, 2014), p. 2.
7 Katinka Barysch and Michael Heise, 'Will TTIP Harm the Global Trading System?', *Yale Global*, January 9, 2014, http://yaleglobal.yale.edu/content/will-ttip-harm-global-trading-system.
8 See, for example, Georg Koopmann and Stephan Wittig, 'Whither WTO – The Multilateral Trading System After Bali', (2014) 49 *Intereconomics* 1, pp. 2–3.
9 ICTSD, 'Success in Bali Sparks Questions over Doha, WTO Future', *Bridges Weekly*, December 12, 2013, p. 3.
10 José Manuel Barroso, EU Commission President, statement on the outcome of the WTO Global Trade talks in Bali, Brussels, December 7, 2013, http://europa.eu/rapid/press-release_MEMO-13-1111_en.htm.
11 Statement by US President, Barack Obama, on the World Trade Organization Trade Agreement, December 8, 2013, https://geneva.usmission.gov/2013/12/09/president-obama-on-world-trade-organization-trade-agreement/.
12 See Bhagwati Jagdish, 'Regionalism Versus Multilateralism', (1992) 15 *The World Economy* 535, pp. 535–555.

13 Roberto Azevêdo, 'World Back in WTO', speech at the ninth WTO Ministerial Conference, December 7, 2013.

14 Ibid.

15 According to Nora Neufeld, 'conventional wisdom in the WTO at that time held that negotiations could only succeed if conducted in small group, such as the infamous Green Room meetings'. See Nora Neufeld, 'The Long and Winding Road: How WTO Members Finally Reached a Trade Facilitation Agreement', WTO Staff Working Paper, ERSD-2014–06 (2014).

16 Nora Neufeld, 'The Long and Winding Road: How WTO Members Finally Reached a Trade Facilitation Agreement', WTO Staff Working Paper, ERSD-2014–06 (2014).

17 The article of 'Economics from a Legal Standpoint' (see (1908) *American Law Review*, 42 Am. L. R. 379) argued that 'relief from this situation might be secured by having our economists become lawyers and our lawyers economists'. Also see W. H. Timlin, 5 (1921) 5 *Marquette Law Review* 177, p. 177.

18 Neufeld, see *supra* note 16.

19 It included Bangladesh, Botswana, Cuba, Egypt, India, Indonesia, Jamaica, Kenya, Malaysia, Mauritius, Namibia, Nepal, Nigeria, the Philippines, Rwanda, Tanzania, Trinidad & Tobago, Uganda, Venezuela, Zambia and Zimbabwe, etc.

20 It was mainly composed of developed country Members.

21 The 'July package' was the Decision Adopted by the General Council on August 1, 2004 (WT/L/579). Its Annex D was the Modalities for Negotiations on Trade Facilitation.

22 WTO, WT/L/579, Annex D, para. 8.

23 The introduction also fills the gap in recounting the trade facilitation course from 1950s to 1990s, as left from the previous chapters.

24 When the TFA was concluded, United Nations Regional Commissions and regional development banks were added, so the 'Annex D plus organizations' replaced the 'Annex D organizations'.

25 See Agreement Establishing the World Trade Organization, Preamble.

26 Miguel de Cervantes Saavedra, *Don Quixote*, Part II, Chapter 3.

27 William Shakespeare, *The Tempest*, Act II, Scene I.

1   Free trade is not for free

In the post-war era, globalization has been a powerful force in shaping the world. Over the course of globalization, a wave of phenomena come to the fore: merchandise and service of various types and of high quality are increasingly available for the diversified choices of people living in different regions; capital flows with unprecedented velocity internationally out of an instinct for optimizing profit margins; labor markets are more open to foreign job hunters to alleviate the skill shortages of the hosting countries; technological innovations, which spill over more rapidly than ever before, enhance productivity; transportation and communication costs have decreased so that it is easier to reach a place or person that is thousands of miles away; natural resources, including raw materials and energy sources, are more efficiently allocated on a global scale; and economies – no matter they are neighboring or geographically distant – are increasingly integrated or connected by trade and investment.

Globalization has brought far-reaching impacts worldwide. Incontrovertibly, this revolutionary process has fundamentally transformed societies and changed everyday life for many people. At the same time, there are of course critics. Anti-globalization campaigners are vocal in their criticism that globalization concurrently has caused negative side-effects, such as inequality, marginalization of small and vulnerable economies, shrinkage of traditional industries and damage to the environment. While some may contend that 'it is the best of times', it could also be 'the worst of times'[1] in the eyes of others. Nevertheless, '[t]oday globalization is fact of life, so the question is less about whether or not we like globalization – it is more about how we should respond'.[2] At the dawn of the new millennium, world leaders declared that 'the central challenge we face today is to ensure that globalization becomes a positive force for all the world's people'.[3] As Margaret Thatcher conveyed, 'there is no alternative'.

The calls for free trade

Free trade (also known as 'trade liberalization') is the enduring and dynamic engine that has driven globalization forward.[4] Liberalizing trade entails eliminating restrictions and barriers on the exchange of goods and services between countries. Among the restrictions and barriers, tariffs and non-tariff measures (NTMs) are the most salient. In the modern world where countries are tightly connected by international trade, if we are committed to steering globalization towards a promising trajectory, we should accelerate the momentum of free trade. At least, what generations of theorists have advocated is still worth heeding.

The notion of free trade can be traced back to the *Grotian tradition*. Hugo Grotius, in *The Free Sea* (1609), articulated the rule of international law as the foundation: 'it is lawful for any nation to go to any other and to trade with it'.[5] On free trade, he wrote in *Commentary on the Law of Prize and Booty* (1605):

> Freedom of trade, then, springs from the primary law of nations, which has a natural and permanent cause, so that it cannot be abrogated. Moreover, even if its abrogation were possible, such a result could be achieved only with the consent of all nations. Accordingly, it is not remotely conceivable that one nation may justly impose any hindrance whatsoever upon two other nations that wish to enter into a contract with each other.[6]

Grotius, however, lived in an age when *Mercantilism*[7] was dominant in Europe (from the sixteenth to the eighteenth century). Against the 'encouraging exportation, discouraging importation'[8] *mercantile system*, Adam Smith, through the *principle of absolute advantage*, argued that unrestricted trade and free international competition were more beneficial to a country.[9] For instance, if the wine of France was better and cheaper than that of Portugal, it would be advantageous for Great Britain to purchase the French wine;[10] Great Britain should hence relax the discriminatory restraints on the importation of French wine (e.g., higher tariffs than on Portuguese wine).[11] As a proponent of free trade, Adam Smith explained the rationale for international trade in his magnum opus – *the Wealth of Nations* (1776):

> In every period, indeed, of every society, the surplus part both of the rude and manufactured produce, or that for which there is no demand at home, must be sent abroad, in order to be exchanged for something for which there is some demand at home.[12]

Following Smith, David Ricardo propounded the *theory of comparative advantage*. According to the 'two-goods, two-country' *Ricardian model*, there is scope for mutually beneficial trade even when one country is more productive in every possible area (viz. that country can produce more goods with one unit of labor in both modeled lines of production than its trading counterpart), as long as each country specializes in its pattern of comparative advantage. Ricardo, in *On the Principles of Political Economy and Taxation* (1817), also advocated free trade:

> Under a system of perfectly free commerce, each country naturally devotes its capital and labour to such employments as are most beneficial to each. This pursuit of individual advantage is admirably connected with the universal good of the whole. By stimulating industry, by regarding ingenuity,

and by using most efficaciously the peculiar powers bestowed by nature, it distributes labour most effectively and most economically. While, by increasing the general mass of productions, it diffuses general benefit, and binds together by one common tie of interest and intercourse, the universal society of nations throughout the civilized world. It is this principle which determines that wine shall be made in France and Portugal, that corn shall be grown in America and Poland, and that hardware and other goods shall be manufactured in England.[13]

John Stuart Mill, subsequently, enriched the Ricardian model. In *Principles of Political Economy* (1848), Mill explicated that the countries with more elastic demands for other countries' goods tend to benefit more in a system of comparative-advantage-based trade.

On January 23, 1860, Great Britain and France concluded a free trade treaty (usually called 'the Chevalier-Cobden treaty').[14] Under this treaty, Great Britain and France reduced their tariffs substantially, abolished import prohibitions and granted each other unconditionally most-favored-nation (MFN) status.[15] As a result, the value of British exports to France more than doubled in the 1860s, and the increase was mainly in manufactured goods; the importation of French wines into Britain also doubled.[16] The Chevalier-Cobden treaty was a signal that the sentiment of free trade had reached ascendancy.[17]

Since then (except for those periods of depressions and wars), free trade remained the universal basis of commercial relations between countries. A wave of theorists continued to advocate this sentiment. At the beginning of the twentieth century, Eli Heckscher and Bertil Ohlin, with their *Heckscher-Ohlin model*, found that a country which is well endowed with a factor (e.g., capital, labor) tends to export the goods whose production is intensive in that factor. This theorem empirically verifies the pattern of trade between developed and developing countries (i.e., the exports of developed countries are concentrated in sectors with higher skill intensity; the exports of developing countries are concentrated in sectors with lower skill intensity).[18]

In the 1980s, Paul Krugman developed the *new trade theory*. Traditional trade theories had suggested that international trade is based on the production of different goods in each country to satisfy unmet needs in others. Krugman's new trade theory, however, presented models that explain how countries benefit from producing and trading in similar goods and how production facilities are globally distributed,[19] by taking broader account of the updated trends of international trade (e.g., increased production of goods leading to economies of scale and increased diversity of products leading to greater choice for consumers).

Many theorists, indeed, contend that free trade is an ideal towards which trade policies should strive; in reality, few countries have fully achieved free trade.[20] As international trade is becoming increasingly complex and elusive, free trade sentiment frequently drops and *trade protectionism* recurs, when crisis or depression strikes. From November 2008 to September 2013, for example, 2134 government policy measures, which affected large categories of trade and discriminated against foreign commercial interests, were reportedly implemented by countries.[21] Would this situation evoke *déjà vu* of the archaic mercantile system? 'If governments have not been scrambling to raise new barriers to trade, they have not exactly been rushing to agree to new liberalization either'.[22] In the event, free trade 'has irretrievably lost its innocence' and 'has shifted from optimum to reasonable rule of thumb'.[23]

Nevertheless, the basic politics of the world trading system and trade policies of most countries have not deviated from the spirit of free trade; even many of those who consider free trade as less-than-perfect still believe that free trade is usually better than any other trade policy a government is likely to follow.[24] 'Free trade is not passé', as Krugman asserted.[25] At least, 'there is still a case for free trade as a good policy, and as a useful target in the practical world of politics'.[26]

Free trade per se costs

Free trade is of course not free. In practice, international trade today is organized – under the auspices of globalization – within the global value chains (GVC) where different countries located at different stages of the production process contribute integrant values to a final product. At the same time, international trade is operationally carried by the global supply chains (GSC), which 'encompass freight transportation, warehousing, border clearance, payment systems and increasingly many other functions outsourced by producers and merchants to dedicated service providers'.[27] In operating trade, goods need to be moved from a factory to a seaport, land port, or airport, processed at the border and loaded onto a cargo ship or airplane, transported an often long distance to another country, unloaded and processed again at the border, then transferred onto a truck or train and put into a local distribution network, so that they can finally reach the consumer.[28] Accordingly, every trade transaction includes not only the value of the goods but also the costs of moving the goods.

Therefore, the concept of *trade costs* arises. Trade costs refer to the costs rendered in getting a product to the final consumer other than the marginal costs of producing it.[29] The movement of goods along the global supply chains – 'the backbone of international trade and commerce'[30] – is essentially a process where trade costs cumulate. This is in keeping with the facts: (i) trade transactions are usually contracted following the INCOTERMS[31] modes (e.g., FOB, CIF) that indicate at which agreed stage in a supply chain a consignment of goods shall be handed over from the seller to the buyer; and (ii) the more rearward in a supply chain the handover is arranged, the more determinants of trade costs (e.g., carriage, freight, insurance, port charges, border clearance fees, duties and taxes) should be specified in the contract.

Figure 1.1 reflects that determinants of trade costs are miscellaneous. Those determinants ubiquitously exist throughout the global supply chains: before the border, at the border and behind the border.[32] Some of the determinants (e.g., carriage, freight, insurance) are market-priced, so the costs for them are subject

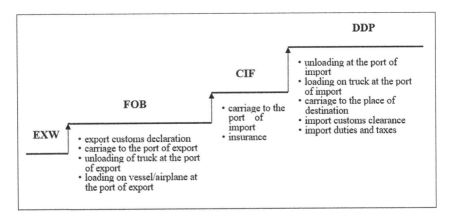

Figure 1.1 Trade costs creeping along a supply chain

to bargaining with the relevant service providers and can be dealt with in commercial terms (e.g., a trader can choose the cheapest carrier to ship his goods). We may call them the *commercial part* of trade costs. Meanwhile, the prices for other determinants of trade costs (e.g., port charges, border clearance fees and import duties and taxes) are not commercially negotiable, because (i) they are fixed by monopoly (e.g., the port authority may *ex parte* charge the containers stacked on its wharf); or (ii) complexity on the site (e.g., border clearance is a complex process) makes pricing unattainable; or (iii) the rates of the determinants (e.g., import duties and taxes include tariff, excise, value-added tax and so on) are lawfully set at all. These determinants obviously have administrative features, so we call them the *administrative part* of trade costs. The commercial part of trade costs obtains the services which are worth the expenses (e.g., the goods are shipped or insured upon the payment); in contrast, the administrative part is like the peel of an orange: the peel itself is of no utility to the payer but the whole orange has to be paid for without peeling it.

In the administrative part, tariffs, which are applied at the border, are distinctive in several respects: (i) it accounts for a considerable proportion of trade costs; and (ii) it can be used discriminatorily against any country. For instance, in 1696, Great Britain levied 25 percent tariffs upon all imported French goods (except brandy), while the goods imported from other countries were subject to lighter tariffs, seldom exceeding 5 percent.[33] In this case, (i) tariffs, which equaled one-quarter of the value of nearly all French goods, resulted in higher trade costs per consignment from France; and (ii) French goods were disadvantaged in comparison to the goods of other countries, if they were imported to Great Britain. As a result, France retaliated against British goods with high tariffs; the mutual restraints put an end to almost all normal trade between the two countries and smugglers became the principle importers of British and French goods.[34] As the simplest and oldest form of trade policy,[35] tariffs were competitively employed by countries for centuries with the aim of protecting their domestic markets and collecting revenue until the prevalence of another trade costs driver – NTMs. Unlike tariffs, NTMs extensively straddle the areas before, at and behind the border. Port charges and border clearance fees (at the border) and import duties and taxes (behind the border), for example, fall under NTMs, which contain a wider range of trade costs determinants (mostly the administrative part).

In economic terms, trade costs (mainly the administrative part) engenders an ad valorem tariff equivalent effect. As calculated, trade costs in developing countries in 2010 was equivalent to a 219 percent ad valorem tariff – this implies that, if it costs 1 USD to manufacture a product, another 2.19 USD will be added in the form of trade costs; even in high-income countries, the same product faced the 134 percent ad valorem tariff equivalent in trade costs.[36] Under globalization, goods are usually produced under 'the multi-stage production framework'. For example, some auto parts are made in the US; the auto parts are exported to Mexico where they are assembled into engines; the engines are then exported back from Mexico to the US where they are installed in cars; these cars are finally exported to Canada for consumption. After the goods pass through stages in different countries, the tariff equivalent effect will be magnified.[37] At this rate, given that the global costs of cross-border trade have reached 2 trillion USD,[38] its tariff equivalent would be immense.

From a historical point of view, trade costs over the long run impact trade booms and busts. Through investigation into the 130-year evolution of trade costs in three eras of globalization – the pre-World War I Belle Époque (1870–1913), the fractious interwar period (1921–1939) and the post-World War II resurgence of global trade (1950–2000), it is inferred that (i) from 1870 to 1913 declines in trade costs resulted in 290 percent of the growth in international trade; (ii) in the period from 1950 to 2000, declines in trade costs were responsible for 148 percent of trade growth; (iii) the 1870s and the 1970s were the periods when the relevant contribution of trade costs declines to world trade growth was at its greatest; and (iv) the interwar trade bust could be explained largely by the precipitous rise in trade costs associated with the Great Depression, where the collapse of the gold standard and the evaporation of trade credit were highlighted.[39]

Since trade is sensitive to its costs, trade costs exert a comprehensive influence on trade in a variety of aspects (e.g., how global trade flows and grows, who is involved in doing trade, what trade policies a country is supposed to adopt). Exorbitant trade costs make a dent in a country's comparative advantage and are inimical to the country's economic competitiveness by means of, for example, isolating this country from world markets, limiting its economic development opportunities, aggravating burdens on the poor, undermining economic welfare and preventing its business community from engaging with the world economy.[40] For example, according to the World Bank statistics (2014), Tajikistan, a landlocked country, had export/import costs of 9,050/10,650 USD per container; by comparison, in coastal Singapore, the costs for export/import per container were only 460/440 USD.[41] *Ceteris paribus* (other things being equal), Singapore will generally drum up more trading opportunities than Tajikistan.[42]

Thus, trade costs matter. According to the OECD and the WTO, 'keeping trade costs at reasonable levels and reducing them as far as possible in some key areas is essential to enjoying comparative advantage and the gains from trade'.[43]

Externality of trade costs

When we speak about free trade, it is essential, first of all, to scrutinize the traders struggling at the grass-roots level. What is a trader then? A trader (no matter a natural person or a legal person) is a *homo economicus* (economic human) in the sense of economics. According to Lionel Robbins, 'economics is the science which studies human behavior as a relationship between ends and scarce means which have alternative uses'.[44] This pattern of behavior, as interpreted by Milton Friedman and *the rational choice theory*, reflects the *rationality* that a human in a society applies in balancing costs against benefits to arrive at an action that maximizes personal returns;[45] in other words, a human is naturally liable to make decisions on how he acts out of the mind of maximizing his benefits and minimizing his costs through the action. A hypothetical feature of *homo economicus* is therefore created to epitomize the miscellaneous individuals who perform various economic behaviors every day in a society. Albeit critics stress that a human in the economics context must be also equipped with morality[46] (e.g., Adam Smith by himself held that 'how selfish soever man may be supposed, there are evidently some principles in his nature'),[47] a *homo economicus*, depicted by John Stuart Mill as rational and self-interested, normally 'desires to possess wealth, and is capable of judging the comparative efficacy of means for obtaining that end'.[48]

In the real world, a trader, as a *homo economicus*, breaks a sweat to earn more on the one hand, and pinches pennies to incur less costs on the other, because 'the exposure to trade, or increases in this exposure, forces the least efficient firms out of the industry'.[49] As Friedrich Hayek described:

> In a competitive industry at any rate [. . .] the task of keeping cost from rising requires constant struggle, absorbing a great part of the energy of the manager. [. . .] The very strength of the desire, constantly voiced by producers and engineers, to be able to proceed untrammeled by considerations of money costs, is eloquent testimony to the extent to which these factors enter into their daily work.[50]

In terms of economics, trade costs, if excessive, would have the property of *externality*, where 'the utility of one or more individuals is dependent upon, among other things, one or more activities which are under the control of someone else'.[51] The externality of trade costs is basically negative (namely, 'external diseconomy'), because a trader[52] has to pay for the trade costs (if more excessive than normal) that (i) bring about nuisance (harmful effect) to his profit margins,[53] and (ii) are externally imposed on him (out of his control). As to the question of nuisance, it is already clear, from Hayek's description, that a trader is anxious about trade costs. Then, as to the question of external imposition, we need to explore the concept of business environment which determines trade costs externally.

Business environment is 'the quality of a country's government, including the regulatory and security environment affecting the business of importers and exporters active in the country'.[54] Features of a poor business environment usually, for example, include: deficient logistics infrastructures that sluggishly move goods and services; asymmetry and inadequacy of market information that misleads traders and causes loss of business opportunities; gray zones in regulating and enforcing trade policies; widespread rent-seeking activities that add 'rent' to trade costs; deterioration of business ethics that impairs the doctrine of good faith and fair dealing; excessive or undue fees and charges that overload traders with financial burdens; and red tape that makes the processing of trade transactions oppressively complex and time-consuming.

Alternatively, there are healthy business environments that have, for example, these positive features: an inclusive and open environment for establishing, running and closing a business; transparent and reasonable laws, policies and rules, as well as proper enforcement; standardized administrative procedures that enable business operations to go swimmingly; availability of important knowledge and information needed by traders either for seizing market opportunities or for legal compliance; and business-friendly governance that spares traders from red tape and needless expense. Empirically, a poor business environment implies higher trade costs and thereby enervates operating trade; on the contrary, a healthy business environment facilitates trade by making it more efficient, easy, cheap and joyful.

Box 1.1   Surveys on business environment

To diagnose the health of national business environments, several international institutions conduct surveys with different methodologies. The World Bank, OECD and World Economic Forum surveys are the most prominent.

The World Bank publishes Doing Business annually. This survey is focused on the regulatory and institutionary environment for business and is founded on the premise that 'economic activity requires good rules that are transparent and accessible to all, and such regulations should be efficient, striking a balance between safeguarding some important aspects of the business environment and avoid distortions that impose unreasonable costs on businesses'.[55] Doing Business compares across 189 economies and measures the regulations on their domestic companies from 11 respects through their business lifecycle. Summing up countries' experiences globally, Doing Business reveals the good practices in common (e.g., providing online filling and one-stop service, streamlining regulatory processes, using risk-based inspections, allowing electronic submission and processing, reducing financial burdens).[56]

OECD has developed a family of regulation indicators, including Product Market Regulation (PMR) Indicator and Foreign Direct Investment (FDI) Restrictiveness Index, with a view to quantitatively measuring regulations that undermine market competitiveness.[57]

The World Economic Forum in its Transportation Industry Partnership Programmed creates the Enabling Trade Index (ETI). The ETI is composed of four sub-indexes: market access, border administration, infrastructure, operating environment. The ETI measures to what extent individual economies have developed institutions, policies and services facilitating the free flow of goods over borders. Consequently, individual economies are ranked according to their ETI scores.[58]

Business environment is vitally important to the success of a trader. A trader – out of rationality – may vote with his feet on the externality of trade costs: (i) opting for a better business environment to engage in trade; or (ii) abandoning it all together if the business environment is poor. In fact, few traders have the capability of placing themselves in an ideal business environment; the majority of traders, especially small and medium-sized enterprises (SMEs), are confined to a business environment in their home countries and can only choose between 'trading' and 'not trading'.

According to Paul Krugman, when there are trade costs, a small subset of more productive enterprises export; the remaining only serve their domestic market.[59] Moreover, this situation corroborates *the puzzle of home bias in trade*,[60] which finds that *intra-national* trade is much larger than *international* trade because of the presence of trade costs (in particular tariffs and NTMs); that is to say, trade costs discourage most of the traders from trading abroad. For instance, in 2000, only 4 percent of the 5.5 million firms operating in the US engaged in exporting; the top 10 percent of US trading firms by value (the sum of imports and exports) accounted for over 95 percent of the total value of US foreign trade[61] – this means that almost 90 percent of firms had nothing to do with international trade.

How can we diminish the externality of trade costs then? Ronald Coase in *The Problem of Social Cost* (1960)[62] drew up treatments of externality. The *Coase theorem*, primarily points out that bargains between the parties in the presence of externality would anyhow attain an efficient outcome (desirably an optimum allocation of resources, viz. *Pareto optimality*) on the premise that the bargains (described as 'market transactions' in Coase' literature) are carried out costlessly.[63] Accordingly, a trader may bargain with relevant parties for lower costs. This treatment, however, is only applicable to the commercial part of trade costs which is priced by markets. For example, an exporter may negotiate with a trucker on a concessional rate for carrying his goods from the factory to the port if they have a long-term commercial partnership. But this treatment would not be efficacious in coping with the administrative part of trade costs. For example, if a trader decides to bargain with the party that imposes a NTM (e.g., consular invoice fees)[64] on him, he, as a private entity, would find it difficult and extremely costly to conduct such bargains (with the embassy or any consular office issuing the consular invoice). In this case, he would have to identify with whom and on what terms to bargain; the bargaining process also costs time, manpower and money that would overburden him.

At any rate, a society is not a state of *laissez faire* or an ideal world; any society has its own government. The Coase theorem helpfully provides another treatment by advocating the selection of appropriate *social arrangements* ('government regulations') for handling the externality. As Coase argued, the government has a variety of capacities which the individual traders do not have: the government 'may impose regulations which state what people must or must not do and which have to be obeyed'; the government 'is able to influence the use of factors of production by administrative decisions'; the government 'has powers to enable it to get some things done at a lower cost than could a private organization' (though 'the governmental administrative machine is not itself costless').[65] Hence, diminishing the externality of trade costs (mainly the administrative part) at a social level falls on the government. Ironically, the government (to be more accurate, some specific government agencies) itself is the initiator of the administrative part of trade costs (e.g., the foreign ministry may endorse consular invoice fees to replenish its own budget). Business environment, which is highly policy-based and in return reflects the quality of the government, is the cause of externality of trade costs. A government shall embark on harnessing its business environment to make it a better place. At this point, it is crucial that a government adopts appropriate trade policies that trim trade costs in a universal way (as a social arrangement). A government in pursuit of free trade normally starts its trade policies with focus on two matters – cutting tariffs and NTMs.

Cutting tariffs and NTMs for freer trade

The course of cutting tariffs

Tariffs once played both a political and economic part in making history. For instance, the Tariff Act of July 4, 1789 became the first substantive legislation passed by the first US Congress and (together with a collection of subsequent acts)[66] set up tariffs as the prime source of the federal government's revenue for the newly independent nation that was 'teetering on the brink of bankruptcy'.[67]

Notwithstanding its effects of protecting domestic industries and securing the government's revenue, tariffs may distort markets. The majority of theorists (typically the *neoclassical* economists) have demonstrated that tariffs result in deadweight loss, where the gains in both of producers' surplus and government's revenue cannot redeem the decrease in consumers' surplus. This means cutting tariffs would ideally generate a net gain for the society as a whole.

A lesson painfully learned from World War II is that unilaterally raising tariffs, which is intended to curb foreign cheaper imports and then protect domestic industries, is an impolitic move. As evidenced by the Smoot-Hawley Act of 1930,[68] a country initiating this beggar-thy-neighbor action would possibly face retaliation from its trading partners. Reversal of this failed act by the US Congress set an example that negotiating tariff cuts with trading partners on a recipro-cal basis was more pragmatic than applying high tariffs. In opposition to the tit-for-tat tariff conflicts, Sumner Welles, the US Undersecretary of State during Franklin D. Roosevelt's Administration, concluded that:

> The high-tariff policies pursued by the Harding, Coolidge, and Hoover Administrations killed any chance of debt payments. They also rolled up unemployment in Great Britain and in Western Europe. They encouraged the German Government to adopt its autarchic economic policy, which in turn was a contributing factor in bringing about World War II.[69]

Bearing this lesson in mind, a new generation of leaders gathered after the war and discussed establishing a mechanism whereby tariffs could be reduced in a non-discriminatory, negotiable, reciprocal and binding manner. Due to the abortion of the International Trade Organization (ITO), which was originally designed as one of the three pillars (the other two known as IMF and the World Bank) to sustain the 'Bretton Woods' system, the General Agreement on Tariffs and Trade (GATT) turned out to be the mechanism governing the multilateral trading system for almost half a century until the birth of the WTO. Over the erstwhile years of GATT, tariff cuts remained the mainstream for every round of negotiations, because the GATT was 'launched as a tariff agreement' that favored tariffs – a form of protection 'fairer' than other protectionist measures.[70]

Following the previous rounds of GATT negotiations, which had already low-ered the average of tariffs in GATT participants from over 40 percent at the end of the war down to less than 5 percent after the Tokyo Round (1973–1979),[71] the Uruguay Round (1986–1993) ended with further tariff cuts, which were negotiated line by line rather than through formulas, to the extent that:

(i)   99 percent industrial tariff lines for developed countries and 73 percent for developing countries were subject to bound tariffs;[72]
(ii) The weighted average level of tariffs applicable to industrial products was supposed to fall from 6.3 percent to 3.8 percent in developed countries, from 8.6 percent to 6 percent in transition economies and from 15.3 percent to 12.3 percent in developing countries, when the process of staged reduc-tions in tariffs agreed in this round was completed by January 1, 1999;[73]
(iii) Developed countries and certain developing countries agreed to eliminate all tariffs in certain sectors – the so-called 'zero-for-zero' sectors, which included pharmaceuticals, agricultural equipment, construction equipment, medical equipment, furniture, paper, steel and toys.[74]

The course of cutting NTMs

Besides tariffs, there is another type of potent trade barriers – the NTMs. 'Unlike tariffs, NTMs are not mere numbers – they are complex legal texts that are not eas-ily amenable to quantification, comparison, or even standard formatting'.[75] Hence, it is critically essential to spell out the discernible measures that constitute NTMs. The Multi-Agency Support Team (MAST),[76] convened by the United Nations Conference on Trade and Development (UNCTAD), has developed a classification of NTMs. This tree-structured classification encompasses 16 'branches' (chapters) of NTMs, and each chapter is comprised of in-depth groupings at the 'sub-branch' (1-digit), 'twig' (2-digit) and 'leaf' (3-digit) levels.[77] In total, nearly 250 individual non-tariff measures are specified in the MAST's classification (see Tables 1.1 and 1.2).

Table 1.1 Classification of non-tariff measures (2012 version)

	Classification	*Description*
A	**Sanitary and Phytosanitary Measures**	Measures that are applied: to protect human or animal life from risks arising from additives, contaminants, toxins or disease-causing organisms in their food; to protect human life from plant- or animal-carried diseases; to protect animal or plant life from pests, diseases, or disease-causing organisms; to prevent or limit other damage to a country from the entry, establishment or spread of pests; and to protect bio-diversity. These include measures taken to protect the health of fish and wild fauna, as well as of forests and wild flora.
B	**Technical Barriers to Trade**	Measures referring to technical regulations, and procedures for assessment of conformity with technical regulations and standards, excluding measures covered by the SPS Agreement.
C	**Preshipment Inspection and Other Formalities**	Measures that cover preshipment inspection, direct consignment requirement, requirement to pass through a specified customs port, import monitoring and surveillance requirements and other automatic licensing measures, etc.
D	**Contingent Trade Protective Measures**	Measures implemented to counteract particular adverse effects of imports in the market of the importing country, including measures aimed at 'unfair' foreign trade practices, contingent upon the fulfillment of certain procedural and substantive requirements.
E	**Non-automatic Licensing, Quotas, Prohibitions and Quantity-control Measures**	Control measures generally aimed at restraining the quantity of goods that can be imported, regardless of whether they come from different sources or one specific supplier. These measures can take the form of non-automatic licensing, fixing of a predetermined quota, or through prohibitions. All measures introduced for SPS and TBT reasons are classified in Chapters A and B above.

(Continued)

Table 1.1 (Continued)

	Classification	Description
F	Price-control Measures, including Additional Taxes and Charges	Measures implemented to control or affect the prices of imported goods in order to, inter alia: support the domestic price of certain products when the import prices of these goods are lower; establish the domestic price of certain products because of price fluctuation in domestic markets, or price instability in a foreign market; or to increase or preserve tax revenue. This category also includes measures, other than tariffs measures, that increase the cost of imports in a similar manner, i.e., by fixed percentage or by a fixed amount: they are also known as para-tariff measures.
G	Finance Measures	Financial measures are intended to regulate the access to and cost of foreign exchange for imports and define the terms of payment. They may increase import costs in the same manner as tariff measures.
H	Measures Affecting Competition	Measures to grant exclusive or special preferences or privileges to one or more limited group of economic operators.
I	Trade-related Investment Measures	Measures that include local content measures, trade-balancing measures, etc.
J	Distribution Restrictions	Distribution of goods inside the importing country may be restricted. It may be controlled through additional license or certification requirements.
K	Restriction on Post-sales Services	Measures restricting producers of exported goods to provide post-sales service in the importing country.
L	Subsidies	Financial contribution by a government or public body, or via government entrustment or direction of a private body (direct or potential direct transfer of funds: e.g., grant, loan, equity infusion, guarantee; government revenue foregone; provision of goods or services or purchase of goods; payments to a funding mechanism), or income or price support, which confers a benefit and is specific (to an enterprise or industry or group thereof, or limited to a designated geographical region).
M	Government Procurement Restrictions	Measures controlling the purchase of goods by government agencies, generally by preferring national providers.
N	Intellectual Property	Measures related to intellectual property rights in trade: intellectual property legislation covers patents, trademarks, industrial designs, lay-out designs of integrated circuits, copyright, geographical indications and trade secrets.
O	Rule of Origin	Rules of origin cover laws, regulations and administrative determinations of general application applied by government of importing countries to determine the country of origin of goods. Rules of origin are important in implementing such trade policy instruments as anti-dumping and countervailing duties, origin marking and safeguard measures.
P	Export-related Measures	Measures applied by the government of the exporting country on exported goods.

Source: UNCTAD, International Classification of Non-Tariff Measures (2012 Version)

Table 1.2 Chapter F: Price–control measures including additional taxes and charges (as an example of the 'twig' and 'leaf' levels of NTMs)

F. Price-control Measures including Additional Taxes and Charges
  F1 Administrative measures affecting customs value
    F11 Minimum import prices
    F12 Reference prices
    F19 Other administrative measures affecting the customs value
  F2 Voluntary export price restraints (VEPRs)
  F3 Variable charges
    F31 Variable levies
    F32 Variable components
    F39 Variable charges
  F4 Customs surcharges
  F5 Seasonal duties
  F6 Additional taxes and charges levied in connection to services provided by the government
    F61 Custom inspection, processing and servicing fees
    F62 Merchandise handling or storing fees
    F63 Tax on foreign exchange transactions
    F64 Stamp tax
    F65 Import license fee
    F66 Consular invoice fee
    F67 Statistical tax
    F68 Tax on transport facilities
    F69 Additional charges
  F7 Internal taxes and charges levied on imports
    F71 Consumption taxes
    F72 Excise taxes
    F73 Taxes and charges for sensitive product categories
    F79 Internal taxes and charges levied on imports
  F8 Decreed customs valuations
  F9 Price control measures

Source: UNCTAD, International Classification of Non-Tariff Measures (2012 Version)

The MAST's classification reveals a strong affinity between the various NTMs and a broad spread of trade policies. Indeed, many of the NTMs are neutral and legitimate, especially when they are designed to safeguard public interests.[78] However, a country's government, for any protectionist purpose, may pick from the pool of accredited NTMs and build them into its trade policies invisibly. For example, in a survey carried out by the International Trade Center (ITC) in 2015–2016, the traders in the European Union reportedly experienced 7,264 issues relating to NTM regulations when they were exporting; most of the NTM regulations were burdensome, regardless of their purposes.[79] In the economists' eyes, 'a NTM generates a wedge between the domestic and world prices of one or several traded goods or services'.[80] NTMs, therefore, are often seen 'as inherently more discriminatory, more varied and more disruptive of market forces' than tariff.[81] Thus, NTMs should be cut, or constrained at least. But tackling the NTMs requires a deep understanding of a country's regulatory culture and background.[82]

The debate on NTMs was no less intense than on tariffs at the time of constructing the post-war world trading system. The US was intent on prohibiting most of the NTMs (except the quotas and restrictions that buttressed its own agricultural support programmes).[83] In both the Suggested Charter for an International Trade Organization of the United Nations (1946) proposed by the US and the ensuing Havana Charter for an International Trade Organization (1948), there were a mass of articles on NTMs. Owing to the complexity of NTMs (e.g., the various forms they take, their relevance to trade and the accountability of countries for using them), the world trading system eventually failed to deeply embrace them. In the early GATT rounds, NTMs were left as nuts to crack instead of being picked as low-hanging fruits.[84] Even so, some general rules in the GATT (e.g., Article VII, VIII, X and XI) have lightly touched upon NTMs.

The Kennedy Round in the 1960s started to pluck NTMs from obscurity. Despite the stillbirth of the 'Anti-dumping Code' and the American Selling Price Agreement – the potential fruit of the Kennedy Round – due to objection from the US Congress, the trade ministers' agreement that the forthcoming negotiations 'should deal not only with tariffs but also with non-tariff barriers'[85] was nonetheless a good sign of enriching the multilateral trading system. The Tokyo Round in the 1970s ended with a set of agreements on NTMs (e.g., Agreement on Import Licensing Procedures,[86] Agreement on Technical Barriers to Trade,[87] Agreement on Implementation of Article VII of GATT),[88] 'in some cases interpreting the existing GATT rules, in others breaking entirely new ground'.[89] These agreements were known as 'the Tokyo Round Codes',[90] but they were only signed by some of the GATT participants. Then, the Uruguay Round (1986–1994) carried forward NTMs (including 'the Tokyo Round Codes') and boldly declared at its launch that 'negotiations shall aim to reduce or eliminate non-tariff measures [. . .] without prejudice to any action to be taken in fulfillment of the rollback commitments'.[91] Besides creating the WTO, the Uruguay Round not only resulted in some emerging agreements on NTMs (e.g., Agreement on Sanitary and Phytosanitary Measures, Agreement on Preshipment Inspection) but also renovated some of 'the Tokyo Round Codes' and made them new agreements fully in force (e.g., Agreement on Technical Barriers to Trade, Agreement on Implementation of Article VII of GATT).[92]

Table 1.3 Subjects covered by the GATT Rounds

Year	Round	Subjects Covered	Countries
1947	**Geneva**	Tariffs	23
1949	**Annecy**	Tariffs	13
1951	**Torquay**	Tariffs	38
1956	**Geneva**	Tariffs	26
1960–1961	**Dillon**	Tariffs	26
1964–1967	**Kennedy**	Tariffs, Anti-dumping measures	62
1973–1979	**Tokyo**	Tariffs, Non-tariff measures, 'Framework' Agreements	102
1986–1994	**Uruguay**	Tariffs, Non-tariff measures, Rules, Services, Intellectual Property, Dispute Settlement, Textiles, Agriculture, Creation of WTO, etc.	123

Source: WTO

At present, the WTO system contains a number of agreements pertaining to certain types of NTMs – e.g., Agreement on the Application of Sanitary and Phytosanitary Measures (cf. Chapter A under the NTM Classification), Agreement on Technical Barriers to Trade (cf. Chapter B), Agreement on Trade-related Investment Measures (cf. Chapter I), Agreement on Implementation of Article VI of the GATT 1994 (cf. Chapter D1, 'Anti-dumping Measure'), Agreement on Implementation of Article VII of the GATT 1994 (cf. Chapter F8, 'Decreed Customs Valuations'), Agreement on Preshipment Inspection (cf. Chapter C), Agreement on Rules of Origin (cf. Chapter O), Agreement on Import Licensing Procedures (cf. Chapter E1), Agreement on Subsidies and Countervailing Measures (cf. Chapter L and D2), Agreement on Safeguards Agreement on Trade-related Aspects of Intellectual Property Rights (cf. Chapter N) and Agreement on Government Procurement (cf. Chapter M). That said, NTMs are still drawing more attention than ever before, because 'the expansion of world trade, the deepening integration of economies and the widening and strengthening of trade rules have inevitably resulted in NTMs emerging as an increasingly salient feature of the international trade landscape'.[93] Different from the case that tariffs (and quotas) are able to be progressively zeroed through mutual exchanges of market access commitments, bringing NTMs to zero is not applicable.[94] In fact, the WTO agreements only constrain (or partially cut) the relevant NTMs rather than cut them thoroughly. 'Looking ahead, [. . .] with NTMs, we need to reflect more carefully on our core culture and approach to trade opening. A new horizon and context must be defined', stated Pascal Lamy, former Director-General of the WTO.[95]

Notes

1 Charles Dickens in his *A Tale of Two Cities* wrote 'it was the best of times, it was the worst of times'.
2 Roberto Azevêdo, 'Let's Make Nairobi a Success', speech in Costa Rica on August 25, 2015, www.wto.org/english/news_e/spra_e/spra77_e.htm.
3 UN, A/RES/55/2 (2000), para. 5.
4 The drivers of globalization may also include technical advances, open market, integration in trade, liberalization of capital flows, free movement of labor, etc. See, for example, Tatyana P. Soubbotina, *Beyond Economic Growth: An Introduction to Sustainable Development* (World Bank, 2004), p. 66.
5 Hugo Grotius, *The Free Sea* (Richard Hakluyt trans., Liberty Fund, 2004), p. 10.
6 Hugo Grotius, *Commentary on the Law of Prize and Booty* (Martine Julia van Ittersum ed., Liberty Fund, 2006), p. 356.
7 The Mercantilists argued that it was necessary to impose strict government regulation on foreign trade (e.g., encouraging exports and discouraging imports, prohibiting export of gold and silver and requiring all domestic money to be kept in circulation) in order for a state to accumulate the 'favorable balance of trade' (namely, exports greater than imports).
8 Adam Smith wrote that there were two engines for enriching a country under the *Mercantile System: Restraints upon Importation and Encouragement to Exportation*. See Adam Smith, *The Wealth of Nations* (1776, London: Methuen & Co., Ltd., 5th edn, 1904), Book IV, Chapter I.
9 Reinhard Schumacher , 'Adam Smith's Theory of Absolute Advantage and the Use of Doxography in the History of Economics', (2012) 5 *Erasmus Journal for Philosophy and Economics* 54, pp. 54–80.

10 According to the treaty of commerce between Great Britain and Portugal at that time, British imports of Portuguese wine should be more preferential than its imports of French wine. See Smith, *The Wealth of Nations*, Book IV, Chapter VI.

11 See Smith, *The Wealth of Nations*, Book IV, Chapter III. Adam Smith also argued that the trade between Great Britain and France at that time was subject to many discouragements and restraints; if the two countries considered their real interests without either mercantile jealousy or national animosity, the trade with France might be more advantageous to Great Britain than that of any other country, and for the same reason that of Great Britain to France.

12 Ibid., Book III, Chapter I.

13 David Ricardo, *On the Principles of Political Economy and Taxation* (1817, London: John Murray, 3rd edn, 1821), Chapter 7: 'On Foreign Trade'.

14 The treaty was named after the main British and French originators: Richard Cobden and Michel Chevalier.

15 Endre Ustor, 'First Report on the Most-Favored-Nation Clause', (1969) 2 *The Yearbook of the International Law Commission* 159, p. 162.

16 Llewellyn Woodward, *The Age of Reform: 1815–1870* (Oxford University Press, 2nd edn, 1962), p. 179. See also Arthur Louis Dunham, *The Anglo-French Treaty of Commerce of 1860 and the Progress of the Industrial Revolution in France* (Russell & Russell, 1971).

17 See *supra* note 16.

18 Paul Krugman, Maurice Obstfeld and Marc Melitz, *International Economics: Theory and Policy* (Pearson, 10th edn, 2015), pp. 116–145.

19 See 'Modelling Trade in a World of Plenty', press release of the 2008 Nobel Prize in Economics, www.nobelprize.org/nobel_prizes/economic-sciences/laureates/2008/speedread.html.

20 Krugman, Obstfeld and Melitz, see *supra* note 18, p. 269.

21 Kent Jones, *Reconstructing the World Trade Organization for the 21st Century: An Institutional Approach* (Oxford University Press, 2015), pp. 18–19.

22 Christophe Bellmann, Trineesh Biswas and Marie Chamay, 'Recent Trends in World Trade and International Negotiations', (2010) 1 *Revue internationale de politique de développement* 161, pp. 161–187.

23 Paul Krugman, 'Is Free Trade Passé?' (1987) 1 *The Journal of Economic Perspectives* 131, pp. 131–144.

24 Krugman, Obstfeld and Melitz, see *supra* note 18, p. 269.

25 Krugman, see *supra* note 23, pp. 131–144.

26 Ibid.

27 World Bank, *Connecting to Compete 2014: Trade Logistics in the Global Economy*, p. iii.

28 OECD and WTO, *Aid for Trade at a Glance 2015: Reducing Trade Costs for Inclusive, Sustainable Growth*, p. 39, https://www.wto.org/english/res_e/booksp_e/aid4trade15_e.pdf.

29 James E. Anderson and Eric van Wincoop, 'Trade Costs', (2004) 42 *Journal of Economic Literature* 691, pp. 691–751.

30 Jean-François Arvis et al., *Connecting to Compete 2014: Trade Logistics in the Global Economy* (World Bank, 2014), p. iii.

31 INCOTERMS (International Commercial Terms) are a set of pre-defined commercial terms published by the International Chamber of Commerce (ICC) to be used in international commercial transactions. The updated version is INCOTERMS 2010.

32 OECD, 'Trade Costs: What Have We learned? A Synthesis Report', TAD/TC/WP(2013)3/FINAL, p. 12.

33 Smith, *The Wealth of Nations*, Book IV, Chapter III.

34 Ibid.

35 Krugman, Obstfeld and Melitz, see *supra* note 18, p. 239.
36 WTO, *World Trade Report 2015 - Speeding up trade: Benefits and challenges of implementing the WTO Trade Facilitation Agreement* (WTO, 2015), p. 75.
37 Kei-Mu Yi, 'Can Multistage Production Explain the Home Bias in Trade?' (2010) 100 *American Economic Review* 364, pp. 364–393.
38 Pascal Lamy, 'A Trade Facilitation Deal Could Give a $1 Trillion Boost to World Economy', speech to the Chittagong Chamber of Commerce in Bangladesh on February 1, 2013, www.wto.org/english/news_e/sppl_e/sppl265_e.htm.
39 David S. Jacks, Christopher M. Meissner and Dennis Novy, 'Trade Booms, Trade Busts, and Trade Costs', (2011) 83 *Journal of International Economics* 185, pp. 185–201.
40 OECD and WTO, *Aid for Trade at a Glance 2015: Reducing Trade Costs for Inclusive, Sustainable Growth*, pp. 36–46.
41 World Bank, *Doing Business 2015: Going Beyond Efficiency* (World Bank, 2014).
42 Tajikistan still has advantages in some categories of goods, e.g., ferrous metals, clothing, organic fruits and vegetables, and crops. There are considerable volumes of trade between Tajikistan and countries geographically nearby, including China, Kazakhstan, Russia and Turkey. See website of Chamber of Commerce and Industry of the Republic of Tajikistan, http://tpp.tj/en/.
43 See *supra* note 40, p. 36.
44 Lionel Robbins, *An Essay on the Nature and Significance of Economic Science* (Palgrave MacMillan, 1932), p. 15.
45 Milton Friedman, *Essays in Positive Economics* (University of Chicago Press, 1953), pp. 3–43.
46 Thus evolved a wave of concepts and models, e.g., *homo reciprocans* and *homo sociologicus*.
47 Adam Smith, *The Theory of Moral Sentiments* (London: A. Millar, 6th edn, 1790), para. II 1.
48 John Stuart Mill, *Essays on Some Unsettled Questions of Political Economy* (London: Longmans, Green, Reader & Dyer, 2nd edn, 1874), 'Essay 5: On the Definition of Political Economy, and on the Method of Investigation Proper to It', para. 38 and para. 48.
49 Marc J. Melitz, 'The Impact of Trade on Intra-Industry Reallocations and Aggregate Industry Productivity', (2003) 71 *Econometrica* 1695, pp. 1695–1725.
50 Friedrich Hayek, 'The Use of Knowledge in Society', (1945) 35 *The American Economic Review* 519, p. 523.
51 Alan Randall, 'Market Solutions to Externality Problems: Theory and Practice', (1972) 54 *American Journal of Agricultural Economics* 175, p. 175; James M. Buchanan and Wm. Craig Stubblebine previously elaborated this definition in their article, see 'Externality', (1962) 29 *Economica* 371, p. 372.
52 According to Gregory Mankiw, the externality arises when the well-being of a bystander is influenced by another person's activity. See Gregory Mankiw, *Principles of Microeconomics* (Cengage Learning Publishers, 7th edn, 2015), p. 196. In doing trade, however, a trader is one of the parties that decides the commercial part of trade costs (e.g., he pays a trucker for delivering his goods to the port at an agreed price) so he is not a bystander. However, if the commercial part of trade costs is excessive (e.g., the truckers' association increases the market price to an unreasonable level), the trader then becomes a bystander. With regard to the administrative part of trade costs (e.g., tariffs), the trader is by nature a bystander because his well-being is ex parte influenced by the administration.
53 According to the argument of Paul Krugman et al., trade costs reduce the profitability of exporting for all firms; and for some, that reduction in profitability makes exporting unprofitable. See Krugman, Obstfeld and Melitz, *supra* note 18, p. 218.

54 World Economic Forum, *Enabling Trade: Valuing Growth Opportunities* (World Economic Forum, 2013), p. 8.

55 World Bank, *Doing Business 2012: Doing Business in a More Transparent World* (World Bank, 2012), p. 1.

56 See World Bank, *Doing Business 2014: Understanding Regulations for Small and Medium-Size Enterprises* (World Bank, 2013), *Doing Business 2015: Going Beyond Efficiency* (World Bank, 2014), *Doing Business 2016: Measuring Regulatory Quality and Efficiency* (World Bank, 2016).

57 See OECD, *Economic Policy Reforms 2014: Going for Growth Interim Report* (OECD Publishing, 2014), *Economic Policy Reforms 2015: Going for Growth* (OECD Publishing, 2015), *Economic Policy Reforms 2016: Going for Growth Interim Report* (OECD Publishing, 2016).

58 See World Economic Forum, *Global Enabling Trade Report 2014, 2015, 2016* (World Economic Forum, 2014, 2015, 2016).

59 Krugman, Obstfeld and Melitz, see *supra* note 18, pp. 217–233.

60 First raised by John McCallum in 1995. See John McCallum, 'National Borders Matter: Canada-U.S. Regional Trade Patterns', (1995) 85 *The American Economic Review* 615, pp. 615–623. Maurice Obstfeld and Kenneth Rogoff then identified this as one of the six major puzzles in international economics. See Maurice Obstfeld and Kenneth Rogoff, 'The Six Major Puzzles in International Macroeconomics: Is There a Common Cause?' in Ben Bernanke and Kenneth Rogoff (eds.), *NBER Macroeconomics Annual 2000, Volume 15* (MIT Press, 2001), pp. 339–412.

61 Andrew B. Bernard et al., 'Firms in International Trade', (2007) 21 *Journal of Economic Perspectives* 105, pp. 105–130.

62 Ronald Coase, 'The Problem of Social Cost', (1960) 3 *The Journal of Law and Economics* 1, pp. 1–44.

63 Ibid., Chapter V and VI.

64 No. F66 of the International Classification of Non-tariff Measures (2012 Version).

65 Coase, 'The Problem of Social Cost', Chapter VI.

66 The Acts included the Act of July 20 imposing duties on tonnage and the Act of July 31 that established port districts in each state and created the US Customs Service.

67 Raj Bhala, *International Trade Law: Interdisciplinary Theory and Practice* (LexisNexis, 3rd edn, 2008), pp. 614–615.

68 Smoot-Hawley Tariff or Hawley-Smoot Tariff, was an act sponsored by Senator Reed Smoot and Representative Willis C. Hawley, and signed into law on June 17, 1930, which raised US tariffs on imports by nearly 60 percent. In response, 60 other countries retaliated against the US by raising their own tariffs. At last the Act was replaced with the Reciprocal Trade Agreement Act of 1934.

69 Sumner Wells, 'The Tragic Years: In America', *The Argus* (Melbourne), July 18, 1944, at page 2.

70 WTO, *World Trade Report 2012 – Trade and public policies: A closer look at non-tariff measures in the 21st century* (WTO, 2012), p. 39.

71 Sherry M Stephenson, 'The United Nation System and International Trade', in Martin Ira Glassner (ed.), *The United Nations at Work* (Praeger Publishers, 1998), p. 110.

72 Marc Bacchetta and Bijit Bora, 'Post-Uruguay Round Market Access Barriers for Industrial Products', UNCTAD/ITCD/TAB/13 (2001), pp. 1–2.

73 Great Britain Commonwealth Secretariat and International Trade Centre, *Business Guide to the World Trading System* (International Trade Centre, 1999), p. 183.

74 Ibid.

75 Olivier Cadot, Mariem Malouche and Sebastián Sáez, *Streamlining Non-Tariff Measures: A Toolkit for Policy Makers* (World Bank, 2012), p. 9.
76 Institutional members of MAST as of July 2008 were: Food and Agriculture Organization of the United Nations (FAO), International Monetary Fund (IMF), International Trade Centre UNCTAD/WTO (ITC), Organization for Economic Cooperation and Development (OECD/TAD), United Nations Conference on Trade and Development (UNCTAD), United Nations Industrial Development Organization (UNIDO), World Bank (WB), World Trade Organization (WTO). Observers: European Commission (EC), United States International Trade Commission (USITC), United States Department of Agriculture (USDA). The MAST was jointly coordinated by UNCTAD and World Bank. MAST reported to the Group of Eminent Persons, which was convened by the director general of UNCTAD. MAST submitted a first report in July 2008.
77 See UNCTAD, *International Classification of Non-tariff Measures (2012 Version)*; *Non-Tariff Measures: Evidence From Selected Developing Countries and Future Research Agenda*, UNCTAD/DITC/TAB/2009/3 (2010).
78 Jones, *Reconstructing the World Trade Organization for the 21st Century: An Institutional Approach*, p. 13.
79 International Trade Centre (ITC) and European Commission (EC), *Navigating Non-Tariff Measures: Insights From a Business Survey in the European Union* (2016), p. 7.
80 Cadot, Malouche, and Sáez, *Streamlining Non-Tariff Measures: A Toolkit for Policy Makers*, p. 10.
81 WTO, *supra* note 70, p. 40.
82 Sungjoon Cho, *The Social Foundations of World Trade: Norms, Community, and Constitution* (Cambridge University Press, 2015), p. 16.
83 WTO, *supra* note 70, p. 40.
84 Cho, *The Social Foundations of World Trade: Norms, Community, and Constitution*, p. 16.
85 WTO, *supra* note 70. See also US Department of State, *General Agreement on Tariffs and Trade: Analysis of United States Negotiations, 1960–61 Tariff Conference* (1971), p. 203.
86 GATT, LT/TR/A/4.
87 GATT, LT/TR/A/5.
88 GATT, LT/TR/A/2.
89 WTO, *Understanding the WTO*, (WTO, 4th edn, 2008), p. 16.
90 The Tokyo Round Codes covered Subsidies and Countervailing Measures (interpreting GATT Articles 6, 16 and 23), Technical Barriers to Trade (sometimes called the Standards Code), Import Licensing Procedures, Government Procurement, Customs Valuation (interpreting GATT Article 7), Anti-dumping (interpreting GATT Article 6, replacing the Kennedy Round code), Bovine Meat Arrangement, International Dairy Arrangement, Trade in Civil Aircraft.
91 Ministerial Declaration on the Uruguay Round, September 20, 1986.
92 The contents of these agreements are different from what they were in the 'Tokyo Round Codes'.
93 WTO, *supra* note 70, p. 45.
94 Pascal Lamy, 'The Universe of Non-Tariff Measures Has Changed', speech on July 16, 2012, www.wto.org/english/news_e/sppl_e/sppl243_e.htm.
95 Ibid.

2 Rise of trade facilitation

If liberalizing a country's trade is like opening its door to world markets, the cuts of tariffs and NTMs, as well as other market access measures, basically determine the degree of the opening. For instance, at the end of the Uruguay negotiations, trade negotiators predicted that the proportion of industrial products entering developed country markets on the MFN duty-free basis would increase from 22 percent to 44 percent.[1] This implied that the door of a developed country would doubly open for the entry of industrial products. There is, however, usually beneath the door a threshold that people stumble on when moving inward and outward. Likewise, in the context of free trade, there are also 'thresholds' that cannot prohibit the entry of goods into a country but can impede the movement of goods across its border. In the day-to-day trading operations, the 'thresholds' become tangible problems for traders.

What after the cuts of tariffs and NTMs?

Regardless of how trading operations evolve (e.g., paperless trading, E-commerce, just-in-time delivery), a typical trading transaction consists of two contrary flows: the flow of money and the flow of goods.[2] Online payment instruments (e.g., PayPal), using simple mouse clicks and the swift remittance of money by banking networks, enable an international trading transaction to take mere minutes. In contrast, the goods need to be manufactured, packaged, warehoused, loaded, transported, inspected, released, distributed and delivered incrementally through the supply chains before they arrive at last at the buyer's location. The flow of goods consequently can take days (or weeks or months) and involves dozens of participants. The 'upstream' flow of goods is thus more time-consuming and taxing than the 'downstream' flow of money. Friedrich Hayek pertinently described:

> The continuous flow of goods and service is maintained by constant deliberate adjustments, by new dispositions made every day in the light of circumstance not known the day before, by B stepping in at once when A fails to deliver. Even the large and highly mechanized plant keeps going largely

because of an environment upon which it can draw for all sorts of unexpected needs: tiles for its root, stationery for its forms, and all the thousand and one kinds of equipment in which it cannot be self-contained and which the plans for the operation of the plant require to be readily available in the market.[3]

Goods flow relatively slowly through the supply chains. Any 'threshold'[4] in a supply chain makes the flow of goods slower. Tariffs and NTMs are typical 'thresholds'. NTMs per se are official regulations in a country with which traders must comply.[5] Nevertheless, if the NTMs adopted by governments are for protectionist purposes and impose burdens on traders, they by definition constitute *regulatory obstacles*.[6] Besides, *procedural obstacles* are another type of NTM-related obstacles and are 'hurdles that companies face in complying with these [NTM] regulations'.[7] For example, a country may promulgate a stringent regulation on 'licensing procedure with no specific *ex ante* criteria' (E111 under the NTM Classification), under which, for each import, a trader shall apply for licensing that might or might not be granted at the discretion of the issuing authority. The trader, even if he has endeavored to comply with the regulation, might still face problems. For instance, he may have limited access to relevant information and therefore does not know how to proceed; he may be required to submit excessive documents, which he cannot prepare immediately; or he may face delays in obtaining licensing approval if the conditions for his transaction have changed.

In the case of promulgating the NTM regulation, a trader could perceive the NTM itself as a regulatory obstacle; in the case of complying with the NTM regulation, however, the trader would substantially experience the procedural obstacles. Thus, procedural obstacles concern the process of applying a given NTM regulation rather than the stringency of the regulation itself.[8] Procedural obstacles, indubitably, also come under 'thresholds' in the supply chains. An equivalent to procedural obstacles is *red tape*. According to the taxonomy developed by the International Trade Center (ITC), procedural obstacles take the form of administrative burdens related to regulations, information and transparency issues, inconsistent or discriminating behavior of officials, time constraints, unusually high payment and infrastructural challenges (see Table 2.1).

Concerning the manifestation and effect of the specific procedural obstacles posed by a 'large number of different documents' (A1 of the NTM Classification) and 'documentation [that] is difficult to fill out' (A2 of the NTM Classification), for example, the UK Simpler Trade Procedures Board (SITPRO)[10] presented a pithy summary:

A minimum of 12 participants are involved in the simplest international trade transaction. All want information about what is being moved or paid for and the core of that information is the same. Vast amounts of time and resources

Table 2.1 Procedural obstacles

A	**Administrative burdens**	A1	Large number of different documents
		A2	Documentation is difficult to fill out
		A3	Difficulties with translation of documents from or into other languages
		A4	Large number of checks (e.g., inspections, checkpoints, weighbridges)
		A5	Numerous administrative windows/organizations involved
B	**Information/ transparency issues**	B1	Information is not adequately published and disseminated
		B2	No due notice for changes in procedure
		B3	Regulations change frequently
		B4	Requirements and processes differ from information published
C	**Inconsistent or discriminatory behavior of officials**	C1	Inconsistent classification of products
		C2	Inconsistent or arbitrary behavior of officials
D	**Time constraints**	D1	Delay in administrative procedures
		D2	Delay during transportation
		D3	Deadlines set for completion of requirements are too short
E	**Payment**	E1	Unusually high fees and charges
		E2	Informal payment (e.g., bribes)
		E3	Need to hire a local customs agent to get shipment unblocked
F	**Infrastructural challenges**	F1	Limited/inappropriate facilities (e.g., storage, cooling, testing, fumigation)
		F2.	Inaccessible/limited transportation system (e.g., poor roads, road blocks)
		F3	Technological constraints (e.g., information and communications)
G	**Security**	G1	Low security level for persons and goods
H	**Legal constraints**	H1	No advance binding ruling procedure
		H2	No dispute settlement procedure
		H3	No recourse to independent appeal procedure
		H4	Poor intellectual property rights protection, (e.g., breach of copyright, patents, trademarks)
		H5	Lack of recognition (e.g., of national certificates)
I	**Other**	I1	Other obstacles

Source: International Trade Centre (2016)[9]

are spent transferring the information from one document to another. Errors occur frequently; for example, 123 becomes 213, 'car parts' becomes 'car ports'. Error rates in excess of 50% have been consistently recorded in Letters of Credit. Error rates of 30% are not uncommon in manual processing of Customs entries. (123 to 213 sounds a small problem. However, if a ship or aircraft manifest, based on an inaccurate waybill, contains wrong information, time and money would be spent looking for the missing 90 packages; probably claims letters and repudiations would have been sent before the mistake was realized).

UK research has indicated that over 50% of the documents lodged in respect of documentary credits contained errors which delayed settlement by at least two weeks, with the result that exporters lost £70 million per annum. Research in other countries shows a similar situation.

There is no more irate customer than the one who knows that the goods he has ordered are nearby, but the paperwork isn't. In fact, with the growing trend towards purchasing 'just-in-time', delays are likely to mean lost business. If 'local' suppliers can make goods and deliver in a certain time, the 'remote' supplier must compete – or have significant advantages on price, quality or uniqueness.

So trade procedures and related information handling have a decisive effect on the speed, efficiency and reliability of delivery of goods to the buyer and payment to the seller. Complexities and inefficiencies in them create a formidable 'invisible barrier' to improved export performance. This problem is seriously under-estimated in most countries and requires more attention by traders, service industries and governments.

Constant additional costs on transactions to represent the buyer (and their national economies) higher 'arrived' prices of goods; to the seller, at the least, repeated arguments with his customer and loss of profit; in the end probably loss of business.[11]

After rounds of cutting but not eradicating tariffs and NTMs, the global costs of cross-border trade remain a sizeable 2 trillion USD.[12] Procedural obstacles, which entail the application of NTMs, account for a considerable part of this amount. An ITC survey of 8,100 companies across 26 sectors in the European Union's (EU) 28 member states in 2015 and 2016 provided even more evidence. The ITC found that (i) an EU trader faces on average 1.31 procedural obstacles per transaction when exporting to developed countries and 1.52 procedural obstacles per transaction when exporting to developing countries; and (ii) during that period, EU traders experienced 8,649 issues relating to procedural obstacles. The NTM-related burdens on the traders, as the ITC found, are due to procedural obstacles rather than the NTMs.[13]

As procedural obstacles raise trade costs, they become a nuisance (*externality* caused by trade costs) suffered by traders. In other words, procedural obstacles sabotage business environments. Where procedural obstacles abound, trading operations are far from efficient, easy, cheap and joyful. EU traders vividly told their stories in the aforementioned ITC survey:

A British exporter of lamb to Ghana: We have to provide a Health Certificate issued by a vet. The certificate has to be immaculate, as even a small typo could result in the goods being rejected despite there being no threat to human life. There is no possibility to amend the error, and we are given two options – either destroy the goods or return them, both of which cost roughly the same. It is a hit or miss situation, and it can be arbitrary.[14]

An Italian company: We are required to provide a non-preferential certificate of origin but we usually need to wait up to 30 days for it to be issued from the Chamber of Commerce, especially if it needs to obtain several certificates at the same time. To facilitate that process, we would like to be able to retrieve the certificate online, which is currently not possible. Moreover, while it only costs €5, we need to obtain 1,000 certificates each year, which amounts to €5,000 annually, about 2% of the value of the exported product.[15]

A Belgian exporter to Dominican Republic: We have an authorization to put an origin declaration EUR.1 stamp on our invoices instead of sending a EUR.1 certificate[16] with our shipments. However, Dominican Republic Customs officials still want to see the EUR.1 certificate, and it takes 14 days for them to accept the authorized origin declaration EUR.1 stamp on the documents.[17]

A Romanian company: In accordance with EU regulation, when exporting fabricated metal products, we are required to get an export permit from Department of Export Controls (ANCEX) of the Ministry of Foreign Affairs. Getting the results of the application takes 30 days, which results in delays. The document is requested at the Romanian Customs for each exported product regardless of the destination.[18]

Procedural obstacles closely correlate with the performance of customs. 'Every international trade transaction involves at least two customs interventions, one at export and one at import. It is clear, therefore, that the manner in which customs conducts its business has a substantial impact on the movement of goods across international borders'.[19] Customs, which is one of the oldest fiscal machineries, has a rich history that can be traced to the Hellenistic period.[20] As a national gatekeeper, customs works at the front door of a country, which opens to the world. Customs plays a unique role not only in implementing tariffs and other trade policies but also in protecting the borders of its territory. On the one hand, customs applies procedures and documentation requirements in order to control the cross-border movement of goods; these procedures and documentation requirements constitute red tape and impose compliance costs on traders.

Customs compliance costs can be more burdensome than customs duties. For example, reportedly, a large North American automotive exporter's internal costs of preparing separate customs paperwork for exports to various Asian and Pacific countries might exceed the duties paid for the exports.[21] As estimated, costs engendered by customs and related import formalities could be 2 to 5 percent of the merchandise trade value.[22] According to Asia-Pacific Economic Cooperation (APEC), the impact of streamlining customs procedures is larger than that of tariff reductions.[23]

Notably, customs is not the only party responsible for red tape; other border agencies such as licensing authorities, sanitary and phytosanitary inspections, transport and shipping administrations could also be inefficient.

Procedural obstacles, which are emblematic of how poor a business environment is, have a corrosive impact on enterprises' engagement in trade. UNCTAD opined that 'in all countries, potential traders, especially SMEs, are confined to the margins of international trade because of lack of efficient procedures, lack of access to information and information networks, or inadequate support services or trade logistics'.[24] Indeed, enterprises (especially SMEs) that are on the margins of international trade are mostly prone to retreat. 'Greater participation in international trade is a prerequisite for development'[25] so 'ensuring that no potential trader is excluded from international trade is a priority objective for the international community as a whole'.[26]

Undoubtedly, 'the historic signing of the Final Act of the Uruguay Round [. . .] marked the successful conclusion of many years of negotiations on the macro-economic framework required for the emergence of an open, predictable, secure and non-discriminatory trading system'.[27] The international community, however, is conscious that 'efforts made to secure an open trade environment will not bear their full benefits unless the enterprises of all nations can import and export efficiently'.[28] In other words, the prevalent procedural obstacles that impair the efficiency of operating trade would erode the gains from the Uruguay Round. After cutting tariffs and NTMs, it is vital to reduce procedural obstacles, though these 'micro-economic issues of international trade'[29] were 'not of interest to senior management' for a long time.[30]

The international community has embarked on taking measures to overcome procedural obstacles. A collection of measures (e.g., 'simplifying the requirements', 'harmonizing the procedures and the documentation', 'standardizing commercial practices', [and] 'introducing agreed codes for the representation of information elements')[31] prove to be most viable. These measures fall under a concept – *trade facilitation*.

Rise of trade facilitation

In aggregating the measures that diminish procedural obstacles to international trade, the concept of trade facilitation emerges. The concept is indeed a tautology, because the multilateral trading system is at its core 'all about facilitating trade'.[32] In this sense, trade facilitation is an end rather than a means.

The concept of trade facilitation, however, was polysemous under different frameworks. The United Nations Economic Commission for Europe (UNECE) was one of the forerunners in this field. In the 1960s, UNECE established the Working Party on Simplification and Standardization of External Trade Documents. In 1972, UNECE renamed it the Working Party on Facilitation of International Trade Procedures (the well-known 'WP.4'). The International Maritime Organization (IMO) used 'facilitation of international maritime traffic' to title its endeavor 'to prevent unnecessary delays in maritime traffic [. . .] and to secure the highest practicable degree of uniformity in formalities and other procedures'.[33] The World Customs Organization (WCO)[34] focused on 'simplification and harmonization of customs procedures', which is embodied in the International Convention on the Simplification and Harmonization of Customs Procedures (also known as 'Revised Kyoto Convention', or 'RKC'). Those complex headings – no matter how they were titled (e.g., 'facilitation of international trade procedures', 'facilitation of international maritime traffic', 'simplification and standardization of external trade documents', or 'simplification and harmonization of customs procedures') – only concerned parts of trade facilitation.

'All the great things are simple, and many can be expressed in a single word', said Winston Churchill, former British Prime Minister. Eventually, UNCTAD, another trailblazer in this domain, condensed the lengthy terminologies to 'trade facilitation'. 'The United Nations Conference on Trade and Development held in Geneva in the spring of 1964 ushered in a new chapter in the history of United Nations endeavors to accelerate the economic development of developing countries'.[35] The Conference recommended that UNCTAD 'should promote, within the United Nations family, arrangements for [. . .] intergovernmental action for research into [. . .] the simplification of formalities relating to customs procedure [. . .]'.[36] In the 1960s, UNCTAD established the Interregional Advisory Services on Trade Facilitation.[37] Then in 1975, UNCTAD launched a Special Program on Trade Facilitation (FALPRO).[38] However, in the 1990s, UNCTAD was dedicated to facilitating trade in the name of a slightly changed concept – *trade efficiency*. UNCTAD put trade efficiency high on its agenda since its eighth session held in Cartagena, Colombia, in 1992. In the Cartagena Commitment heralded at the session, UNCTAD counted trade efficiency as one component of the betterment of countries' trade conditions[39] that would enhance participation of developing countries and transition economies in the world economy.[40] Therefore, UNCTAD established an *ad hoc* working group on trade efficiency and prepared for an international symposium on trade efficiency in 1994, as the culmination of all related efforts. In the context of UNCTAD, trade efficiency, 'which allows faster, simpler, broader and less costly trade',[41] pursued the same objective as trade facilitation did. UNCTAD made explicit reference to the term of trade facilitation in its official documents during that time. For example, the 1992 Cartagena Commitment stated:

> The Conference acknowledges the efforts made by many countries to increase *trade efficiency* through the use of information technology. Countries are urged to continue such efforts, especially in areas of *trade facilitation* and customs automation. All countries are encouraged to adopt laws, regulations and policies that would reduce barriers to *trade facilitation* through the use of information technology.[42]

The 1994 Columbus Ministerial Declaration on Trade Efficiency stated that '[w]e agree that technical assistance programmes in the following areas deserve immediate attention: training and awareness in the main areas of *trade facilitation* and trade efficiency'.[43] UNCTAD, however, did not elaborate on the meaning of trade facilitation and its relation to trade efficiency. Though its resolute argument that 'trade efficiency can be achieved as a result of trade facilitation' might imply a causality between trade facilitation and trade efficiency, UNCTAD failed to definitely distinguish between the two concepts.

UNECE, however, dissented from propagating the concept of trade efficiency. It argued in an official document in 1996 that 'In the first place 'trade efficiency' is never defined. It may be pretty well what WP.4 understands by trade facilitation'.[44] UNECE further questioned: '[i]s this a good argument for more of the same, even if labeled 'trade efficiency'?' Indeed, the reason why UNECE was in such a huff was that '[i]t is also inherent, in the case presented by UNCTAD, that some thirty years work on facilitation by the [UN]ECE has had no appreciable beneficial effect on costs'. In that year, UNECE transformed WP.4 into the United Nations Center for Trade Facilitation and Electronic Business (UN/CEFACT). WP.4 and UN/CEFACT have developed over 40 recommendations on such issues as the UN Layout Key (UNLK) for Trade Documents, establishment of National Trade Facilitation Bodies (also known as 'PRO Committees'), codes and standards for international trade, UN/EDIFACT (the United Nations Directories for Electronic Data Interchange for Administration, Commerce and Transport) and legal aspects of E-commerce.

The debate subsided by the end of 1996 when the issue of trade facilitation, instead of trade efficiency, was formally tabled at the first session of WTO Ministerial Conference.[45] Even so, the WTO Singapore Ministerial Declaration still underlined the crucial role of UNCTAD, stating that 'careful attention will be given to [. . .] coordinating meetings with those of relevant UNCTAD bodies'.[46]

Since many parties are involved in the movement of goods through the supply chains, a score of institutions with different portfolios play a part in the domain of trade facilitation. These institutions include (i) UN bodies and commissions (e.g., UNCTAD, UNCITRAL,[47] and UNECE); (ii) the 'Bretton Woods' institutions (World Bank and IMF); (iii) specialized international organizations (e.g., IMO, ICAO, OECD and WCO);[48] (iv) regional fora or entities (e.g., APEC, ASEM, MERCOSUR, COMESA, EU and ASEAN); (v) national agencies (e.g., SWE-PRO);[49] and (vi) organizations representing the private sector or relevant industries (e.g., ICC, CIPE,[50] IRU). Regional trade agreements (RTAs) – including free trade agreement (FTA), preferential trading agreement (PTA), customs union and economic integration agreement – are increasingly absorbing trade facilitation provisions with a view to facilitating the bilateral or plurilateral trade between countries.

Box 2.1   Some of the institutions engaged in trade facilitation

International organizations

International Air Transport Association (IATA)
International Civil Aviation Organization (ICAO)
International Chamber of Commerce (ICC)
International Chamber of Shipping (ICS)
International Federation of Freight Forwarders Associations (FIATA)
International Monetary Fund (IMF)
International Maritime Organization (IMO)
International Organization for Standardization (ISO)
International Road Transport Union (IRU)
International Trade Centre UNCTAD/WTO (ITC)
Organization for Economic Co-operation and Development (OECD)
United Nations Conference on Trade and Development (UNCTAD)
United Nations Economic Commission for Europe (UNECE)
United Nations Commission on International Trade Law (UNCITRAL)
United Nations Economic and Social Commission for Asia and the
    Pacific (UNESCAP)
World Bank
World Customs Organization (WCO)
World Trade Organization (WTO)

Regional fora or entities

Asia Europe Meeting (ASEM)
Asia-Pacific Economic Cooperation (APEC)
Association of Southeast Asian Nations (ASEAN)
Common Market for Eastern and Southern Africa (COMESA)
European Union (EU)
North American Free Trade Agreement (NAFTA)
South American Common Market (MERCOSUR)

Although the concept of trade facilitation has risen, it remains undefined, except for a frequently quoted metaphor: 'the plumbing of international trade'.[51] Like the saying 'there are a thousand Hamlets in a thousand people's eyes', the definition of trade facilitation is fluid in the eyes of different interpreters. STI-PRO and UNECE were the first to define trade facilitation in the 1990s. STI-PRO described trade facilitation as 'the systematic rationalization of procedures, information flows and documentation'.[52] UNECE originally defined trade facilitation as 'the systematic rationalization of procedures and documentation for international trade (trade procedures being the activities, practices and formalities involved in collecting, presenting, communicating and processing data required for the movement of goods in international trade)'.[53] UNECE later (including UN/CEFACT) fine-tuned the definition to 'the simplification, standardization and harmonization of procedures and associated information flows required to move goods from seller to buyer and to make payment'.[54] These interpretations set the tone for defining trade facilitation so that other institutions followed the keynote in their respective interpretations.

WTO: The simplification and harmonization of international trade procedures that include activities, practices and formalities related to the collection, presentation, communication and processing of data required for the movement of goods in international trade.[55]

OECD: The simplification and standardization of procedures and associated information flows required to move goods internationally from seller to buyer and to pass payments in the other direction;[56] Policies and measures aimed at easing trade costs by improving efficiency at each stage of the international trade chain.[57]

WCO: The avoidance of unnecessary trade restrictiveness. This can be achieved by applying modern techniques and technologies, while improving the quality of controls in an internationally harmonized manner.[58]

ICC: Improving the efficiency of the processes associated with trading in goods across national borders.[59]

APEC: The simplification, harmonization, use of new technology and other measures to address procedural and administrative impediments to trade (2001);[60] The simplification and rationalization of customs and other administrative procedures that hinder, delay or increase the cost of moving goods across international borders, or to put it another way, cutting red tape at the border for importers and exporters so that goods are delivered in the most efficient and cost-effective manner (2007).[61]

COMESA: The coordination and rationalization of trade procedures and documents relating to the movement of goods from their place of origin to their destination. 'Trade procedures' means activities related to the collection, presentation, processing and dissemination of data and information concerning all activities constituting international trade.[62]

An old Chinese proverb says 'the benevolent see it and call it benevolence, the wise see it and call it wisdom'.[63] People – probably from *Platonic realism*[64] – usually define a thing for their own purposes or reasons and within their knowledge, though the thing has its permanent nature of existence. With regard to trade facilitation, it is understandable that those institutions have their distinct interests in this issue so that they choose to tailor an interpretation that is most suitable for them. Additionally, the definition of trade facilitation is evolving in each institution's own context. It does not matter that there is not a standard definition of trade facilitation. Overall, in a narrow sense, trade facilitation refers to the systematic rationalization of trade procedures and documentation; more broadly, it covers all the regulatory measures that facilitate the movement of goods and money between buyers and sellers along the entire global supply chains.

No matter how trade facilitation is defined, the be-all and end-all of this concept is composed of the following discernible themes[65] that determine what governmental measures might be involved and affected:[66]

Simplification: The superfluous requirements shall be eliminated and the complexity and duplications in trading formalities, procedures and documentation shall be reduced.

Harmonization: The trading procedures, requirements and documentation between nations as well as between national agencies shall be aligned.

Standardization: Internationally or regionally agreed standards or formats shall be developed for the purpose of uniform application of trading practices and rules.

Transparency: The laws, regulations and requirements on trade shall be made easily available, predictable and understandable to interested parties.

Consistency: The trading procedures and requirements should be applied in a consistent manner with integrity so as to minimize uncertainty of doing trade.

Non-discrimination: Rules, procedures and requirements relating to trade shall be applied in a manner that does not discriminate between or among like products or services or trading practitioners in like circumstances.

Due process: Interested parties shall have the rights and channels to claim his rights or comments to the relevant governmental agencies either on specific cases or on trade policies.

Cooperation and coordination: Governmental agencies shall cooperate and coordinate with each other nationally or internationally, and cooperate and coordinate with private sectors, in order to maintain a healthy business environment.

Modernization: Updated regimes and technologies shall be utilized by governmental agencies to adapt to the changed trading circumstances.

Under each theme, the governmental measures that facilitate trade are tangible. For example, there are at least *trade-facilitative measures* in pursuit of *simplification* as below:[67]

Simple formalities for goods permits and licenses. E.g., 'A Contracting State which continues to require export licenses or permits for certain types of goods shall establish simple procedures whereby such licenses or permits can be obtained or renewed rapidly'. (ICAO, Convention on International Civil Aviation, Annex 9:4.14)

The minimum number of copies necessary for declaration. E.g., 'The Customs shall require the lodgment of the original Goods declaration and only the minimum number of copies necessary'. (WCO, Revised Kyoto Convention, General Annex, Chapter 3 Standard 15)

License application forms to be as simple as possible. E.g., 'Applicable forms and, where applicable, renewal forms shall be as simple as possible. Such documents and information as are considered strictly necessary for the proper functioning of the licensing regime may be required on application'. (GATT, Agreement on Import Licensing Procedures, Article 1:5)

Use of aligned official forms. E.g., 'Document is intended for application in the designing of documents related to the [. . .] administrative [. . .] activities constituting external trade'. (UNECE, United Layout Key for Trade Documents, paragraph 16)

Limitation on requests for copies of documents. E.g., 'All parties involved in international maritime transport, including shipping lines, shippers, agents, consignees, customs and ports and other authorities, should limit their requests for copies of Bills of Lading and other maritime transport documents to those which are required absolutely'. (UNECE, Working Party on Facilitation of International Trade Procedures, Recommendation No.12, paragraph 22)

Sanitary and other documents to be simple, widely publicized and standardized. E.g., 'Where Sanitary Certificates or similar documents are required in respect of shipments of certain animals, plants or products thereof, such certificates and documents should be simple and widely publicized and Contracting Parties should cooperate with a view to standardizing such requirements'. (IMO, Convention on Facilitation of International Maritime Traffic, 1965, Annex B:4.3, Recommended Practice)

Trade facilitation generates dividends

Some once argued:

> Trade facilitation may have little of the glamour of headline-hitting trade talks, but recent research suggests that it packs a powerful economic punch. Moreover, it may be the best way and perhaps only way forward for the world trade system in today's difficult political climate.[68]

Regardless of whether the profile of trade facilitation is overrated or underestimated in this argument, it is true that trade facilitation is a win-win scenario, which yields gains not only to governments but also to the business community. Australia's submission to the WTO stated:

> There are many benefits of measures to simplify import and export procedures. For governments it is better information and control, revenue protection and more efficient administration. For business and industry, particularly small and medium sized enterprises it is added certainty and transparency, reduced costs and delays and more competitive import and export conditions. For the community it is lower prices and a more efficient public sector.[69]

The outright effect of trade facilitation comes to the elimination of procedural obstacles and therefore reduction of trade costs, which further lead to these results: augmentation of trade flow, government revenue increase, attractiveness to foreign direct investment,[70] increased economic efficiency, better trade control and security,[71] improved trade competitiveness and enhanced economic growth prospects.[72] In particular, trade facilitation encourages the SMEs – often acknowledged as a major economic growth engine – to take part in international trade.[73] As former US Trade Representative Michael Froman stated, 'Trade facilitation, at its core, is about connecting countries – their farmers and businesses – to the global economy. This is most important for small and medium-sized businesses that have the drive to succeed but lack the resources to manoeuver through red tape'.[74] This statement echoes the argument in Chapter I that SMEs lack the capabilities and resources to bargain over the red tape that causes externality.

In the APEC region, which accounts for nearly half of world trade,[75] the dividends of trade facilitation are obvious: (i) trade facilitation efforts would create a gain of about 0.26 percent of real GDP of APEC economies, nearly twice the gain from tariff liberalization (i.e., tariff reduction);[76] (ii) improved customs procedures by 10 percent would boost intra-APEC imports by a minimum of 0.5 percent;[77] and (iii) if port efficiency and customs environment in the below-APEC-average members are brought half-way to the initial APEC-average, intra-APEC trade would increase by 11.5 percent, including a 9.7 percent gain (117 billion USD) from increased port efficiency and a 1.8 percent gain (22 billion USD) from an improved customs environment.[78]

In global terms, every dollar of assistance provided to support trade facilitation reform in developing countries yields a return of up to 70 dollars in economic benefits.[79] If there is a globally collective action (e.g., an international accord) on trade facilitation, it is assessed that (i) it could reduce the average trade costs for all goods by 14.3 percent, with the decrease in trade costs for manufactured goods at 18 percent and for agricultural goods at 10.4 percent;[80] and (ii) it could cut trade costs by 10 percent in advanced economies and by 13–15.5 percent in

Table 2.2 Benefits of trade facilitation

Government's Benefits	Traders' Benefits
increased effectiveness of control methods	cutting costs and reducing delays
more effective and efficient deployment of resources	faster Customs clearance and release through predictable official intervention
correct revenue yields	enhanced competitiveness
improved trader compliance	
accelerated economic development	simple commercial framework for doing
encouragement of foreign investment	both domestic and international trade

Source: UNECE, 'Trade Facilitation: An Introduction to the Basic Concepts and Benefits', ECE/TRADE/289 (2002)

developing countries. In other words, trade facilitation would have an even bigger impact on trade costs than reducing all most-favored-nation (MFN) tariffs (currently estimated to average around 9 percent) to zero would have.[81] As diminution of global trade costs by 1 percent would increase worldwide income by more than 40 billion USD, most of which would accrue in developing countries,[82] this collective action (e.g., an international accord) could also stimulate the 22 trillion USD world economy by more than 1 trillion USD.[83] 'Simply reducing this red tape by half would have the economic effect of removing all tariffs', pointed out Pascal Lamy, former Director-General of the WTO.[84]

Trade facilitation also brings about potential employment gains. As calculated, the pay-off of trade facilitation will be roughly a global employment gain of 21 million, with 2.6 million additional jobs in developed countries and 18 million in developing countries. Among the developing countries who are the largest group of gainers, there will be an 11 million job increase in East Asia, as well as 2.2 million in East Europe and Central Asia, 2.9 million in Latin America and Caribbean, 0.19 million in Middle East and North Africa, 0.61 million in South Asia and 1 million in Sub-Saharan Africa.[85]

These estimations indicate that even small improvements in trade facilitation can generate sizeable increases in trade and national welfare,[86] and explain why trade facilitation over the years remains high on the trade agenda. Countries have been aware that 'trade facilitation contributes to the overall trade development strategy by optimizing the use of the trade infrastructure and complementing the trade promotion efforts by improving the country's image as an efficient trading center',[87] and that 'the general trade facilitation environment is now often characterized as a critical element of a country's economic infrastructure, because it is so closely linked to economic output and growth'.[88]

'Trade facilitation is about easing access to the global marketplace', commented Angel Gurría, Secretary General of OECD.[89] 'Trade facilitation offers a development dividend for all countries', concluded Robert B. Zoellick, former President of the World Bank.[90]

Notes

1 Marc Bacchetta and Bijit Bora, 'Post-Uruguay Round Market Access Barriers For Industrial Products', *UNCTAD/ITCD/TAB/13* (2001), pp. 1–2.
2 The flows of money and goods are usually accompanied with the flow of trading information.
3 Friedrich Hayek, 'The Use of Knowledge in Society', (1945) 35 *The American Economic Review* 519, p. 524.
4 Similarly, APEC uses the term 'chokepoints' to describe supply chain connectivity problems.
5 International Trade Centre (ITC) and European Commission (EC), *Navigating Non-Tariff Measures: Insights from a Business Survey in the European Union* (2016), p. 6.
6 Ibid.
7 Ibid.

8 UNCTAD, *Non-Tariff Measures: Evidence from Selected Developing Countries and Future Research Agenda*, UNCTAD/DITC/TAB/2009/3 (2010), p. xvii.

9 See International Trade Centre (ITC), *Thailand: Company Perspectives – An ITC Series on Non-Tariff Measures* (2016), p. 84; *Mauritius: Company Perspectives – An ITC Series on Non-Tariff Measures* (2014), p. 100. However, in *Navigating Non-Tariff Measures: Insights From A Business Survey in the European Union* (2016), the procedural obstacles itemized by the ITC are slightly different from those as above. For example, in the survey in the European Union, Item G is 'lack of recognition/ accreditations', including G1. 'facilities lacking international accreditation/recognition', G2. 'other problems with international recognition (e.g., lack of recognition of national certificates)'.

10 SITPRO was a non-departmental public body established by the British Government in 1970 to guide, stimulate and assist the rationalization of international trade procedures and documentation and the information flows associated with them. In other words, SITPRO was an advocate for trade facilitation.

11 SITPRO, 'Facilitating Trade: Draft Guidelines on Better Trade Practice', TD/B/WG.2/6/Add.1/Part I (1993), paras. 3.2.6–3.3.5.

12 Pascal Lamy, 'A Trade Facilitation Deal Could Give a $1 Trillion Boost to World Economy', speech to the Chittagong Chamber of Commerce in Bangladesh on February 1, 2013, www.wto.org/english/news_e/sppl_e/sppl265_e.htm.

13 See International Trade Centre (ITC) and European Commission (EC), *Navigating Non-Tariff Measures: Insights From A Business Survey in the European Union* (ITC and EC, 2016).

14 Ibid., p. 9.

15 Ibid., p. 12.

16 To claim preferential treatment under the Generalized System of Preferences or a free trade agreement, traders must justify their claim by requesting a movement certificate named EUR.1 or EUR-MED or Form A (to import under GSP). It is essentially a proof of origin requested by the customs administrations of the importing country and released by the competent national authorities according to the EU regulation. The certificate can occasionally be replaced by other declarations made out by exporters that must be first approved by the customs authorities. See http://ec.europa.eu/taxation_customs/sites/taxation/files/resources/documents/customs/customs_duties/rules_origin/preferential/guidelines_movements_certificates_en.pdf.

17 ITC and EC, See *supra* note 13, p. 12.

18 Ibid, p. 14.

19 UNCTAD, 'Draft Guidelines on Key Sector on Trade Efficiency', TD/B/WG.2/11/Add.1 (1994), para. 1.

20 Hironori Asakura, *World History of the Customs and Tariffs* (WCO, 2003), pp. 19–20.

21 See UNESCAP and ADB, *Designing and Implementing Trade Facilitation in Asia and the Pacific* (UNESCAP and ADB, 2013), p. 3.

22 Brian Rankin Staples, 'Trade Facilitation: Improving the Invisible Infrastructure', in Bernard Hoekman, Aaditya Mattoo and Philip English (eds.), *Development, Trade and the WTO: A Handbook* (World Bank, 2002), pp. 139–148.

23 See APEC, 'Assessing APEC Trade Liberalization and Facilitation', 99-EC-01.1(1999).

24 Columbus Ministerial Declaration on Trade Efficiency, declared at the United Nations International Symposium on Trade Efficiency organized by UNCTAD (1994), para. 4.

25 Ibid., para. 1.

26 Ibid., para. 4.

27 Ibid., para. 2.

28 Ibid., para. 2.
29 Ibid., para. 2.
30 SITPRO, 'Facilitating Trade: Draft Guidelines on Better Trade Practice', TD/B/WG.2/6/Add.1/Part I (1993), para. 1.6.
31 UNCTAD, 'Compendium of Trade Facilitation Recommendations', TD/B/WG.2/6 (1993), para. 1.1.1.
32 Nora Neufeld, 'The Long And Winding Road: How WTO Members Finally Reached A Trade Facilitation Agreement', WTO Staff Working Paper, ERSD-2014–06 (2014).
33 See Convention on Facilitation of International Maritime Traffic.
34 The WCO's formal name is the Customs Cooperation Council (CCC).
35 See United Nations, *Proceedings of the United Nations Conference on Trade and Development*, E/CONF.46/141 Vol. I (1964), p. iii.
36 Ibid., Annex A.II.4, p. 31.
37 The Interregional Advisory Services on Trade Facilitation was initiated under the UNECE Resolution 4(XXIV) which was endorsed by the United Nations Economic and Social Council, and financed by the United Nations Development Programme.
38 See UN Economic Commission for Latin America, 'Trade Procedures in the Caribbean', CARIB/INT/82/12 (1982), pp. 19–20.
39 Other components included access to markets and structural adjustment; effective policies in the field of commodities; further evolution of the international debt strategy; rapid and balanced expansion of the service sectors in developing economies; exploiting the interrelationship between technology and investment; and strong policies for human resources development.
40 Columbus Ministerial Declaration on Trade Efficiency, para. 63 A (1).
41 Ibid., para. 3.
42 Cartagena Commitment, para. 161.
43 Columbus Ministerial Declaration on Trade Efficiency, para. 11.
44 UNECE, TRADE/WP.4/R.1260 (1996).
45 It already rose in WTO bodies before the ministerial conference, e.g., Council for Trade in Goods, General Council. See WTO, G/C/W/67, G/C/M/15, WT/GC/W/46.
46 WTO Singapore Ministerial Declaration, WT/MIN(96)/DEC.
47 The work of UNCITRAL (The United Nations Commission on International Trade Law) on trade facilitation focuses on electronic commerce and electronic signature, including implementing e-applications such as the single window.
48 IMO and ICAO are UN Specialized Agencies, while the OECD and WCO are independent inter-governmental organizations unaffiliated with the UN.
49 Swedish Trade Procedures Council.
50 Center for International Private Enterprise.
51 Staples, see *supra* note 22, p. 139.
52 SITPRO, see *supra* note 30, para. 3.1.3.
53 UNECE, 'UNECE Facts about the Working Party on Facilitation of International Trade Procedures', TRADE/WP.4/INF.91, TD/B/FAL/INF.91; See also TD/B/WG.2/6.
54 UN/CEFACT, 'An Integrated Strategic Framework for UN/CEFACT Deliverables', ECE/TRADE/C/CEFACT/2013/8/Rev.1.
55 WTO, 'Trade facilitation', http://gtad.wto.org/trta_subcategory.aspx?cat=33121.
56 In fact, OECD used the definition presented by John Raven, former President of the International Express Carriers Conference (IECC), in a communication to the OECD Secretariat on May 18, 2001, see TD/TC/WP(2001)21/FINAL.
57 OECD, 'Trade Facilitation Indicators: The Impact on Trade Costs', TAD/TC/WP(2011)5/FINAL.

58 See WCO, 'What is Securing and Facilitating Legitimate Global Trade', www. wcoomd.org/en/topics/facilitation/overview/customs-procedures-and-facilitation. aspx.

59 See ICC, 'ICC recommendations for trade facilitation through effective customs duty relief programmes', 104–29 (2004); 'Updated ICC recommendations for a WTO agreement on trade facilitation', 104–53 (2007).

60 See APEC Principles on Trade Facilitation (2001).

61 See APEC Second Trade Facilitation Action Plan (2007).

62 COMESA Treaty, Chapter 2, Article 2.

63 It originated from *The Book of Changes (Zhou Yi)*.

64 Platonic realism is a philosophical term referred to as the idea of realism regarding the existence of universals or abstract objects. The philosophy is expounded in the Theory of Forms, which reflects the belief expressed by Socrates in some of Plato's dialogs. According to Socrates, solutions to the problems of the universal are roughly archetypes or abstract representations of the many types of things, and properties we feel and see around us, that can only be perceived by reason.

65 The themes of trade facilitation are not exhaustive. There might be other themes, e.g., efficiency, protection and compliance, integrity. See WTO, G/C/W/126 (1998).

66 Krista Lucenti, 'Is There a Case for More Multilateral Rules on Trade Facilitation?', Chapter IV of *The Singapore Issues and The World Trading System: The Road to Cancun and Beyond*, a volume edited by Simon J. Evenett and the Swiss State Secretariat of Economic Affairs.

67 See UN/CEFACT, *Compendium of Trade Facilitation Recommendations* (2001).

68 Gary Clyde Hufbauer, Martin Vieiro and John S.Wilson, 'Trade facilitation matters!' September 2012, www.voxeu.org/article/trade-facilitation-matters.

69 WTO, G/C/W/443 (2002).

70 OECD, TD/TC(2005)12/FINAL.

71 UNECE, 'Trade Facilitation: An Introduction to the Basic Concepts and Benefits', ECE/TRADE/289 (2002).

72 ADB, *Designing and Implementing Trade Facilitation in Asia and Pacific* (ADB, 2009), pp. 5–8.

73 Ibid.

74 Michael Froman, keynote remarks at the World Trade Organization Public Forum on Innovation and the Global Trading System on October 1, 2013, https://ustr. gov/about-us/policy-offices/press-office/speeches/transcripts/2013/october/ froman-wto-innovation-global-trade.

75 APEC economies account for approximately 59 percent of world GDP, and about 49 percent of world trade in 2016. See the White House, 'Fact Sheet: 24th Annual APEC Economic Leaders' Meeting', November 20, 2016, www. whitehouse.gov/the-press-office/2016/11/20/fact-sheet-24th-annual-apec-economic-leaders-meeting.

76 APEC, *The Impact of Trade Liberalization in APEC* (1997), p. iii.

77 See OECD, TD/TC/WP(2005)12/FINAL, p. 16.

78 Ibid.

79 Robert B. Zoellick et al., 'How to Make Trade Easier', June 27, 2012, www. project-syndicate.org/commentary/how-to-make-trade-easier.

80 WTO, *World Trade Report 2015 – Speeding up trade: benefits and challenges of implementing the WTO Trade Facilitation Agreement* (WTO, 2015), p. 70.

81 Ibid., p. 78.

82 OECD, 'Trade facilitation agreement would add billions to global economy, says OECD', March 5, 2013, www.oecd.org/trade/trade-facilitation-agreement-would-add-billions-to-global-economy-says-oecd.htm.

83 Pascal Lamy, see *supra* note 12.
84 Ibid.
85 Gary Hufbauer and Jeffrey Schott, *Payoff from the World Trade Agenda* (The Peterson Institute for International Economics, 2013), p. 12.
86 Krista Lucenti, *Is There a Case for More Multilateral Rules on Trade Facilitation? (2004)*, p. 24.
87 UNESCAP, *Trade Facilitation Handbook for the Greater Mekong Subregion* (United Nations, 2002), p. 2.
88 WTO, WT/GC/W/254 (1999).
89 OECD, 'Trade Facilitation Agreement Would Add Billions to Global Economy, says OECD', March 5, 2013, http://www.oecd.org/trade/trade-facilitation-agreement-would-add-billions-to-global-economy-says-oecd.htm.
90 Robert B. Zoellick et al., see *supra* note 79.

3 An international accord on trade facilitation?

Trade facilitation, together with cuts of tariffs and NTMs, serves as a solution to the externality of trade costs. According to the Coase theorem, the government is responsible for building up a healthy business environment that benefits traders. Therefore, there are normally two forces that propel the trade facilitation agenda ahead: one is the business community; and the other is the government. However, neither of the two forces would carry out those trade facilitation initiatives which only prevail within a country's own territory. A trader not only has stout interests in relishing a trade-facilitative business environment in his country but also is keen on seeing expeditious, predictable and cheap delivery of its goods to foreign markets. At the same time, the governments of those countries, whose trade accounts for a considerable portion of its economy, are correspondingly inclined to 'sell' their home-made trade facilitation initiatives abroad. In this regard, trade facilitation entails multinational engagement, as well as universal rules for countries. An international accord on trade facilitation is therefore essential.

Business community's call for an international accord on trade facilitation

The concept of 'public sphere', created by the *Constructivists*, sets the scene for a business community's call for an accord on trade facilitation. As the *Constructivists* argue:

> The idea of the public sphere [. . .] designates a theater in modern societies in which political participation is enacted through the medium of talk. It is the space in which citizens deliberate their common affairs, hence, an institutionalized arena of discursive interaction. This arena is conceptually distinct from the state; it is a site for the production and circulation of discourses that can in principle be critical of the state.[1]

Immediately after World War II, the International Trade Organization (ITO) and the General Agreement on Tariffs and Trade (GATT) under construction afforded the most capacious 'public sphere' for trade talks.

Meanwhile, there need to be discussants in the 'public sphere'. The International Chamber of Commerce (ICC),[2] founded in the early twentieth century by a handful of entrepreneurs as 'the merchants of peace',[3] has been representing the business community in a range of United Nations and its specialized agencies' activities since 1946 and holding 'top-level consultative status'.[4] On trade facilitation, the ICC always acts as the most eloquent discussant. Speaking for the world business community, the ICC claimed to be a stakeholder on this subject (though not in the name of trade facilitation) in the 1940s:

[The ICC] believes that the expansion of world trade demands a drastic simplification of administrative procedure and formalities whatever the policy followed. The importance of this to the future development of world trade and travel cannot be over-emphasized. Cumbersome, costly, obscure and changeable regulations and formalities are often as severe a hindrance as the policies from which they arise. The policies are usually subject to public discussion and control and are enforced by the normal legislative process. The administrative procedure is too frequently devised ad hoc, without proper consultation of the interests concerned, and goes far beyond the purpose for which it was originally designed. It acts as an additional obstacle or an additional protection, rather than simply as a mechanism for giving effect to the control or protection established by law.[5]

In June 1947, the ICC's Montreux Congress, as its first post-war gathering,[6] endorsed the report on Barriers to the International Transport of Goods (ICC Brochure 121), which primarily brought forward recommendations for the simplification and standardization of administrative formalities and regulations connected with international trade and transport.[7] The ICC urged that 'immediate action be taken by governments, both nationally and internationally, to give effect to these recommendations which are of particular importance to trading and transport interests throughout the world'.[8] For example, in respect of documentary requirements, it recommended:

Reduction of the number of documents required in the international transport of goods to the following three or at most four, which should be sufficient for all legitimate governmental requirements as well as for the needs of the trader and carrier:

a) transport document (bill of lading, consignment note);
b) commercial invoice in standardized form;
c) packing list when necessary (it obviously serves no useful purpose in the case of goods in bulk like grain);
d) in the case of sea and air transport, the manifest.

Only a reasonable number of copies of such documents should be required.[9]

In 1949, the ICC's Quebec Congress adopted the resolution on Invisible Barriers to Trade and Travel (ICC Brochure 130) on the basis of a report prepared by its Committee on Customs Technique. The ICC Brochure 130 encompassed 'nine questions of outstanding importance which it believes governments might usefully select as a starting point for immediate action',[10] including (i) formalities and regulations connected with the administration of import quotas, licensing systems and exchange control; (ii) the nationality of goods; (iii) methods of ad valorem valuation; (iv) documentary requirements and consular formalities; (v) publicity for regulations and charges; (vi) treatment of samples and advertising material; (vii) marks of origin; (viii) standardization of customs nomenclatures; and (ix) temporary admission of imports.[11] The ICC brought forward recommendations regarding those questions, for example:

Publicity for Regulations and Charges

The competent authorities of each country should publish promptly, and in an easily accessible and understandable form, not only its tariff of customs duties but also all accessory charges and taxes levied in connection with the goods. This should be accompanied by a clear and binding statement of the regulations and formalities which importers and exporters are obliged to observe, covering not only customs matters but also any requirements arising out of quota, licensing, or exchange control regulations.

At that moment, the ICC pinned its faith on the Havana Charter for an International Trade Organization ('the Havana Charter' for short) and the GATT, which predominated in constituting the post-war world trading system. The Brochure 130 stated:

The ICC welcomes the provisions of Section E of Chapter IV and other relevant provisions of the Havana Charter[12] as well as the corresponding articles of the General Agreement on Tariffs and Trade. Although there are points of detail on which it dissents from these provisions, it believes that their application, in the spirit as well as in the letter, by all governments would be a useful step forward.[13]

Then, the 1951 ICC Lisbon Congress published its resolution on International Trade and Governmental Regulations (ICC Brochure 153), which covered the questions: (i) valuation of goods for customs purposes; (ii) nationality of manufactured goods; (iii) documentary requirements; (iv) consular formalities; (v) formalities connected with quantitative restrictions; and (vi) customs treatment of samples and advertising material. The Brochure 153 was aimed at amplifying, completing and clarifying the ICC's previous recommendations for the relevant questions.[14] Convinced that the simplification of formalities could not go without administrative reforms, the ICC proposed to create not only an independent committee in each country to overhaul the administrative machinery but also an international committee to start work on standardizing the reforms.[15] When it appeared certain that the Havana Charter would not come into effect, the ICC had recourse to the GATT and argued that '[t]he prime responsibility is placed squarely on the shoulders of the Contracting Parties to GATT, who have signed a definite undertaking[16] to proceed rapidly with reforms of administrative procedure'.[17] The ICC subsequently submitted its Brochure 130 and Brochure 153, together with a dozen of other documents, to the sixth Session of GATT Contracting Parties for their consideration.[18] Because the GATT was a 'provisional agreement', the ICC yet reaffirmed in its communication to the GATT Contracting Parties that 'an intergovernmental organization for the promotion of world trade on a multilateral basis would be of great value' and further suggested that 'the organization thus created give particular attention to bringing about as rapidly as possible a far-reaching simplification of administrative procedure and formalities in international trade'.[19]

With the stillbirth of the ITO and the entry into force of the GATT at last, the ICC's discourse on trade facilitation in the 'public sphere' of multilateral trading system settled. Some of the ICC's recommendations were laid aside, while some (e.g., valuation of goods for customs purposes, reduction of the number of documents, publicity for regulations and charges) were absorbed by relevant GATT articles (e.g., Article VII, VIII and X).

Establishment of the WTO turned the page on the history of the post-war world trading system which had been governed by the GATT for almost 50 years. On the occasion of the first WTO Ministerial Conference in 1996, the ICC was a strong supporter of putting trade facilitation on the WTO agenda.[20] In 1997, the ICC underlined to WTO Member governments that 'world business urgently needs a comprehensive set of rules for ensuring high standards for customs procedures and practices in the form of a binding, enforceable and truly multilateral agreement'.[21] In 2001, the ICC consolidated its call for an international accord on trade facilitation in its policy statement that '[p]olitical commitment to multilaterally binding rules on trade facilitation, administered by the WTO, would steer reform in a consistent direction and benefit all parties in international transactions'.[22] In 2007, the ICC, in light of the substantive progress in WTO negotiations on trade facilitation, stated:

> An important role for an International Trade Facilitation Agreement (ITFA) will be to define the responsibilities of governments involved in complex transactions covering export, transit, and final import of the goods. ICC's aim is to encourage the establishment of a trade facilitation agreement [. . .] through the establishment of mutually agreed rules covering trade procedures that improve the management of traded goods as they cross national borders.[23]

International accords on trade facilitation in history

At source, a country's initiative in trade facilitation is mostly spontaneous, because its government adopts trade-facilitative measures out of the pressure at borders brought about by the burgeoning trade volumes. In the parlance of international relations, this is a 'self-help' behavior (viz. the country merely does this domestically rather than requests its trading partners to do so). On a global scale, these spontaneous initiatives, however, are implemented by individual countries in such an 'anarchic' way that they are scattered and leaderless instead of being gathered to allow a universal governance. Even though 'anarchy is what states make of it',[24] trade at any rate links countries – exportation of one country means importation of its trading partner, and *vice versa*. A country whose trade accounts for a considerable portion of its economy is apt to take promoting its own trade facilitation initiatives abroad (mainly to its important trading partners) as one of its state interests. This country, therefore, is usually a proponent of an international accord on trade facilitation.

Constructivism would be instrumental in rationalizing an international record on trade facilitation. The school of Constructivism stems from the *Grotian tradition*, which views that international order is based on norms and rules that guide behaviors of countries in an 'international society'.[25] In the opinion of constructivists, conventions are norms that foster and give rise to games of countries' coordination.[26] Constructivists provide a relatively peaceful perception that state interests are given their meanings and constructed as a result of social interaction in an international society.[27] In the process of social interaction, two basic tenets of Constructivism 'that the structures of human association are determined primarily by shared ideas rather than material forces, and that the identities and interests of purposive actors are constructed by these shared ideas rather than given by nature'[28] are increasingly accepted. When it comes to trade facilitation – an issue not about power or values but of economic meaning, this perception sets the stage for envisaging the construction of trade facilitation accords by virtue of sharing ideas, taking collective actions and furthermore setting up universal rules in the context of international relations. Immediately after World War I ended, the international community had started such efforts.

In 1920, the League of Nations was founded. According to Article 23 (e) of the Covenant of the League of Nations, 'the Members of the League will make provision to secure and maintain freedom of communications and of transit and equitable treatment for the commerce of all Members of the League'. This article, as a compromise, reconciled the conflicting views regarding whether the most-favored-nation (MFN) treatment should only be limited to a state's allies or be operated in international harmony.[29] This article was seemingly in line with the third of the Fourteen Points presented by then US President Woodrow Wilson:

> The removal, so far as possible, of all economic barriers and the establishment of an equality of trade conditions among all the nations consenting to the peace and associating themselves for its maintenance.

'With a view to applying between themselves the principle and the stipulations of Article 23 of the Covenant of the League of Nations with regard to the equitable treatment of commerce',[30] over 30 countries held a conference on November 3, 1923 in Geneva, and concluded the International Convention Relating to the Simplification of Customs Formalities.[31] In this Convention, those countries undertook that 'their commercial relations shall not be hindered by excessive, unnecessary or arbitrary customs or other similar formalities',[32] and therefore figured out a broad range of disciplines that would simplify customs formalities. There were two remarkable articles in this Convention: (i) Article 4 which was about publication of regulations relating to customs formalities; and (ii) Article 14 which was about simplification of customs formalities for the purpose of rapid release of goods.

Article 4

The Contracting States shall publish promptly all regulations relating to customs and similar formalities and all modifications therein, which have not been already published, in such a manner as to enable persons concerned to become acquainted with them and to avoid the prejudice which might result from the application of customs formalities of which they are ignorant.

The Contracting States agree that no customs regulations shall be enforced before such regulations have been published, either in the Official Journal of the country concerned or through some other suitable official or private channel of publicity.

This obligation to publish in advance extends to all matters affecting tariffs and import and export prohibitions or restrictions.

In cases, however, of an exceptional nature, when previous publication would be likely to injure the essential interests of the country, the provisions of the second and third paragraphs of this Article will lose their obligatory force. In such cases, however, publication shall, so far as possible, take place simultaneously with the enforcement of the measure in question.

Article 14

The Contracting States shall consider the most appropriate methods of simplifying and making more uniform and reasonable, whether by means of individual or concerted action, the formalities relating to the rapid passage of goods through the customs, the examination of travelers' luggage, the system of goods in bond and warehousing charges [. . .]

Furthermore, Article 14 had an annex that afforded a series of recommendations for the countries' favorable consideration.

Box 3.1   Elements of the Annex to Article 14

A   Rapid passage of goods through the customs

1   Clearance of goods at inland offices or warehouses shall be encouraged.

2   The lead or other customs seals affixed by a State to goods in transit or on their way to warehouses should be recognized and respected by other States.

3   The States should facilitate the clearance of perishable goods outside ordinary office hours and on days other than working days; and authorize the lading and unlading of vessels and boats outside the ordinary customs-house working days and office hours.

4   The consignee should be free to declare goods to the customs in person or by some person designated by him.

5   The States may adopt a printed form, including the customs declaration, for the party concerned to fill in the certificate of verification and the receipt for the payment of the import duties.

6   The States should refrain from inflicting severe penalties for trifling infractions of customs procedure or regulations.

7   The States should consider the possibility of using postal money-orders or cheques for the payment or guarantee of customs duties.

8   The customs authorities should be authorized to refund on re-exportation of goods the duties paid on their importation; no export duties should be imposed when such goods are re-exported.

9   Suitable measures should be taken to avoid delay in the passage intended for advertisement.

10   The office, which grants the consular visa for purposes of customs formalities, should let the hours of business fit in with the local commercial circles.

B   Examination of baggage

11   The practice of examining hand baggage in trains should be generally applied.

12   The examination of travelers' baggage should be extended to journeys by sea and on rivers.

13   Notices stating the charges and duties payable on the chief articles which travelers usually carry and a list of the articles which are prohibited from importation should be posted on the customs-house premises and in railway carriages and on boats.

C   Treatment of goods in warehouses and warehousing charges

14   The States should establish or approve the establishment of warehouses for goods that require special care.

15 Warehouse charges should be drawn up on a reasonable basis to cover general expenses and interest on the capital laid out.

16 All persons having goods in warehouses should be allowed to withdraw damaged goods.

D   Goods shown on the manifest but not landed

17 The payment of import duties should not be required in the case of goods which are not actually introduced into the country.

E   Cooperation of the services concerned

18 It is desirable to develop the system of international railway stations and to obtain effective cooperation among the various national organizations established therein.

In fact, the International Convention Relating to the Simplification of Customs Formalities is still valid today. Even in the 1960s, some countries (e.g., Israel,[33] Malawi,[34] Niger,[35] Singapore)[36] acceded to this Convention; and in the 1990s, some countries (e.g., Slovakia,[37] Zimbabwe)[38] became contracting parties in succession.

Under the auspices of the League of Nations, the World Economic Conference[39] was held in Geneva in May 1927. This conference was not diplomatic and bound no one because the delegates participated in their individual capacities (not on behalf of their countries).[40] Nevertheless, the delegates discussed in great detail the problems of international trade,[41] and advocated collective action 'with a view to encouraging the expansion of international trade on an equitable basis by removing or lowering the barriers to international trade which are set up by excessive customs tariffs'.[42] Besides focus on tariff issues (in particular MFN treatment), the Conference dealt with trade formalities. Regarding the consular fees in connection with the issuance of visas for commercial travelers and consignments of goods, for example, the Conference pertinently recommended:

Consular fees should be a charge, fixed in amount and not exceeding the cost of issue, rather than an additional source of revenue. Arbitrary or variable consular fees cause not only an increase of charges, which is at times unexpected, but also an unwarrantable uncertainty in trade.

In spite of the occurrence of war afterwards, much of the spirits embodied in the accords on trade facilitation at the time of League of Nations were resurrected in the course of building up the post-war world trading system. Some of the legalese used in the 1920s was carried forward – almost intact – by the succeeding Suggested Charter for an International Trade Organization of the United Nations (the

1946 US proposal) and the 1948 Havana Charter (instituted largely on the basis of American and British proposals). For example, the Havana Charter stipulated:

Article 38

Publication and Administration of Trade Regulations

1   Laws, regulations, judicial decisions and administrative rulings of general application made effective by any Member, pertaining to the classification or the valuation of products for customs purposes, or to rates of duty, taxes or other charges, or to requirements, restrictions or prohibitions on imports or exports or on the transfer of payments therefor, or affecting their sale, distribution, transportation, insurance, warehousing, inspection, exhibition, processing, mixing or other use, shall be published promptly in such a manner as to enable governments and traders to become acquainted with them. Agreements affecting international trade policy which are in force between the government or governmental agency of any Member country and the government or governmental agency of any other country shall also be published. Copies of such laws, regulations, decisions, rulings and agreements shall be communicated promptly to the Organization.

2   No measure of general application taken by any Member effecting an advance in a rate of duty or other charge on imports under an established and uniform practice or imposing a new or more burdensome requirement, restriction or prohibition on imports, or on the transfer of payments therefor, shall be enforced before such measure has been officially made public.

Article 36

Formalities Connected with Importation and Exportation

1   The Members recognize that all fees and charges of whatever character (other than import and export duties and other than taxes within the purview of Article 18) imposed by governmental authorities on or in connection with importation or exportation should be limited in amount to the approximate cost of services rendered and should not represent an indirect protection to domestic products or a taxation of imports or exports for fiscal purposes. The Members also recognize the need for reducing the number and diversity of such fees and charges, for minimizing the incidence and complexity of import and export formalities, and for decreasing and simplifying import and export documentation requirements.

Not able to be ratified by the US Congress, the Havana Charter eventually failed to come into force and the defunct ITO became 'the first casualty of the post-war political environment'.[43] But the GATT, which were negotiated during the 1947 Geneva Conference (only intended as a supposedly 'interim' arrangement and with limited purpose of pending approval of the Havana Charter), remained as a treaty that governed the multilateral trading system (without a planned administrative institution) until establishment of the WTO. The GATT also took care of the above issues in its Article X and VIII:

Article X:

Publication and Administration of Trade Regulations

1 Laws, regulations, judicial decisions and administrative rulings of general application, made effective by any contracting party, pertaining to the classification or the valuation of products for customs purposes, or to rates of duty, taxes or other charges, or to requirements, restrictions or prohibitions on imports or exports or on the transfer of payments therefor, or affecting their sale, distribution, transportation, insurance, warehousing, inspection, exhibition, processing, mixing or other use, shall be published promptly in such a manner as to enable governments and traders to become acquainted with them.
   Agreements affecting international trade policy which are in force between the government or a governmental agency of any contracting party and the government or governmental agency of any other contracting party shall also be published.

2 No measure of general application taken by any contracting party effecting an advance in a rate of duty or other charge on imports under an established and uniform practice, or imposing a new or more burdensome requirement, restriction or prohibition on imports, or on the transfer of payments therefor, shall be enforced before such measure has been officially published.

[. . .]

Article VIII:

Fees and Formalities connected with Importation
and Exportation

3 (a) All fees and charges of whatever character (other than import and export duties and other than taxes within the purview of Article III) imposed by contracting parties on or in connection with importation or exportation shall be limited in amount to the approximate cost of services rendered and shall not represent an indirect protection to domestic products or a taxation of imports or exports for fiscal purposes.

[. . .]

4 The provisions of this Article shall extend to fees, charges, formalities and requirements imposed by governmental authorities in connection with importation and exportation, including those relating to:

   (a) consular transactions, such as consular invoices and certificates;

[. . .]

A renovated accord for today?

There had already been the case of constituting international accords on trade facilitation nearly a century ago, albeit they were not under the title of trade facilitation. However, business environment today is more complex than it was decades ago. The early international accords, such as the International Convention Relating to the Simplification of Customs Formalities and the GATT 1947 (later translated into the GATT 1994), turn out to be deficient when they are governing trade facilitation, which has its contemporary meanings. For example, the GATT Article X provides that:

1   Laws, regulations, judicial decisions and administrative rulings of general application [. . .] shall be published [. . .] in such a manner as to enable governments and traders to become acquainted with them.
2   No measure of general application [. . .] shall be enforced before such measure has been officially published.

Legal text in this article is disputable: Article X:1 refers to 'laws, regulations, judicial decisions and administrative rulings of general application', and Article X:2 talks about 'measure of general application'; Article X:1 does not have the word 'officially' which is present in Article X:2. Thus, several questions arise, for example: (i) why shall the two subparagraphs have subjects in different wordings – what are the distinctions between 'laws, regulations, judicial decisions and administrative rulings of general application' (q.v. Article X:1) and 'measure of general application' (q.v. Article X:2); is there any 'measure of general application' that does not take the form of 'laws, regulations, judicial decisions and administrative rulings of general application'? (ii) what if the 'laws, regulations, judicial decisions and administrative rulings of general application' (q.v. Article X:1) are not published 'officially' (q.v. Article X:2)? (iii) considering the emergence of new media and information technology (e.g., internet) since the 1940s, in what manner shall the publication be appropriately done today – does a trader who is used to searching information from websites need to stand in front of a bulletin board to see what is published? and (iv) how long is the interval between the official publication and the enforcement of the 'measure of general application' (q.v. Article X:2) – are two weeks too short or are six months too long?

Regarding Question (ii), the Panel on *EC – IT Products* concluded the finding:

> While Article X:1 requires that measures be 'published,' Article X:2 refers to measures having been 'officially published.' The absence of the adverb 'officially' in Article X:1, which is present in Article X:2, clarifies that the publication of the relevant measure does not need to be in an 'official' publication in order to satisfy Article X:1.[44]

But for the rest of the questions, there are no answers thus far. Aware that 'within this new trading environment, the regulatory infrastructures of all [. . .]

developed and developing economies alike [. . .] need to more actively keep pace with the technological advancements and developments in logistical practices',[45] some countries' governments hence advocate to revamp the existing international accords or to dedicatedly constitute a new one for this traditional subject.

Why the WTO?

Where is the suitable institution to administer this accord?

International accords are multifarious. An international accord might be a convention globally applicable to a wide range of states, or a regional deal adopted by limited participants; it might be an independent treaty, or the one annexed to a family of agreements; it might be mandatory on a *pacta sunt servanda* (treaties should be observed) basis, or be a 'soft' law that is not enforceable.

In light of the one-century spadework done by the international community, the accord on trade facilitation, which is of compelling significance for today's world trade, should not be a modest one. When drawing up an accord, the elements, such as the scope of participants, institutional arrangement for administering the accord and enforceability of the rules, that characterize this accord are essential. The new accord on trade facilitation is supposed to be at least endowed with the following merits:

(i) **Political engagement is firmly in place.** A thoroughgoing trade facilitation initiative should be based on some prerequisites (such as a top-down reform on trade and customs regimes, mobilization of border management resources and readiness for formulating or amending the legislation), which all in all cannot go without political engagement. If this accord is infused with a firm political engagement (hopefully at the ministerial or even cabinet level), it will ensure a robust trade facilitation campaign.

(ii) **A large number of countries contract in.** The more signatories this accord has, the more influential it will be. It is better to encourage as many countries as possible to contract into the accord, or to find an existing host where plenty of countries have already been gathered, so that the broadest joint effect can be reached.

(iii) **A broad range of issues can be covered.** Trade facilitation is a cross-cutting subject covering a series of issues like transparency, simplification of trade procedures, customs modernization, standardization, border cooperation and coordination, etc. Those concrete issues relevant to trade facilitation should comprehensively blend into this accord.

(iv) **Rules are binding and enforceable.** The rules set up in this accord shall bind any of its signatory to fulfillment of its obligations in order for this accord to take effect. Otherwise, a signatory would be subject to other signatories' remonstrance, as prescribed in the accord, for its non-compliance with the rules.

(v) **The administrative institution can take on a role in the synergy with other stakeholders.** Trade facilitation is an area in which various stakeholders (public or private) have different interests and propositions. The institution that administers this accord shall have the capability of synergizing the stakeholders involved towards an agreed scheme.

(vi) **Sufficient resources are within the reach of the administrative institution.** If this accord universally applies to countries on different development levels, implementation of the accord by developing countries and least developed countries logically entails assistance and support. The institution that administers this accord should be able to obtain resources (such as funds, experts and knowledge) to make sure that the assistance and support to developing countries and least developed countries are available.

It is usually the case that an international accord is administered by a certain international institution. To determine an institution that administers an international accord, there are two options: (i) an international accord creates an institution (e.g., Convention Establishing A Customs Cooperation Council gave birth to the Customs Cooperation Council, whose working name is the World Customs Organization) that administers it; or (ii) an international accord is drawn up under an existing institution that can appropriately administer it (e.g., Convention on Facilitation of International Maritime Traffic was drafted under the Inter-Governmental Maritime Consultative Organization, which is currently the International Maritime Organization). For option (i), creating a special international trade facilitation institution might be too idealistic at present. The contemporary global governance system stingily leaves little room for late entrants (although it deserves fresh blood). Then, option (ii) is more feasible: an existing international institution would be the most realistic solution for administering the new accord on trade facilitation. But the candidate institutions in line with the set of merits above are rare.

We can screen the existing international institutions (e.g., APEC, UNECE, WCO, UNCTAD, WTO) to single out the most suitable one for administering a new accord on trade facilitation. Regional fora on trade facilitation, like APEC, have been working as laboratories that introduce new initiatives to the multilateral trading system.[46] The trade facilitation programmes administered by APEC (especially embodied in the 1994 Bogor Declaration and the 1995 Osaka Action Agenda) are ambitious, but they are confined to a collective action plan (instead of an agreement) and only have a regional influence. A global institution, therefore, is more relevant. UNECE has figured out more than 30 trade facilitation recommendations, but these recommendations are far from being binding international agreements. WCO remarkably governs the International Convention on the Simplification and Harmonization of Customs Procedures (previously the 1974 Kyoto Convention and then the 1999 Revised Kyoto Convention, 'RKC' for short), but the RKC is a customs convention other than a trade deal and falls under a 'soft' law at last due to its feeble treatment of non-compliant situations. With the outstanding experience of convening international trade accords – e.g., United Nations Convention on a Code of Conduct for Liner Conferences (1974), United Nations Convention on the Carriage of Goods by Sea (Hamburg Rules, 1978), United Nations Convention on International Multimodal Transport of Goods (1980), International Convention on Maritime Liens and Mortgages (together with IMO, 1993) and International Convention on Arrest of Ships (together with IMO, 1999) – UNCTAD, theoretically, should be an eligible institution for administering the international accord on trade facilitation. Since the establishment of the WTO in 1996, however, UNCTAD has placed an emphasis on carrying out 'groundwork covering the identification and normative/analytical exploration of the issues and the policy options – particularly in their developmental aspects – as well as the building of consensus on the basic parameters of possible international agreements' for trade issues 'to the point where they can be fruitfully negotiated in WTO'.[47] In other words, UNCTAD leaves 'the implementation and negotiation of contractual trading rules and disciplines'[48] to the WTO in view of the complementarity between the two leading institutions in trade. 'The question is where – not whether – work on trade and investment should take place', said Mr. Renato Ruggiero, the first Director-General of the WTO.[49]

Where to find an institution that lends itself to such an ambitious trade facilitation accord then? The merits, which have been identified as above, together point at one place – the WTO. Some states deem:

> WTO rules are the surest way to ensure the political commitment needed to turn trade facilitation into reality. By setting a framework of rules one ensures, at the highest political level, that the importance to development of trade facilitation is recognized, and the necessary reforms begun.[50]

It is, *quoad hoc*, firmly believed that the development of trade facilitation commitments by the WTO will work as a means to provide both high level political impetus and an overall trade policy framework to ensure that countries will follow a consistent approach to trade facilitation.[51]

Knowing about the WTO

Born out of the 8-year Uruguay Round negotiations (September 1986 – April 1994), the WTO came into being in 1995 and has displaced the GATT in terms of multilaterally governing the rules for today's world trade. As declared by trade ministers in Marrakesh, 'the establishment of the WTO ushers in a new era of global economic cooperation, reflecting the widespread desire to operate in a fairer and more open multilateral trading system for the benefit and welfare of their peoples'.[52] Over the 20-odd years of its presence, this international body has made the grade. As Pascal Lamy, former Director-General of the WTO, described, the WTO has become:

> a laboratory for harnessing globalization and contributing to the construction of a system of global governance; a place where evolving global governance can find some roots in ensuring legitimate decision-making; an institution that can also evolve in providing for the increasing participation of non-traditional international and domestic actors; a forum where values can be discussed; a fundamental player in the building of a system of global governance.[53]

Being still a young on paper but 'both traditional and modern' institution,[54] the WTO has already acted as 'a part of a global system in which countries are aligned very differently than they had been in the GATT period, both in trade and in other matters' and constituted a large membership of 164 players,[55] where 'some that had once been outside the global market economy are now among its most active Members, and others have moved from the periphery towards the center'.[56] The WTO's system of rules and disciplines has covered around 98 percent of global trade.[57] 'It is difficult to imagine a world without the WTO and the system of rules and structures that the organization embodies', asserted Roberto Azevêdo, Director-General of the WTO.[58]

The WTO at bottom is a rule-based system, whose framework is sustained by an artful set of legal texts, contracted by the governments of a number of economies. Regardless of the forms the legal texts may take, including agreements (general agreements dealing with broad principles, or extra agreements falling to specific issues), annexes, decisions, understandings, accession protocols and schedules/lists of commitments by individual Members, they are essentially contracts, which bind the contracting parties' trade policies to the agreed limits.

Table 3.1 The basic structure of the WTO Agreements in a nutshell

AGREEMENT ESTABLISHING WTO

Annex 1A: Multilateral Agreements on Trade in Goods	**Annex 1B:** General Agreement on Trade in Services (GATS)	**Annex 1C:** Trade-Related Aspects of Intellectual Property Rights (TRIPS)
- GATT - other goods agreements and annexes - Member' schedules of commitments	- services annexes - Members' schedules of commitments (and MFN exemptions)	

Annex 2: Dispute Settlement Understanding
Annex 3: Trade Policy Review Mechanism
Annex 4: Plurilateral Trade Agreements
ministerial decisions and declarations, understandings, accession protocols, etc.

The WTO becomes a 'modern' institution because of the innovative features of its system. One innovative feature is the dispute settlement system, rooted in the Understanding on Rules and Procedures Governing the Settlement of Disputes (DSU). As a result of the Mid-Term Review of the Uruguay Round, which began in Montreal and was concluded in Geneva at the end of the 1980s, the DSU manages to afford compulsory jurisdiction[59] that is accessible to all Members. Any Member, large or small, trading with the other challenged Member or not, can trigger easily and quickly a dispute settlement procedure by means of a claim that another Member is running afoul of the WTO rules, while no Member may oppose the triggering. After adjudication, the implementation of dispute rulings, made by Panels (the jurisdiction of first instance) or the Appellate Body (the appeal stage), is subject to continuous multilateral monitoring until full satisfaction of the complainant in cases where a violation has been found; if rulings are not implemented, the membership must authorize retaliatory actions (i.e., counter-measures), the level and application of which still remain under WTO multilateral surveillance.[60] Over the past 20 years, this mechanism has successfully dealt with almost 500 trade disputes and won 'a highly enviable track record on the international stage'.[61]

Another innovative feature is the Trade Policy Review Mechanism (TPRM) – a 'peers' review process',[62] which enables the regular collective appreciation and evaluation (conducted by the entire membership) of the full range of individual Members' trade policies and practices, as well as their impact on the functioning of the multilateral trading system. The TPRM is not limited to generating information; it also helps in improving trade policymaking.[63] The 'father' of TPRM, Julius Katz, former Deputy US Trade Representative,[64] argued in the 1980s:

> The overall aim of the review procedure was [. . .] not intended purely to serve purposes of information, but to enable contracting parties collectively to survey the course of trade policies and to assess what should be done, as well as to assist government administrators in taking stock of how national policies should evolve. In this context, transparency was not a modest objective.[65]

The TPRM in practice ensures 'greater transparency in, and understanding of, the trade policies and practices of the Members' thereby to improve 'adherence by all Members to rules, disciplines and commitments made under the multilateral trading system'.[66] The DSU and TPRM, respectively attached to the Agreement Establishing the WTO, work as the two cornerstones for constituting powerful mechanisms that make sure all the rules are equally enforceable to all Members, and further demonstrate how the principle of *pacta sunt servanda* comes into play.

At the dawn of the new millennium, world leaders gathered to reaffirm their faith in a more peaceful, prosperous and just world at the 55th UN General Assembly, where the United Nations Millennium Declaration was released.[67] In the Declaration, leaders resolved

> to ensure greater policy coherence and better cooperation between the United Nations, its agencies, the Bretton Woods Institutions and the World

Trade Organization, as well as other multilateral bodies, with a view to achieving a fully coordinated approach to the problems of peace and development.

Based on a global action plan subsequently rolled out, the leaders committed their own countries to the Millennium Development Goals (MDG) – a series of time-bound targets with a deadline of 2015. Goal 8 of the MDG (viz. Develop a Global Partnership for Development) set forth a specific target to 'develop further an open, rule-based, predictable, non-discriminatory trading and financial system', which correlates with what the WTO (together with other organizations) stands for. With the expiry of the MDG in 2015, the international community's resolution to 'promote a universal, rules-based, open, non-discriminatory and equitable multilateral trading system under the World Trade Organization'[68] is renewed by the 2030 Agenda for Sustainable Development. In this regard, the WTO is a driving force of world peace and development, as well as 'one part of the scheme with responsibility for the governance of international trade relations',[69] more than just 'a place where Member governments go to try to sort out the trade problems they face with each other'.[70] Notably, Goal 17 (Strengthen the Means of Implementation and Revitalize the Global Partnership for Sustainable Development) of the 2030 Agenda for Sustainable Development, *inter alia*, aims to 'significantly increase the exports of developing countries, in particular with a view to doubling the least developed countries' share of global exports by 2020'. This is the place where trade facilitation plays a pertinent role.

Notes

1 Nancy Fraser, 'Politics, Culture and the Public Sphere: Toward a Postmodern Conception', in Linda Nicholson and Steven Seidman (eds.), *Social Postmodernism: Beyond Identity Politics* (Cambridge University Press, 1995), p. 287.
2 It is also self-called 'the World Business Organization'.
3 See the ICC website, www.iccwbo.org/about-icc/policy-commissions/trade-and-investment-policy/.
4 The Economic and Social Council of the United Nations granted the ICC category 'A' – the highest consultative status. See ICC Resolutions of Lisbon Congress (Brochure 161) (1951).
5 See ICC Brochure 130, pp. 5–6.
6 Frank Schipper, *Driving Europe: Building Europe on Roads in the Twentieth Century* (Aksant Academic Publishers, 2008), p. 241.
7 See ICC Brochure 161, p. 48.
8 See ICC Brochure 130, pp. 13–14.
9 Ibid.
10 Ibid.
11 ICC Brochure 130 included some recommendations in the ICC Brochure 121 in a revised and condensed form.
12 Section E of Chapter IV in the Havana Charter was about General Commercial Provisions, including articles on Freedom of Transit, Anti-dumping and Countervailing Duties, Valuation for Customs Purposes, Formalities connected with Importation and Exportation, Marks of Origin, Publication and Administration of Trade Regulations, Information, Statistics and Trade-Terminology.

13 ICC Brochure 130, p. 6.
14 ICC Brochure 161, p. 49.
15 Ibid., p. 12.
16 ICC referred the undertaking to the GATT Article VIII. See ibid., p. 49.
17 ICC Brochure 161, p. 12.
18 See GATT/CP.6/7Add.1 (1951). The ICC therefore earnestly requested both the Economic and Social Council of the United Nations and the Contracting Parties to the GATT to give the documents favorable consideration.
19 GATT/CP/98 (1951), p. 3.
20 Maria Livanos Cattaui, 'The Importance of Trade Facilitation to Business', in Carol Cosgrove-Sacks and Mario Apostolov (eds.), *Trade Facilitation: The Challenges for Growth and Development* (United Nations, 2003), p. 186. See also Maria Perez-Esteve, 'The Influence of International Non-State Actors in Multilateral and Preferential Trade Agreements: A Question of Forum Shopping?' in Ann Capling and Patrick Low (eds.), *Governments, Non-State Actors and Trade Policy-Making: Negotiating Preferentially or Multilaterally?* (Cambridge University Press, 2010), p. 288.
21 See 'ICC recommendations to member governments of the World Trade Organization on customs modernization and the simplification of trade procedures', 103–32/57 (1997).
22 See 'ICC recommendations to WTO members on trade facilitation', 103–32/91 (2001).
23 See 'Updated ICC recommendations for a WTO agreement on trade facilitation', 104–53 (2007).
24 Alexander Wendt, 'Anarchy Is What States Make of It: The Social Construction of Power Politics', (1992) 46 *International Organization* 391, pp. 391–425.
25 The 'international society' is assumed by Hedley Bull, a scholar of the English School. The English School of international relations theory assumes this notion and largely applies the Grotian tradition to rationalize how cooperation is possible under the conditions of international anarchy.
26 See Rodney Bruce Hall, 'Constructivism', in Thomas G. Weiss and Rorden Wilkinson (eds.), *International Organizations and Global Governance* (Routledge, 2014), pp. 144–156.
27 Martha Finnemore, *National Interests in International Society* (Cornell University Press, 1996), p. 2.
28 Alexander Wendt, *Social Theory of International Politics* (Cambridge University Press, 1999), p. 1.
29 Endre Ustor, 'First Report on the Most-Favoured-Nation Clause', UN, A/CN.4/213 (1969), paras. 30–34.
30 See Article 1 of the International Convention Relating to the Simplification of Customs Formalities.
31 See League of Nations, Treaty Series (1923), No. 775.
32 See Article 1 of the International Convention Relating to the Simplification of Customs Formalities.
33 It acceded to the Convention on August 29, 1966.
34 It acceded to the Convention on February 16, 1967.
35 It acceded to the Convention on March 14, 1966.
36 It acceded to the Convention on December 22, 1967.
37 It acceded to the Convention on May 28, 1993.
38 It acceded to the Convention on December 1, 1998.
39 See *Report of the Proceedings of the World Economic Conference*, League of Nations, Doc. C.356. M.129.1927. II, para. 5 (1).
40 Jacob Viner, *The Customs Union Issue* (1950, Paul Oslington ed., Oxford University Press, 2014), p. 31.

41 Endre Ustor, 'First Report on the Most-Favored-Nation Clause', UN, A/CN.4/213 (1969), paras. 70.
42 See 'Report of the World Economic Conference adopted on May 23, 1927', (1927) 134 *The Annals of the American Academy of Political and Social Science* 174, p. 185.
43 Craig VanGrasstek, *The History and Future of the World Trade Organization* (WTO, 2013), p. 10.
44 WTO, WT/DS375/R (2010), para. 7.1082.
45 US Communication on Preparations for the 1999 Ministerial Conference, WT/GC/W/254 (1999).
46 Roberto Azevêdo, 'WTO 20th Anniversary – Building a Stronger Global Trading System', public lecture at S. Rajaratnam School of International Studies on May 25, 2015, www.wto.org/english/news_e/spra_e/spra61_e.htm.
47 UN, A/51/152 (1996), para. 48.
48 Ibid, para. 47.
49 UNCTAD, 'UNCTAD and WTO: A Common Goal in a Global Economy', TAD/INF/PR/9628 (1996).
50 Communication of European Community, WTO, G/C/W/143 (1999).
51 Communication of Australia, WTO, G/C/W/443 (2002).
52 See Marrakesh Declaration of 15 April 1994, para. 2.
53 Pascal Lamy, 'The WTO Is a Laboratory for Harnessing Globalization', speech at Harvard University on November 1, 2006, www.wto.org/english/news_e/sppl_e/sppl47_e.htm.
54 Pascal Lamy, 'The Place of the WTO in the International Legal Order', lecture to the UN Audiovisual Library of International Law on June 15, 2008, www.wto.org/english/news_e/sppl_e/sppl94_e.htm.
55 As of 29 July, 2016.
56 See *supra* note 43, p. X.
57 Roberto Azevêdo, 'Let's Make Nairobi a Success', speech in Costa Rica on August 25, 2015, www.wto.org/english/news_e/spra_e/spra77_e.htm.
58 Roberto Azevêdo, 'WTO at 20: What Challenges for the Future?' speech at Annual Parliamentarians Workshop on May 25, 2015, www.wto.org/english/news_e/spra_e/spra62_e.htm.
59 Debra Steger, 'The WTO Dispute Settlement System: Jurisdiction, Interpretation and Remedies', in Harald Hohmann (ed.), *Agreeing and Implementing the Doha Round of the WTO* (Cambridge University Press, 2008), pp. 294–307.
60 See *supra* note 54.
61 See *supra* note 46.
62 See *supra* note 54.
63 WTO, *WTO Public Forum 2007: How Can the WTO Help Harness Globalisation?* (WTO, 2008), p. 10.
64 He was then the chairperson of Negotiating Group on Functioning of the GATT System.
65 GATT, MTN.GNG/NG14/4 (1987).
66 WTO TPRM legal text, para. A (i).
67 UN, A/RES/55/2 (2000).
68 UN, A/RES/70/1 (2015), para. 17.10.
69 Pascal Lamy, 'Global Governance Requires Localising Global Issues', speech at the Oxford Martin School, Oxford University on March 8, 2012, www.wto.org/english/news_e/sppl_e/sppl220_e.htm.
70 WTO, 'What is the World Trade Organization?', www.wto.org/english/thewto_e/whatis_e/tif_e/fact1_e.htm.

4 The long and arduous journey of trade facilitation in the WTO

The WTO, as foregoing, is the ideal institution that administers an international accord on trade facilitation. However, a WTO agreement cannot be reached at a single stroke; it involves the sequence of jobs: conceptualizing the subject for negotiations, studying the feasibility of launching negotiations on the subject, formulating the negotiating modalities, carrying out negotiations, nailing down the trade deal, ratifying the agreement, etc. It was a long and arduous journey from putting trade facilitation on the WTO agenda to concluding the Agreement on Trade Facilitation at last. The important events of the WTO (e.g., the General Council meetings, the Ministerial Conferences) consecutively marked the mileposts along the journey of trade facilitation.

1996 Singapore Ministerial Conference: trade facilitation kicked off

The WTO held its first Ministerial Conference in Singapore on December 9–13, 1996. The Conference 'brought together 127 countries in a single undertaking and under a set of fundamental rules shared by all'[1] in order to 'assess the implementation of Members' commitments under the WTO agreements and decisions, review the ongoing negotiations and Work Program, examine developments in world trade and address the challenges of an evolving world economy'.[2]

The Singapore Ministerial Conference took place at the time when 'our world of deepening integration and interdependence is demanding a new unity of vision'.[3] In that sense, the Conference opened a 'new chapter in economic history' and signified that 'a world trading system [. . .] will be in a far stronger position to manage the forces of globalization for everyone's benefit'.[4] On account of the Conference, this neonate organization set off on track, though it did not have an independent secretariat.[5]

In the delegations' eyes, however, they were attending this event not only to celebrate the inauguration of the renewed world trading system, but to speak up for their own diplomacies and trade interests. The four days were not breezy for the delegations, most of who were fully engaged in the tight schedules of plenary, bilateral consultations and breakfast meetings, as well as the 'green room' meetings, in which a small part of Members were carefully selected to participate.

The issues of 'observance of core labor standard', 'marginalization for least developed countries', 'relationship between trade and environment', and 'trade in information technology products' were top of the Singapore agenda. The 'WTO work program' and the 'built-in agenda', which coped with those accords agreed during the Uruguay Round and specified future dates for continuous overseeing or negotiations, also took an important place among the Singapore agenda items. Besides, four new issues – 'relationship between trade and investment', 'interaction between trade and competition policy', 'transparency in government procurement' and 'trade facilitation' – were proposed mainly by the US and the European Communities (EC)[6] to be brought into the Singapore agenda. Several developing country Members, including India, Indonesia, Malaysia and Tanzania, strenuously opposed introducing negotiations for new agreements. The opponents argued: the priority for the WTO Members should be implementing the 27,000 pages of Uruguay Round agreements and dealing with problems arising from that implementation; developing country Members were not ready to start negotiations that would lead to new obligations that they were still unable to understand. Renato Ruggiero, then Director-General of the WTO, wrote a cover letter to the trade ministers and suggested: though there was no consensus in the WTO General Council on these new issues, the ministers might still wish to discuss them at the Ministerial Conference.[7] Consequently, the four new issues were put into the agenda and later on collectively dubbed the 'Singapore issues'.

Among the 'Singapore issues', the US and the European Communities laid different emphasis on each individual issue. It was the European Communities that initially presented trade facilitation to the WTO forum. Prior to Singapore, the European Community had raised 'the question [. . .] as to whether steps should also be taken to develop a future multilateral discipline in the trade facilitation area' to the Council for Trade in Goods in November 1996; the European Community further proposed:

> Ministers in Singapore should give a new political impulse to simplification and harmonization of trade procedures in view of its impact on trade. [. . .] Ministers should invite the WTO in cooperation with relevant bodies to undertake exploratory and analytical work [. . .] the Council decides on how to proceed and whether a code should be developed within structures to be defined.[8]

The proposal was echoed by Australia, Colombia, Morocco, Norway, Switzerland, etc.[9]

Thanks to the ministers' graciousness, trade facilitation was eventually kicked off to the field of WTO. The Singapore Ministerial Declaration wrote the kick-off of trade facilitation down in an unobtrusive subparagraph:

> We further agree to: [. . .] direct the Council for Trade in Goods to undertake exploratory and analytical work, drawing on the work of other relevant international organizations, on the simplification of trade procedures in order to assess the scope for WTO rules in this area.[10]

1998 Trade Facilitation Symposium:
a leap to the phase of analytical work

Upon the initiative of the Council for Trade in Goods, the Trade Facilitation Symposium was convened on March 9–10, 1998 in Geneva in order to 'help identify the main areas where traders faced obstacles when moving goods across borders'.[11] The Symposium provided 'a direct interface between the practical level (traders) and the trade policy level (officials in capitals and in Geneva)',[12] where representatives from the private enterprises, Member governments and relevant intergovernmental organizations (such as IMF, ITC,[13] UNCTAD, UNECE, WCO and the World Bank) gave an overview of the key issues and reported on their experiences in respect of trade facilitation.[14]

At the Symposium, 'the greatest attention was given to problems of official procedural requirements for the import and export of goods, in particular in relation to customs and border-crossing'.[15] Issues related to 'import and export procedures and requirements', including 'customs and border-crossing problems', were specified under five headings: (i) documentation requirements; (ii) official procedures; (iii) automation and use of information technology; (iv) transparency, predictability and consistency; and (v) modernization of border-crossing administration. At the same time, suggestions to governments in terms of 'physical movement of consignments (transport and transit)', 'payments, insurance and other financial requirements', and 'electronic facilities and their importance for facilitating international trade' were presented. The Symposium also acknowledged:

> [The WTO] takes a leading role in rationalizing the international regulatory framework by putting trade facilitation on its work programme and committing itself to cutting business and consumer costs and removing barriers in the trade process – an area not covered by current WTO rules. [. . .] [The WTO] should integrate existing standards and recommendations on aligned documents, customs and other procedures into a comprehensive, binding and enforceable WTO agreement, involving international trade bodies, businesses and governments in formulating new global rules.[16]

The Symposium successfully prompted the WTO Members to 'move to the phase of analytical work on trade facilitation and assess the scope for WTO rules in this area, as set out in the Singapore Declaration'.[17]

1998 Geneva Ministerial Conference:
trade facilitation in obscurity

The second Ministerial Conference, held on May 18–20, 1998 in Geneva, took place 'at a time when the economies of a number of WTO Members are experiencing difficulties as a result of disturbances in financial markets'[18] – the 1997 Asian Financial Crisis. However, '[t]he turmoil in Asian economies has reminded us how interdependent our world is', so '[m]ore than ever, the multilateral trading system offers a force for stability and cooperation'.[19] In this context, Renato

Ruggiero brought forward the caveat of increasing trade protectionist pressures and advocated trade ministers to release a signal that they intended to resist these pressures and committed themselves to keeping markets open.[20]

The Conference, however, occurred 'at a particularly significant time for the multilateral trading system, when the fiftieth anniversary of its establishment is being commemorated'.[21] This made the Conference a pageantry, where trade ministers, as well as presidents and prime ministers of almost 20 influential Members, gathered in Geneva to acknowledge the system's most tangible achievements:

> The dramatic rise in world trade, the widening and deepening of the rules, or our rapid expansion towards a truly global trading system and to commemorate the success of three central ideas: the idea that open borders and non-discriminatory trade can be a force for international stability and peace, as well as prosperity.[22]

Holding the view that 'the best way of advancing multilateral liberalization is to start a new round',[23] the European Communities then called for the 'Millennium Round', which incorporated a comprehensive scope of new issues beyond the 'built-in agenda'.[24] The European Communities stated that '[d]uring the new round of negotiations, the Community would like to address [. . .] the subjects identified in Singapore'.[25] The idea of embarking on new negotiations, as before, did not acquire concurrence of the developing country Members, whose focus was still on implementing the Uruguay agreements. Moreover, taking the new round of talks as 'not the way to go', the US was not content with the proposed 'Millennium Round' and, instead, wanted 'a very broad directive to the General Council of the WTO to look at the full range of substantive areas'.[26]

Except voicing panegyric to the multilateral trading system and renewing Members' commitment to reinforce this system, the Geneva Ministerial Declaration, without touching upon the concrete issues, was seemingly uncommitted to the negotiations for new rules, albeit works in those areas were underway. Nevertheless, at the Geneva Ministerial Conference, 'the decision was taken to initiate a preparatory process that many countries understood to be leading to the possible launch of a new round of multilateral trade negotiations at the third Ministerial Conference'.[27] The Geneva Ministerial Declaration implicitly took up trade facilitation, by evoking results of the Singapore Ministerial Conference:

> The General Council's work program shall encompass the following:
>
> (b) recommendations concerning other possible future work on the basis of the work program initiated at Singapore.[28]

Members, at the technical level, did not slack off on their exploratory and analytical work on trade facilitation under the Council for Trade in Goods. They submitted proposals on the scope for WTO rules related to trade facilitation, concerning (i) government mandated information requirements; (ii) official procedures; (iii) transparency and related issues; (iv) transport and transit; and (v) payment, insurance and other financial requirements.[29] Within those proposals, a communication by the European Community particularly suggested:

> Consideration could be given to making [GATT] Article VIII:1(c) fully operational by a provision to expand and elaborate on it;
> We could, in addition, given the demand by business of appropriate judicial or administrative procedures, study the way in which the provisions of [GATT] Articles VIII:3 and X:3 have been implemented by WTO members.[30]

1999 Seattle Ministerial Conference: trade facilitation brushed past

The third session of WTO Ministerial Conference moved to Seattle, from November 30 to December 3, 1999, at the invitation of then US President Clinton, when he was attending the 1998 Ministerial Conference.[31]

Preparations for this Conference had already begun at full blast since September 1998, following the mandate defined in Paragraph 9 of the Geneva Ministerial Declaration, and had gathered pace in the special session of General Council. Members thereby brought to the table more than 150 communications, which submitted 'recommendations regarding the WTO's work program that would enable ministers to take decisions at this Session'.[32] The General Council compiled the various ideas together and earnestly drafted a ministerial text to be issued in Seattle, which would encompass the agenda for a new round of negotiations. The preparatory work for Seattle also took care of trade facilitation. The European Communities, Japan, Korea, Switzerland and the US, in their communications on trade facilitation,[33] proposed to develop a balanced set of commitments for the Members and build up effective and adequate multilateral framework of rules in the WTO system.

In front of the upcoming Millennium when 'too much is at stake',[34] 'it has not proved possible to produce a comprehensive consensus text'[35] for trade ministers in Seattle, due to divergences among Members on an array of issues such as 'core labor standards', 'agriculture' and 'anti-dumping measures'. The ambitious and demanding Seattle Ministerial Conference ended in such a failure that no agreed declaration was issued. 'It would be best to take a time out', stated then Conference Chair, Charlene Barshefsky, at her closing remarks in the Washington State Convention and Trade Center. In the meanwhile, outside the Center, the massive 'Battle in Seattle' campaign against liberalization and globalization was ongoing and somewhat overshadowed the Conference. Consequently, the initiatives of new trade negotiations, which had been thoughtfully incubated, were wrecked.

The opportunity for trade facilitation to rise in Seattle was fleeting. The European Communities had been at the forefront of taking efforts to start off the 'Millennium Round' of trade negotiations in the year of 2000 and to turn trade facilitation into a negotiable subject within its approach to that round.[36] Owing to the deadlock of new trade talks, trade facilitation, which once appeared in the draft Ministerial Declaration, languished at that moment.

Prior to Seattle, the international community had ambitiously envisioned the new round on various occasions (including APEC, OECD,[37] G8)[38]. For instance, APEC leaders declared that 'we will give the strongest possible support at Seattle to the launch of a new Round of multilateral negotiations within the WTO, and endorse the positions adopted by Ministers'.[39] At the working level in the WTO, discussions on 'follow-up to the Seattle Ministerial Conference'[40] proceeded in the General Council shortly after the stalled third Ministerial Conference. Two negotiations respectively on 'Agriculture under Article 20 of the Agreement on Agriculture' and on 'Service under Article XIX of the General Agreement on Trade in Services' were mandated to start technically on January 1, 2000. The momentum for a new round remained slow during a certain period of time.

Fortunately, the work on trade facilitation went on after Seattle under the leadership of Council for Trade in Goods. Members shared their national experiences and bit by bit reified part of the themes of trade facilitation (e.g., simplification and transparency).[41] GATT Article VIII and X were regarded by Members as the most fundamental WTO principles related to trade facilitation.[42] Additionally, the communication by Paraguay emphasized that trade facilitation was of significance in alleviating the landlocked developing countries' disadvantage of having no access to the sea, and argued that GATT Article V was most relevant.[43]

2001 Doha Ministerial Conference: trade facilitation vitalized

On November 9–14, 2001, the fourth Ministerial Conference was hosted by the State of Qatar in Doha. This was a celebrated Conference in the WTO archives, because it initiated 'the next stage in the development of the trading system'.[44]

The setback of Seattle on the other hand generated the confidence-building process in the WTO, which took center stage at the General Council meetings in 2000. Chairperson of the General Council and Director-General of the WTO, immediately after Seattle, announced a set of confidence-building measures, which included specific initiatives to identify the difficulties faced by the least developed country (LDC) Members in the WTO, a comprehensive reassessment of technical cooperation and capacity building activities, a separate mechanism to deal with implementation-related issues and concerns and a dedicated process to seek improvements in WTO procedures to ensure the greater inclusiveness and more effective participation of all Members.[45] Meanwhile, the two negotiations on 'agriculture' and 'service' proceeded relatively well on their own tracks. On this basis, the preparatory process for the Doha Ministerial Conference had been optimistic but sober. Although well-known and well-defended positions still dominated the 'reality check' discussions (Mike Moore, then WTO Director-General, referred to the informal 2001 July General Council meeting as such), which dealt with the scope of the agenda for Doha, the arguments in favor of opening a new round appeared to gain ground and the tone of consultations around was largely constructive.[46]

The Doha Ministerial Conference no doubt came to be one of the most conspicuous fruitions in the history of multilateral trading systems. 'This Conference is the culmination of more than three years of discussions and negotiations about the future work and direction of this Organization'.[47] The Doha Ministerial Declaration was issued, accompanied by the Decision on Implementation-related Issues and Concerns.[48] Additionally, the Conference reached Declaration on Trade-related Aspects of Intellectual Property Rights (TRIPS) and Public Health, Decision on Waiver for EU-ACP Partnership Agreement and Decision on EU Transitional Regime for Banana Imports.

Through the Ministerial Declaration, the ninth round of multilateral trade negotiations – the Doha Round – was kicked off. The Doha Round is also semi-officially called the 'Doha Development Agenda', because trade ministers in the first place declared their awareness:

> The majority of WTO Members are developing countries. We seek to place their needs and interests at the heart of the Work Programme adopted in this Declaration. Recalling the Preamble to the Marrakesh Agreement, we shall continue to make positive efforts designed to ensure that developing countries, and especially the least-developed among them, secure a share in the growth of world trade commensurate with the needs of their economic development.[49]

The Doha Ministerial Declaration was thoroughly written in development-friendly language that spelled out considerations for developing country Members (especially LDC Members) in various dimensions (e.g., 'technical cooperation and capacity building', 'special and differential treatment' and 'small economies'). The considerations were instrumental in having developing country Members get on board.[50] Notably, the mandate for negotiations on each individual subject contained phrases which explicitly claimed to take into account the special needs and interests of developing country Members. This well-turned Declaration, by resolving and re-balancing the developing country participants' concerns about their future implementation, at last drove the whole WTO membership to come around to the consensus of launching the Doha Round. In this sense, 'development is the *raison d'être* of the Doha Round'.[51]

The Doha Ministerial Declaration, in result, managed to set forth a 'broad and balanced Work Programme' that incorporated 'an expanded negotiating agenda'[52] with nearly 20 items – part of those were traditionally inherited from the 'built-in agenda', such as 'agriculture' and 'services; and others were groundbreaking, such as 'duty-free quota-free market access for LDCs' products'. Trade facilitation, as well as other 'Singapore issues', was among those items. The mandate for trade facilitation therein was:

> Recognizing the case for further expediting the movement, release and clearance of goods, including goods in transit, and the need for enhanced technical assistance and capacity building in this area, we agree that negotiations will take place after the Fifth Session of the Ministerial Conference

on the basis of a decision to be taken, by explicit consensus, at that session on modalities of negotiations. In the period until the Fifth Session, the Council for Trade in Goods shall review and as appropriate, clarify and improve relevant aspects of Articles V, VIII and X of the GATT 1994 and identify the trade facilitation needs and priorities of members, in particular developing and least-developed countries. We commit ourselves to ensuring adequate technical assistance and support for capacity building in this area.[53]

After Doha, the Council for Trade in Goods structured 'the work programme on trade facilitation for the year 2002', which contained three core agenda items: (i) GATT Articles V, VIII and X; (ii) trade facilitation needs and priorities of Members, particularly of developing and least-developed countries; and (iii) technical assistance and capacity building.[54] By then, the shape of trade facilitation in the WTO context became clear-cut, but not full-fledged yet. The negotiations on trade facilitation were expected to take place after the fifth Ministerial Conference, if a decision was to be taken by explicit consensus.

Additionally, the Doha Ministerial Conference also 'set the seal on a major historic event: the accession of China and Chinese Taipei to the WTO'.[55] With 'more than one billion people representing new Members of the Organization', the WTO took 'a significant step on the path to making it a global Organization'.[56]

2003 Cancún Ministerial Conference: 'Singapore issues' being an issue

The fifth Ministerial Conference was held on September 10–14, 2003 in Cancún, Mexico.

According to the Doha Ministerial Declaration, the fifth Ministerial Conference should 'take stock of progress in the negotiations, provide any necessary political guidance and take decisions as necessary'.[57] The WTO Secretariat elaborately prepared the Director-General's reports to the Conference, especially pursuant to the Doha Ministerial Declaration Paragraph 41 (technical cooperation and capacity building on various issues)[58] and Paragraph 43 (issues affecting LDCs).[59] This push corroborated the determination that the Doha Round would be truly a development round. Regarding trade facilitation, the report, pursuant to Doha Ministerial Declaration Paragraph 41, stated:

> Members embarked on a large number of assistance activities at the bilateral, regional and sometimes multilateral level. And technical assistance and capacity-building has become one of the three pillars of the Trade Facilitation Work Programme. The Goods Council was regularly briefed and updated on the respective trade-facilitation-related assistance activities by the Secretariat, donor Members, as well as by UNCTAD, the OECD and the World Customs Organization (WCO).

Technical assistance in the area of trade facilitation is often part of another activity covering customs valuation or market access. The objective is to enhance participants' understanding of trade facilitation concepts, the Doha Development Agenda mandate on trade facilitation and the follow-up work on the subject.

This Conference should have been 'an important stop on the road to completing the Doha Development Agenda (DDA) round of trade negotiations',[60] if it gained any consensus. But like Seattle, it abruptly collapsed.

Members' positions widely diverged on a range of issues not only in the draft Ministerial Declaration submitted by then General Council Chairperson, Carlos Pérez del Castillo, and then WTO Director-General, Supachai Panitchpakdi, but also in the revised draft Ministerial Text distributed by then Conference Chair, Mexican Foreign Minister Luis Ernesto Derbez (unofficially called the 'Derbez Text'). At the end of consultations, the question of launching negotiations on the 'Singapore issues' became a bone of contention.

Pierre Pettigrew, then International Trade Minister of Canada, was designated as 'friend of the chair' to facilitate consultations on the 'Singapore issues' at the ministerial conference. Two options for the 'Singapore issues' were in front of the Members: (i) to embark on negotiations in Cancún; or (ii) to refer the issues back to the working groups in Geneva. Indeed, an intermediate solution was figured out – unbinding the 'Singapore issues'. Unbinding the 'Singapore issues' implied that some mature issues therein would be singled out for earlier negotiations on their own merits. Some Members were in favor of letting 'trade facilitation' and 'transparency in government procurement' lift off at Cancún.[61] As the time left before the closing session wore on, the intermediate solution didn't overcome the 'take it or leave it' positions that had hardened. Seeing no signals for reconciling the entrenched positions on the 'Singapore issues', the Conference Chair called off the consultations.[62]

Without any decisions reached, the Cancún Ministerial Conference ended by adopting a six-paragraph Ministerial Statement. The Conference Chair blamed part of the collapse of the Conference on a failure to move away from rhetoric. 'No one can live off rhetoric', he commented.

2004 July General Council: trade facilitation negotiations eventually unveiled

Notwithstanding the Cancún setback, Members in the Ministerial Statement still reaffirmed all their declarations and decisions in Doha, and recommitted themselves to working to implement the declarations and decisions fully and faithfully.[63] After Cancún, consultations went on in Geneva with the aim of bridging the existing gaps between Members to 'maintain a high level of convergence' and 'work for an acceptable overall outcome'.[64]

The General Council meeting held in July 2004 – albeit it was not a ministerial event – gave epoch-making meaning to trade facilitation. Then WTO Director-General Supachai stated:

> There were certain times in the world of multilateral trade negotiations when decisions had to be taken. This was one such time. [. . .] Members needed to consolidate these gains and not lose this great opportunity to take a decision that the whole world was anxiously awaiting.[65]

At that moment, Members were on the verge of taking an historic decision that would provide a strong foundation for the negotiations to advance.[66] On August 1, 2004, after the *nuit blanche* of consultations, the General Council adopted by consensus the decision on the Doha Agenda work programme (usually referred to as the 'July package'), which contained instructions for driving each topic in the Doha Round to a new phase and frameworks for establishing modalities in certain negotiations.[67] The 'July package' detached 'relationship between trade and investment', 'interaction between trade and competition policy' and 'transparency in government procurement' from the Doha Round, stating that these issues would not form part of the work programme set forth in the Doha Ministerial Declaration and therefore no work towards negotiations on any of these issues would take place within the WTO during the Doha Round.[68] Fortunately, trade facilitation remained. The 'July package' in its Annex D defined the Modalities for Negotiations on Trade Facilitation:

1   Negotiations shall aim to clarify and improve relevant aspects of Articles V, VIII and X of the GATT 1994 with a view to further expediting the movement, release and clearance of goods, including goods in transit.[1] Negotiations shall also aim at enhancing technical assistance and support for capacity building in this area. The negotiations shall further aim at provisions for effective cooperation between customs or any other appropriate authorities on trade facilitation and customs compliance issues.
2   The results of the negotiations shall take fully into account the principle of special and differential treatment for developing and least-developed countries. Members recognize that this principle should extend beyond the granting of traditional transition periods for implementing commitments. In particular, the extent and the timing of entering into commitments shall be related to the implementation capacities of developing and least-developed Members. It is further agreed that those Members would not be obliged to undertake investments in infrastructure projects beyond their means.
3   Least-developed country Members will only be required to undertake commitments to the extent consistent with their individual development, financial and trade needs or their administrative and institutional capabilities.
4   As an integral part of the negotiations, Members shall seek to identify their trade facilitation needs and priorities, particularly those of developing and

least-developed countries, and shall also address the concerns of developing and least-developed countries related to cost implications of proposed measures.

5 It is recognized that the provision of technical assistance and support for capacity building is vital for developing and least-developed countries to enable them to fully participate in and benefit from the negotiations. Members, in particular developed countries, therefore commit themselves to adequately ensure such support and assistance during the negotiations.[2]

6 Support and assistance should also be provided to help developing and least-developed countries implement the commitments resulting from the negotiations, in accordance with their nature and scope. In this context, it is recognized that negotiations could lead to certain commitments whose implementation would require support for infrastructure development on the part of some Members. In these limited cases, developed-country Members will make every effort to ensure support and assistance directly related to the nature and scope of the commitments in order to allow implementation. It is understood, however, that in cases where required support and assistance for such infrastructure is not forthcoming, and where a developing or least-developed Member continues to lack the necessary capacity, implementation will not be required. While every effort will be made to ensure the necessary support and assistance, it is understood that the commitments by developed countries to provide such support are not open-ended.

7 Members agree to review the effectiveness of the support and assistance provided and its ability to support the implementation of the results of the negotiations.

8 In order to make technical assistance and capacity building more effective and operational and to ensure better coherence, Members shall invite relevant international organizations, including the IMF, OECD, UNCTAD, WCO and the World Bank to undertake a collaborative effort in this regard.

9 Due account shall be taken of the relevant work of the WCO and other relevant international organizations in this area.

10 Paragraphs 45–51 of the Doha Ministerial Declaration shall apply to these negotiations. At its first meeting after the July session of the General Council, the Trade Negotiations Committee shall establish a Negotiating Group on Trade Facilitation and appoint its Chair. The first meeting of the Negotiating Group shall agree on a work plan and schedule of meetings.

Note:

1 It is understood that this is without prejudice to the possible format of the final result of the negotiations and would allow consideration of various forms of outcomes.

2 In connection with this paragraph, Members note that paragraph 38 of the Doha Ministerial Declaration addresses relevant technical assistance and capacity building concerns of Members.

The 'July package' eventually unveiled negotiations on trade facilitation. From the contents of Annex D of 'July package', what the future Agreement on Trade Facilitation would mostly look like could be envisioned.

2005 Hong Kong Ministerial Conference: negotiations going on

The sixth WTO Ministerial Conference headed to Hong Kong, China, on December 13–18, 2005. Before that time, the negotiating work on trade facilitation had been ongoing for a year.

According to Pascal Lamy, then Director-General of the WTO, the Conference was 'intended to be an important stop along the road to completing the Doha Round at end of 2006' – before the mid-2007 expiry of 'trade promotion authority' of the US George W. Bush's Administration in fact.[69] He also claimed:

> We had sought to use this meeting as a means of moving two-thirds of the way to a final accord, and while we may not achieve that at this Conference, we will use this occasion to build a platform for the negotiations next year.[70]

After six days of haggling, a Ministerial Declaration was agreed. According to Pascal Lamy, the Conference made a progress by moving from 55 percent to 60 percent of the Doha Round.[71] Major achievements of this Conference, as summed up by then Conference Chair, John Tsang, were an end date for all forms of export subsidies in agriculture, an explicit decision on 'cotton', a very solid duty-free and quota-free access for the 32 LDCs, a significant framework for full modalities in 'agriculture' and 'non-agricultural market access' (NAMA) and an agreed text that pointed positively to the way forward in 'services'.[72] In a sense, the most notable accomplishment of the Hong Kong Ministerial Conference might be that '[w]e have managed to put the Round back on track after a period of hibernation'[73] rather than let it collapse like Seattle and Cancún.

On trade facilitation, the Hong Kong Ministerial Declaration stated:

> We recall and reaffirm the mandate and modalities for negotiations on Trade Facilitation contained in Annex D of the Decision adopted by the General Council on 1 August 2004. We note with appreciation the report of the Negotiating Group, attached in Annex E to this document, and the comments made by our delegations on that report as reflected in document TN/TF/M/11. We endorse the recommendations contained in paragraphs 3, 4, 5, 6 and 7 of the report.[74]

The aforementioned Annex E (Report by the Negotiating Group on Trade Facilitation to the Trade Negotiations Committee) stated:

1   Since its establishment on 12 October 2004, the Negotiating Group on Trade Facilitation met eleven times to carry out work under the mandate contained in Annex D of the Decision adopted by the General Council on 1

August 2004. The negotiations are benefiting from the fact that the mandate allows for the central development dimension of the Doha negotiations to be addressed directly through the widely acknowledged benefits of trade facilitation reforms for all WTO Members, the enhancement of trade facilitation capacity in developing countries and LDCs and provisions on special and differential treatment (S&DT) that provide flexibility. Based on the Group's Work Plan (TN/TF/1), Members contributed to the agreed agenda of the Group, tabling 60 written submissions sponsored by more than 100 delegations. Members appreciate the transparent and inclusive manner in which the negotiations are being conducted.

2 Good progress has been made in all areas covered by the mandate, through both verbal and written contributions by Members. A considerable part of the Negotiating Group's meetings has been spent on addressing the negotiating objective of improving and clarifying relevant aspects of GATT Articles V, VIII and X, on which about 40 written submissions have been tabled by Members representing the full spectrum of the WTO's Membership. Through discussions on these submissions and related questions and answers (JOB(05)/222), Members have advanced their understanding of the measures in question and are working towards common ground on many aspects of this part of the negotiating mandate. Many of these submissions also covered the negotiating objective of enhancing technical assistance and support for capacity building on trade facilitation, as well as the practical application of the principle of S&DT. The Group also discussed other valuable submissions dedicated to these issues. Advances have also been made on the objective of arriving at provisions for effective cooperation between customs or any other appropriate authorities on trade facilitation and customs compliance issues, where two written proposals have been discussed. Members have also made valuable contributions on the identification of trade facilitation needs and priorities, development aspects, cost implications and inter-agency cooperation.

3 Valuable input has been provided by a number of Members in the form of national experience papers describing national trade facilitation reform processes. In appreciation of the value to developing countries and LDCs of this aspect of the negotiations, the Negotiating Group recommends that Members be encouraged to continue this information sharing exercise.

4 Building on the progress made in the negotiations so far, and with a view to developing a set of multilateral commitments on all elements of the mandate, the Negotiating Group recommends that it continue to intensify its negotiations on the basis of Members' proposals, as reflected currently in document TN/TF/W/43/Rev.4, and any new proposals to be presented. Without prejudice to individual Member's positions on individual proposals, a list of (I) proposed measures to improve and clarify GATT Articles V, VIII and X; (II) proposed provisions for effective cooperation between customs and other authorities on trade facilitation and customs compliance; and, (III) cross-cutting submissions; is provided below to facilitate further negotiations. In carrying out this work and in tabling further proposals, Members should be mindful of the overall deadline for finishing the negotiations and

the resulting need to move into focused drafting mode early enough after the Sixth Ministerial Conference so as to allow for a timely conclusion of text-based negotiations on all aspects of the mandate.

5   Work needs to continue and broaden on the process of identifying individual Member's trade facilitation needs and priorities, and the cost implications of possible measures. The Negotiating Group recommends that relevant international organizations be invited to continue to assist Members in this process, recognizing the important contributions being made by them already, and be encouraged to continue and intensify their work more generally in support of the negotiations.

6   In light of the vital importance of technical assistance and capacity building to allow developing countries and LDCs to fully participate in and benefit from the negotiations, the Negotiating Group recommends that the commitments in Annex D's mandate in this area be reaffirmed, reinforced and made operational in a timely manner. To bring the negotiations to a successful conclusion, special attention needs to be paid to support for technical assistance and capacity building that will allow developing counties and LDCs to participate effectively in the negotiations and to technical assistance and capacity building to implement the results of the negotiations that is precise, effective and operational, and reflects the trade facilitation needs and priorities of developing countries and LDCs. Recognizing the valuable assistance already being provided in this area, the Negotiating Group recommends that Members, in particular developed ones, continue to intensify their support in a comprehensive manner and on a long-term and sustainable basis, backed by secure funding.

7   The Negotiating Group also recommends that it deepen and intensify its negotiations on the issue of S&DT, with a view to arriving at S&DT provisions that are precise, effective and operational and that allow for necessary flexibility in implementing the results of the negotiations. Reaffirming the linkages among the elements of Annex D, the Negotiating Group recommends that further negotiations on S&DT build on input presented by Members in the context of measures related to GATT Articles V, VIII and X and in their proposals of a cross-cutting nature on S&DT.

The Annex E also enumerated the proposed measures to improve and clarify GATT Articles V, VIII and X; it also incorporated the proposed provisions about effective cooperation between customs and other authorities on trade facilitation and customs compliance, needs and priorities identification, technical assistance and capacity building and other cross-cutting issues.

2009 Geneva Ministerial Conference: Doha Round ambitions vowed again

In the wake of the Hong Kong Ministerial Conference, 2006 was not a vintage year for the Doha Round. 'Members had collectively faced up to the fact that they had not been able to establish modalities in Agriculture and NAMA nor agree on the [Regional Trade Agreements] Transparency Mechanism'.[75] Responding to 'the persistent impasse on Agriculture and NAMA', Pascal Lamy, then WTO Director-General, 'made a recommendation to participants at an informal meeting of the Trade Negotiations Committee on 24 July – which had been accepted, albeit with regret – that the only course of action available was to suspend the negotiations across the [Doha] Round as a whole to enable the serious reflection by participants that was clearly necessary'.[76]

Article IV:1 of Agreement Establishing the WTO stipulates that the Ministerial Conference shall meet at least once every two years. But, due to that situation in the Doha Round, 'Members were not yet in a position to approach a decision on issues related to the next Ministerial'.[77] As a result, there was no Ministerial Conference in 2007. The impasse in negotiations led the WTO to break its own charter.

From November 30 to December 2, 2009, the WTO held its seventh Ministerial Conference in Geneva. The theme of the Conference was 'the WTO, the Multilateral Trading System and the Current Global Economic Environment'.[78]

This Conference was not designed for negotiations.[79] Ministers were dedicated to two working sessions: (i) 'review of WTO activities, including the Doha Work Program', and (ii) 'the WTO's contribution to recovery, growth and development'.[80] In this non-negotiating Conference, ministers yet reaffirmed the need to conclude the Doha Round in 2010 and the need for a stock-taking exercise to take place in the first quarter of the next year, as Chairperson summarized. This ambition aroused a sense of *déjà vu*: ministers had previously vowed to conclude the talks by the end of 2005, 2006, 2007 and 2008, which were marked with informal or formal deadlines for framework agreements on 'agriculture' and NAMA.[81] Would 2010 likewise be held back?

Besides, two 'moratoriums'[82] – one on 'electronic commerce' and the other on 'intellectual property' – were decided. Under 'electronic commerce', Members agreed to extend the moratorium of not charging import duties on electronic transmissions further until the next Ministerial in 2011. Under 'trade-related aspects of intellectual property rights' (TRIPS), ministers decided to extend the moratorium of not bringing 'non-violation'[83] cases to the WTO dispute settlement process once again and to revisit the matter at the next Ministerial Conference.[84]

At the end of the three-day meeting, then Conference Chair, Chilean Finance Minister Andrés Velasco, pointed out that while priority was being given to 'agriculture' and NAMA, it was important to advance on other areas on the agenda, including 'services', 'rules' and 'trade facilitation'.[85]

Regardless of the inane vows, the negotiations on trade facilitation went on very well: the outlines of a new agreement were beginning to take shape; Members agreed to move to the next level by drafting a consolidated negotiating text; negotiations on the consolidated text would start to narrow down areas of disagreement and produce a consensus result, as Pascal Lamy reported to the General Council.

2011 Geneva Ministerial Conference: trade facilitation not a low-hanging fruit

The 2009 Ministerial Conference's vow of concluding the Doha Round in 2010 was indeed a 'non-event'. At the convening of the eighth Ministerial Conference on December 15–17, 2011 in Geneva, the Doha Round was again at an impasse. Pascal Lamy stated:

> This impasse is already taking its toll on the multilateral trading system. Delays in reaching a deal deprive the world economy of an insurance policy against protectionism which has been estimated at 800 billion USD. [. . .] We have not yet found a way to finish the Doha Development Round. At the heart of the impasse lie differences between advanced economies and emerging countries over what constitutes a fair distribution of rights and obligations within the trading system, among Members with different levels of development.[86]

Two weeks before the Conference, the General Council circulated the document of Elements for Political Guidance, which covered three themes: (i) importance of the multilateral trading system and the WTO; (ii) trade and development; and (iii) Doha Development Agenda. Three working sessions, in parallel with the plenary session of the Conference, took place under those themes. Trade ministers underlined the importance of keeping markets open and the need to resist protectionism particularly in this challenging global economic environment. A number of trade ministers stressed that the WTO needed to address current global challenges, including climate change, energy, food security, trade and exchange rates, competition and investment, etc. The 'role of the Committee on Trade and Development (CTD)', 'Aid for Trade' (AfT) and 'the Enhanced Integrated Framework' (EIF) were touched upon under the development dimension.[87] Regarding the Doha Round, then Conference Chair, Olusegun Olutoyin Aganga, Nigeria's Trade and Investment Minister, stated:

> There was a shared sense that a key question to unlock the current impasse is the balance in contributions and responsibilities between emerging and advanced economies, although there were different views as to what the appropriate shares in this balance should be.[88]

Since April 2011, the Director-General of the WTO had been consulting Members on the elements of the so-called 'LDC Plus package',[89] which could be harvested by the end of that year. One issue being discussed as part of that package was trade facilitation.[90] In spite of the Doha Ministerial Declaration mandates of 'single undertaking' negotiations, its Paragraph 47[91] provided room for 'setting in place a negotiating process to achieve a set of deliverables'[92] at an earlier stage. Could trade facilitation eventually be such a deliverable of the 2011 Ministerial? Except for decisions on TRIPS non-violation and situation complaints (WT/L/842), work programme on electronic commerce (WT/L/843), work programme on small economies (WT/L/844), transition period for LDCs under article 66.1 of the TRIPS agreement (WT/L/845), accession of LDCs (WT/L/846), preferential treatment to services and service suppliers of LDCs (WT/L/847), trade policy review mechanism (WT/L/848), 'many ministers expressed deep regret at the impasse currently facing the Doha Round'.[93] Regardless of the possibility of being early harvested, trade facilitation was not a low-hanging fruit at all.

2013 Bali Ministerial Conference: trade facilitation negotiations sealed

The ninth Ministerial Conference was held in Bali, Indonesia, on December 3–7, 2013. At the Conference, a 'Bali package' was brought from Geneva to the trade ministers. The 'Bali package' 'contains measures which are of great significance, both to Members individually, and to the world economy as a whole', and 'would enable the multilateral system to move forward' and 'enable the WTO to breathe again'.[94] The 'Bali package' comprised 10 draft texts – a draft Agreement on Trade Facilitation (TFA), four texts on 'agriculture' and five texts covering development and LDCs issues.[95]

In the consultations on the 'Bali package', many Members – not only the developed countries but also the developing country Members and LDC Members – highlighted the importance of reaching a deal in Bali. They recognized that the 'Bali package' would preserve the credibility of the WTO and prepare the ground for a Post-Bali Agenda which would include unresolved issues from the Doha Round.[96] After round-the-clock consultations, 'the WTO has truly delivered'.[97] Ministers adopted the 'Bali package', with which they 'reaffirmed not just commitment to the WTO – but also to the delivery of the Doha Development Agenda'.[98]

The most conspicuous component of the 'Bali package' was the Agreement on Trade Facilitation (TFA). It was the centerpiece and far outweighed other parts of the 'Bali package' – not just because of its 30 pages. However, the Agreement was entitled by a Ministerial Decision,[99] which also set forth the procedures to insert the TFA into Annex 1A of the Marrakesh Agreement Establishing the WTO and would enable it to enter into forth. The Ministerial Decision stated:

> The Ministerial Conference,
>   Having regard to paragraph 1 of Article IX of the Marrakesh Agreement Establishing the World Trade Organization (the 'WTO Agreement');
>   Decides as follows:
>
> 1   We hereby conclude the negotiation of an Agreement on Trade Facilitation (the 'Agreement'), which is annexed hereto, subject to legal review for rectifications of a purely formal character that do not affect the substance of the Agreement.

2   We hereby establish a Preparatory Committee on Trade Facilitation (the 'Preparatory Committee') under the General Council, open to all Members, to perform such functions as may be necessary to ensure the expeditious entry into force of the Agreement and to prepare for the efficient operation of the Agreement upon its entry into force. In particular, the Preparatory Committee shall conduct the legal review of the Agreement referred to in paragraph 1 above, receive notifications of Category A commitments and draw up a Protocol of Amendment (the 'Protocol') to insert the Agreement into Annex 1A of the WTO Agreement.

3   The General Council shall meet no later than 31 July 2014 to annex to the Agreement notifications of Category A commitments, to adopt the Protocol drawn up by the Preparatory Committee and to open the Protocol for acceptance until 31 July 2015. The Protocol shall enter into force in accordance with Article X:3 of the WTO Agreement.

The conclusion of negotiations on the TFA was of historical significance – not only for concluding the 17 years of work on trade facilitation since Singapore, but also for marking the first multilateral trade deal since the WTO was formed in 1995. With the 'Bali package' achieved, the multilateral trading system lived up to its name.[100] The decisions would be an important stepping stone towards the completion of the Doha Round.[101]

Post-Bali Agenda:
trade facilitation still on the road

The conclusion of 'Bali package' did not necessarily mean the TFA was validated. A set of procedural requirements were still to be followed on the Post-Bali Agenda.

According to the Bali Ministerial Decision of WT/MIN(13)/36, a Preparatory Committee on Trade Facilitation under the General Council, open to all Members, would be established. Hence, the Negotiating Group on Trade Facilitation then would be dismissed and delegates would attend the trade facilitation meetings no longer as negotiators. In order to 'ensure the expeditious entry into force of the Agreement and to prepare for the efficient operation of the Agreement upon its entry into force', there were mainly three tasks left to the Preparatory Committee: (i) conducting a legal review for rectifications of a purely formal character not affecting the substance of the TFA; (ii) receiving notifications of Category A commitments; and (iii) drawing up a Protocol of Amendment to insert the TFA into Annex 1A of the Agreement Establishing the World Trade Organization.[102]

In January 2014, the Preparatory Committee on Trade Facilitation held its first meeting and elected the Philippines Ambassador, Esteban B. Conejos, Jr. as its Chairperson. Members, as they did during the negotiations, communicated their comments on the text of TFA, which were only about wording, sequencing, placement of some paragraphs and so on. But Members could not propose substantial changes any longer, because the legitimacy of negotiating results would have been otherwise undermined. In July, the Preparatory Committee reached an amended text of the TFA (WT/L/931).[103] At the meantime, many Members also notified their Category A commitments, which would 'thereby be made an integral part'[104] of the TFA.

Though the first two tasks proceeded on the fast track, the third task on the Protocol of Amendment got stuck. A few days before the July 31, 2014 deadline of adopting the Protocol of Amendment, India voiced its veto to the adoption. India insisted that the adoption of the trade facilitation protocol should be postponed unless a 'permanent solution' on 'public stockholding for food security purposes' would be found.[105] The TFA therefore lost its scheduled chance of being brought into the WTO legal framework. The Post-Bali Agenda got bogged down in 'a political link between the Public Stockholding programmes and the Trade Facilitation Agreement', as Roberto Azevêdo pointed out.[106] 'In Geneva, trade facilitation is too often a bargaining chip in the great game of multilateral trade negotiations, a pivot point for tactical maneuvering', as then US Trade Representative Michael Froman commented.[107]

The situation was like arm-wrestling: one 'arm' insisted that 'the decisions that ministers reached in Bali cannot be changed or amended in any way; the other 'arm' retorted that 'we have some who believe that those decisions leave unresolved concerns that need to be addressed in ways that, in the view of others, change the balance of what was agreed in Bali'.[108] Director-General of the WTO warned that the failure in adopting the protocol on the TFA 'would be likely to have an impact on all areas of our work'.[109]

Over the subsequent months, the issues of 'public stockholding for food security purposes' and 'trade facilitation' had risen to the top of leader's agenda. Top-level maneuvering politically untied this knot. At the US-India bilateral summit on September 30, 2014, then US President Barack Obama and Indian Prime Minister Narendra Modi 'discussed their concerns about the current impasse in the World Trade Organization and its effect on the multilateral trading system, and directed their officials to consult urgently along with other WTO Members on the next steps'.[110] Afterwards, US and Indian trade officials consulted intensively to find ways forward on the two issues and reached an agreement[111] that resolved the stand-off two days before the convening of G-20 Brisbane summit on November 15–16.

'On the basis of this breakthrough with India, we now look forward to working with all WTO Members and with Director-General Roberto Azevêdo to reach a consensus that enables full implementation of all elements of the landmark 'Bali package', including the Trade Facilitation Agreement', Michael Froman said.[112] 'This breakthrough represents a significant step in efforts to get the 'Bali package' and the multilateral trading system back on track', Roberto Azevêdo responded.[113]

On November 27, 2014, the General Council immediately adopted the three decisions respectively on 'public stockholding for food security purposes', 'trade facilitation agreement' and 'post-Bali work', which endorsed the approach agreed by the US and India. The General Council's decision on adopting the Protocol of Amending the Marrakesh Agreement Establishing the World Trade Organization (WT/L/940) enabled the TFA to be inserted into Annex 1A of the WTO Agreement and paved the way for the WTO Members' ratification and implementation of the TFA.

After 18 years (1996–2014) of hard work, the Agreement on Trade Facilitation was eventually nailed down. At that moment, the long and arduous journey of trade facilitation in the WTO context – from Singapore to post-Bali – temporarily came to an end. 'But now we must embark on another', called Roberto Azevêdo.[114] In capitals of the 164 WTO Members, there will be still onerous homework ahead – to ratify the TFA and ensure that this Agreement shall take effect upon acceptance by two-thirds of the Members (110 Members at least).

Table 4.1 Chronology of trade facilitation negotiations in the WTO

Time	Event	Progress
December 1996	Singapore Ministerial Conference	Singapore issues, including Trade Facilitation, were launched.
March 1998	Trade Facilitation Symposium	Members moved to the phase of analytical work on Trade Facilitation and assessed the scope of WTO rules on it.
November 2001	Doha Ministerial Conference	Trade ministers launched the Doha Round, which included Trade Facilitation.
July 2004	General Council meeting	The General Council approved the mandates for negotiations on Trade Facilitation in the Annex D of 'July package' and officially launched the negotiations.
November 2004	NGTF meeting	NGTF held its first meeting and adopted its work plan.
June 2005	NGTF meeting	The first edition of compilation of TF proposals (TN/TF/W/43) was issued by the WTO Secretariat.
December 2009	NGTF meeting	The first edition of draft consolidated negotiating text (TN/TF/W/165) was issued by the WTO Secretariat.
December 2013	Bali Ministerial Conference	The Agreement on Trade Facilitation was concluded.
January 2014	Preparatory Committee on Trade Facilitation meeting	The Preparatory Committee on Trade Facilitation held its first meeting and elected its Chairperson.
November 2014	General Council meeting	The Protocol of Amendment to insert the TFA into Annex 1A of the WTO Agreement was adopted.

Notes

1 Renato Ruggiero, address at the 1996 Ministerial Conference, www.wto.org/english/thewto_e/minist_e/min96_e/sing_dg_e.htm.
2 Singapore Ministerial Declaration, WT/MIN(96)/DEC (1996).
3 See *supra* note 1.
4 Ibid.
5 On 16 October 1998, the General Council adopted a Decision on Conditions of Service Applicable to the Staff of the WTO Secretariat, including Staff Regulations and Rules and the Regulations and Rules of the WTO Pension Plan; this Decision provided *inter alia* that 'the WTO Secretariat shall be established on 1 January 1999'. See WTO, WT/L/282 (1998).
6 The European Union became the legal successor of the European Communities upon entry into force of Treaty of Lisbon in 2009.
7 Martin Khor, *The 'Singapore Issues' in the WTO: Evolution and Implications for Developing Countries* (Third World Network, 2007), p. 3.
8 The proposal was originally made in a non-paper. The non-paper was subsequently encompassed in WTO document G/C/W/67 (1996).
9 WTO, G/C/M/15 (1996).
10 WTO, WT/MIN(96)/DEC (1996).
11 WTO, 'Major Companies to participate in WTO Trade Facilitation Symposium', March 3, 1998, www.wto.org/english/news_e/pres98_e/pr93_e.htm.
12 Ibid.
13 International Trade Center.
14 WTO, WT/GC/M/28 (1998).
15 WTO, G/C/W/113 (1998).
16 Ibid.
17 Ibid.
18 WTO, WT/MIN(98)/DEC/1 (1998).
19 Renato Ruggiero, address at the 1998 Ministerial Conference, https://www.wto.org/english/thewto_e/minist_e/min98_e/anniv_e/dg_e.htm.
20 Ibid.
21 WTO, WT/MIN(98)/DEC/1 (1998).
22 Flavio Cotti, then President of Federal Council of Switzerland, statement at the 1998 Ministerial Conference, see WTO, WT/FIFTY/H/ST/10 (1998).
23 Jacques Santer, then President of Commission of the European Communities, statement at the 1998 Ministerial Conference; see WTO, WT/FIFTY/H/ST/5 (1998).
24 Some accords agreed during the Uruguay Round specified future dates for continuing review or negotiations in certain areas (e.g., SPS, TBT). The built-in agenda referred to the work set out in the relevant accords.
25 See *supra* note 23.
26 ICTSD, 'WTO Ministerial and Millennium Round', *Bridges Weekly Trade News Digest*, May 18, 1998, at page 1.
27 UNCTAD, *A Positive Agenda for Developing Countries: Issues for Future Trade Negotiations* (2000), p. vi.
28 WTO, WT/MIN(98)/DEC/1 (1998).
29 WTO, G/C/W/132 (1998); G/C/W/132/Rev.1 (1999).
30 WTO, G/C/W/122 (1998).
31 See WTO, WT/FIFTY/H/ST/8 (1998).
32 See WTO, WT/MIN(99)/16 (2000).
33 See WTO, WT/GC/W/190 (1999); WT/GC/W/257 (1999); WT/GC/W/309 (1999); WT/GC/W/264 (1999); WT/GC/W/254 (1999).

34 Mike Moore, then Director-General of World Trade Organization, statement at the 1999 Ministerial Conference, see WTO, WT/MIN(99)/12 (1999).
35 Ali Mchumo, then Chairman of the General Council of WTO, statement at the 1999 Ministerial Conference, see WTO, WT/MIN(99)/16 (2000).
36 The European Community, *Communication from the Commission to the Council and to the European Parliament: The EU Approach to the Millennium Round*, COM (99) 331 final.
37 See Communiqué of the Meeting of the OECD Council at Ministerial Level, May 26–27, 1999.
38 See G-8 Communiqué Köln, June 20, 1999.
39 See 1999 APEC Leaders' Declaration.
40 'Follow-up to the Seattle Ministerial Conference' discussion was characterized by the question of so-called 'deadline issues', which referred to (i) terms in several key Uruguay Round Agreements and to (ii) deadlines from decisions at the 1996 Singapore and 1998 Geneva Ministerial Conferences which would lapse on 31 December 1999 in the absence of decisions expected from the Seattle Ministerial Conference or this last meeting of the General Council. See ICTSD, 'Après Seattle', *Bridges Weekly Trade News Digest*, 10 January 2000, at page 1.
41 See WTO, G/L/425 (2000).
42 Ibid.
43 See WTO, G/C/W/237 (2000).
44 WTO, WT/MIN(01)/12 (2001).
45 See WTO Background Paper, 'The WTO's 2-year strategy comes to fruition', January 2002.
46 Ibid.
47 WTO, WT/MIN(01)/12 (2001).
48 The decision addressed issues and concerns that had been raised by many developing country Members regarding the implementation of some WTO Agreements and Decisions, including the difficulties and resource constraints that had been encountered in the implementation of obligations in various areas.
49 WTO, WT/MIN(01)/DEC/1 (2001), para. 2.
50 ICTSD, 'Comprehensive Trade Round Broadens Scope of Discussions in the WTO', *Bridges Weekly Trade News Digest*, November 14, 2001, at pages 2–6.
51 Pascal Lamy, Secretariat note on Development Aspects of the Doha Round to the WTO's Committee on Trade and Development on November 28, 2005, www.wto.org/english/news_e/news05_e/stat_lamy_28nov05_e.htm.
52 WTO, WT/MIN(01)/DEC/1 (2001), para. 11.
53 Ibid., para. 27.
54 WTO, G/C/M/59 (2002); G/C/M/61 (2002); G/C/M/64 (2002); G/C/M/65 (2002); G/L/595 (2002).
55 WTO, WT/MIN(01)/12 (2001).
56 WTO, WT/MIN(01)/10 (2001).
57 WTO, WT/MIN(01)/DEC/1 (2001), para. 45.
58 See WTO, WT/MIN(03)/3 (2003).
59 See WTO, WT/MIN(03)/1 (2003).
60 Supachai Panitchpakdi, 'Cancún should pave the way for timely DDA conclusion', Director General's letter to journalists, 2003, www.wto.org/english/thewto_e/minist_e/min03_e/brief_e/brief01_e.htm.
61 At that moment, there was no working group on trade facilitation yet.
62 ICTSD, 'Cancun Collapse: Where There's No Will There's No Way', *Bridges Daily Update*, September 15, 2003.
63 WTO, WT/MIN(03)/20 (2003), para. 6.
64 Ibid., para. 5.

65 WTO, WT/GC/M/87 (2004), para. 93.
66 Ibid., para. 92.
67 See WTO, WT/L/579 (2004).
68 Ibid., p. 3.
69 ICTSD, 'Expectations Low as Hong Kong Ministerial Gets Underway', *Bridges Daily Update*, December 13, 2005.
70 Pascal Lamy, Director-General's letter to journalists at the Hong Kong Ministerial Conference, 2005, www.wto.org/english/thewto_e/minist_e/min05_e/brief_e/brief01_e.htm.
71 See 'Hard Truths in Hong Kong', *The Economist*, December 19, 2005.
72 WTO, 'Day 6: Ministers Agree on Declaration that "puts Round back on track"', December 18, 2005, www.wto.org/english/thewto_e/minist_e/min05_e/min05_18dec_e.htm.
73 Ibid.
74 WTO, WT/MIN(05)DEC (2005).
75 WTO, WT/GC/110 (2006), p. 4.
76 Ibid.
77 WTO, WT/GC/110 (2006), p. 25.
78 Pascal Lamy, Director-General's letter to journalists on November 30, 2009, www.wto.org/english/thewto_e/minist_e/min09_e/dg_letter_e.htm.
79 WTO, 'Day 3: Ministers show 'political energy' for ending Doha Round', December 2, 2009, www.wto.org/english/news_e/news09_e/mn09a_02dec09_e.htm.
80 Ibid.
81 ICTSD, 'Members Aim for Doha 'Stocktaking' in March', *Bridges Daily Update*, December 3, 2009.
82 'Moratoriums' are agreements not to take certain actions.
83 'Non-violation complaints' under TRIPS concerns whether countries should be allowed to bring WTO disputes on the grounds that the spirit, but not the letter, of WTO intellectual property (IP) rules has been violated. The WTO allows such complaints for trade in goods and services, but there has been a ban on IP-related cases since the WTO's founding in 1995. The prohibition was meant to last five years, but it was extended at ministerial conferences ever since.
84 See *supra* note 79.
85 See Chairman's summary of the meeting on December 2, 2009. WTO, WT/MIN(09)/WS/R/1 (2010).
86 Pascal Lamy, 'Director General's Welcome Letter', 15 December 2011, www.wto.org/english/thewto_e/minist_e/min11_e/dg_letter_e.htm.
87 See WTO, WT/MIN(11)/11 (2011).
88 Ibid.
89 LDC Plus package included Duty-Free Quota-Free and the associated rules of origin, a step forward on Cotton and the Services Waiver, Trade Facilitation, Export Competition, S&D Monitoring Mechanism, a step forward on Fisheries Subsidies and a step forward on environmental goods and services.
90 Pascal Lamy, 'WTO Trade Facilitation Deal to Reduce Trade Costs and Boost Trade', speech at the World Customs Organization in Brussels on June 24, 2011, www.wto.org/english/news_e/sppl_e/sppl197_e.htm.
91 Paragraph 47: 'However, agreements reached at an early stage may be implemented on a provisional or a definitive basis. Early agreements shall be taken into account in assessing the overall balance of the negotiations'.
92 Pascal Lamy, statement at the informal Trade Negotiations Committee meeting on June 22, 2011, www.wto.org/english/news_e/news11_e/tnc_infstat_22jun11_e.htm.
93 WTO, WT/MIN(11)/11 (2011).

94 Roberto Azevêdo, opening address at the 9th WTO Ministerial Conference on December 3, 2013, www.wto.org/english/news_e/spra_e/spra14_e.htm.

95 The 10 texts were on Trade Facilitation, General Services, Public Stockholding for Food Security Purposes, Tariff Rate Quota Administration Provisions of Agricultural Products as Defined in Article 2 of the Agreement on Agriculture, Export Competition, Cotton, Preferential Rules of Origin for LDCs, Operationalization of the Waiver Concerning Preferential Treatment to Services and Service Suppliers of LDCs, Duty-Free and Quota-Free Market Access for LDCs, Monitoring Mechanism on Special and Differential Treatment.

96 WTO, 'Day 2: Consultations on 'Bali package' Begin as Yemen's Membership Accepted', December 4, 2013, www.wto.org/english/news_e/news13_e/mc9sum_04dec13_e.htm.

97 Roberto Azevêdo, concluding remarks at the 9th WTO Ministerial Conference on December 7, 2013, www.wto.org/english/news_e/spra_e/spra16_e.htm.

98 Ibid.

99 WTO, WT/MIN(13)/36 (WT/L/911) (2013).

100 Roberto Azevêdo, concluding remarks at the 9th WTO Ministerial Conference on December 7, 2013.

101 See WTO, WT/MIN(13)/DEC (2013).

102 See WTO, WT/MIN(13)/36 (WT/L/911) (2013); WT/PCTF/W/2 (2014).

103 WT/L/931 (2014) was based on WT/PCTF/W/27 (2014).

104 Agreement on Trade Facilitation, Section II, Article 3. Notification and Implementation of Category A.

105 Before the Bali Ministerial Conference, the G-33 coalition, led by India, had called for WTO rules to be updated in order to grant developing countries greater flexibility for food purchased at administered prices when building stocks for food security purposes. There was a stand-off between the US and India. The stand-off had appeared resolved when WTO members committed to undertake a work program that would conclude work on a 'permanent solution' to this issue before the eleventh WTO Ministerial Conference. In the meantime, trade ministers signed off on an interim solution that would provide a 'peace clause' preventing Members from bringing legal disputes against existing public stockholding programmes in this area. Members with such programmes would need to ensure that their programmes do not distort trade or 'adversely affect' the food security of other Members, and to provide information on the programmes.

106 Roberto Azevêdo, report at the informal meeting of Heads of Delegations on October 31, 2014, www.wto.org/english/news_e/news14_e/tnc_infstat_31oct14_e.htm.

107 Michael Froman, keynote remarks at the WTO Public Forum on Innovation and the Global Trading System on October 1, 2013, https://ustr.gov/about-us/policy-offices/press-office/speeches/transcripts/2013/october/froman-wto-innovation-global-trade.

108 Roberto Azevêdo, report to the Trade Negotiation Committee informal meeting on July 31, 2014, www.wto.org/english/news_e/news14_e/tnc_infstat_31jul14_e.htm.

109 Ibid.

110 The White House, 'U.S. – India Joint Statement', September 30, 2014, www.whitehouse.gov/the-press-office/2014/09/30/us-india-joint-statement.

111 The bilateral agreement makes clear that a mechanism under which WTO Members will not challenge such food security programmes under WTO dispute settlement procedures will remain in place until a permanent solution regarding this issue has been agreed and adopted. It also sets out elements for an intensified program of work and negotiations to arrive at such a permanent solution. See USTR, 'Fact Sheet: U.S. – India Agreement on Trade Facilitation', November 2014, https://

ustr.gov/about-us/policy-offices/press-office/fact-sheets/2014/November/
US-India-Agreement-on-Trade-Facilitation.

112 Michael Froman, statement on U.S. – India WTO Trade Facilitation Agreement,
November 13, 2014, https://ustr.gov/about-us/policy-offices/press-office/press-
releases/2014/November/Statement-by-Ambassador-Froman-on-US-India-
WTO-Trade-Facilitation-Agreement.

113 WTO, 'Azevêdo Applauds India – US Agreement on Key Bali Issues', November
13, 2014, www.wto.org/english/news_e/news14_e/dgra_13nov14_e.htm.

114 Roberto Azevêdo, statement at the General Council meeting on November 27,
2014, www.wto.org/english/news_e/news14_e/gc_rpt_27nov14_e.htm.

5 Growth of the Agreement on Trade Facilitation

From a duck-yard-born egg to a swan

From Singapore to Bali, the 18-year journey of trade facilitation was long and arduous. Fortunately, this journey was not futile. Among the 20-odd eggs laid by the Doha Round, trade facilitation was the first one to hatch out and grow up to be a swan. The negotiations on trade facilitation were not concluded by accident. There were a certain set of conditions that enabled the Agreement on Trade Facilitation (TFA) to come true.

The negotiating group on trade facilitation: the hatchery

The multilateral trading system is the case that the negotiations are conducted by a rather large group of negotiators. The WTO has its own way to group the negotiators for each of the trade issues. According to the mandates of the Doha Ministerial Declaration, 'the overall conduct of the negotiations shall be supervised by a Trade Negotiations Committee under the authority of the General Council'.[1] The Trade Negotiations Committee (TNC) is *ex officio* chaired by the WTO Director-General. At the upper level, the General Council undertakes the regular functions of the WTO (including trade negotiations), works as the highest-level decision-making body (as well as a Dispute Settlement Body and a Trade Policy Review Mechanism) and oversees its subsidiary bodies (such as the Council for Trade in Goods, the Council for Trade in Services and the Council for Trade in TRIPS). The whole structure of the WTO is headed by the Ministerial Conference, which convenes at least once every 2 years to take topmost decisions that can be on any matter under the multilateral trading system – this makes it understandable that the negotiations on trade facilitation were primarily concluded in the form of a Ministerial Decision[2] at the ninth Ministerial Conference.

The Doha Ministerial Declaration requires the TNC to 'establish appropriate negotiating mechanisms and supervise the progress of the negotiations'.[3] Negotiations under the Doha Round, therefore, mainly take place in two kinds of loci:[4]

(i) **Special sessions set out in regular councils or committees:** for example, special session of the Committee on Agriculture for negotiations on 'agriculture'; special session of the Council for Trade in Services for negotiations on 'services'; special session of the Council for TRIPS for negotiations on 'geographical indications'; special session of the Dispute Settlement Body for 'DSU negotiations'.

(ii) **Specially-created negotiating groups:** for example, Negotiating Group on Market Access for 'market access for non-agricultural products' (NAMA); Negotiating Group on Rules for 'WTO rules – anti-dumping and subsidies'.

Specific to trade facilitation, the Negotiating Group on Trade Facilitation (NGTF) was established by the TNC according to the Modalities for Negotiations on Trade Facilitation (namely Annex D of the 2004 'July package'). Prior to 2004, however, trade facilitation was disappointingly 'low-born' and was not even allotted a working group, as opposed to the other three 'Singapore issues'. The reason was that supporters of a trade facilitation agreement – all developed country Members plus a few developing country Members – could not yet convince the rest of the membership, who preferred hortatory recommendations to mandatory disciplines, to embark on a multilateral negotiating exercise.[5] 'Being born in a duck yard does not matter, if only you are hatched from a swan's egg', Hans Christian Andersen wrote in this famous fairy tale *the Ugly Duckling*. The duck-yard-born trade facilitation was found out years later indeed to be a swan's egg. Nonetheless, the 1996 Singapore Ministerial Conference agreed to 'direct the Council for Trade in Goods to undertake exploratory and analytical work, drawing on the work of other relevant international organizations, on the simplification of trade procedures in order to assess the scope for WTO rules in this area'.[6] The Council for Trade in Goods (CTG) had been the dwelling of trade facilitation – for the purpose of discussion but not negotiation – until the NGTF took over. The work done by the CTG solidly paved the way for building up the imminent NGTF.

Pursuant to Annex D, the NGTF held its first meeting on November 15, 2004, where the work plan and near-term schedule of meetings were agreed. The work plan left sufficient flexibility to adapt the substantive discussion at each meeting to the NGTF's respective needs, providing a balanced approach to reflect all the elements of the Modalities for Negotiations on Trade Facilitation in an equitable manner with no judgments on priority and letting the process to be member-driven, with work proceeding on the basis of Members' contributions and other input the NGTF might request.[7]

Thus, the NGTF set its sail for the unforeseeable voyage till its arrival in Bali. During the following years, thanks to the chairmanship of the three sequential Chairpersons – Mr. Muhamad Noor Yacob (Malaysia), Mr. Tony Miller (Hong Kong, China) and Mr. Eduardo Ernesto Sperisen-Yurt (Guatemala), the negotiators closely worked together and drove the negotiations forward with robust momentum. Like a family, the negotiators, either capital-based or Geneva-based, were gathered almost every two months under the same roof (because the plenary meetings, except for intensified consultations, were normally held with such a frequency). The NGTF, other than a talking shop, afforded the negotiators a venue to maneuver their trade diplomacies. The NGTF moved like a bus where from time to time some negotiators hopped off while some new faces hopped on.

Groupings and conflicts

The WTO is a place where the negotiators are not speaking in their personal capacities but for the diplomacies of the states that they represent. Being aware that a group of states can shout an individual state down, the WTO Members holding similar positions usually draw on groupings to maneuver their trade diplomacies. As groupings generally help manage the complexity of multilateral negotiations, the WTO Members progressively favor groupings as a means of building consensus, bolstering the legitimacy of negotiation outcomes and satisfying the desires of all Members to be represented in discussions.[8]

Groupings, geographically or politically formed, are ubiquitous in the Doha negotiations. For instance, the Least-developed Countries' (LDCs) Group represents the 'world's poorest countries' as defined by the United Nations, and includes around 50 countries mainly in Africa and Asia; the African Group is generally a regional coalition composed of more than 40 African countries; the African, Caribbean and Pacific (ACP) Group is not only a geographically broader coalition containing 79 states in these regions but also an organization that was created under the Georgetown Agreement in 1975; G-90 holds a wider representation of the African Group plus the ACP Group then plus the LDCs Group; the European Union (EU) speaks uniformly as a customs union on behalf of its 28 member states; the Cairns Group, formed in 1986, represents 19 agricultural exporting countries lobbying for reforming agricultural trade; G-33, also called 'Friends of Special Products', has already expanded to a group of 46 members and is pressing for flexibility for developing countries to undertake limited market opening in terms of agriculture.

These groupings are not allies in a strict political sense. Most of the groupings are open-ended: a grouping may consist of the mass of Members who share common trade diplomacies on a certain subject; a Member is free to go in with or drop out of any groupings for the sake of its own trade diplomacy. Nevertheless, Members are grouped out of conflicts of trade diplomacies. Therefore, there were, likewise, groupings and conflicts in the trade facilitation negotiations.

To negotiate vs. not to negotiate

'To be or not to be, that is the question', Prince Hamlet bemoaned.[9] For trade facilitation, to negotiate or not to negotiate, that was also the question. The debate on this question led to the forming of two groupings at source. One was the Colorado Group,[10] which included all developed country Members as well as a number of developing country Members. In this grouping, the US and the European Communities (EC), which was succeeded by the European Union (EU) in 2009, were the mainstay. The other one was the Core Group,[11] whose regular participants were developing country Members and LDC Members.[12] Malaysia and the Philippines chaired this grouping.

The debate on whether to negotiate or not was in essence about whether to draw up new WTO rules on trade facilitation. In the Colorado Group's view, a set of multilateral rules, 'thus being of complementary nature rather than involving different reform approaches',[13] would enable the pushes for domestic trade facilitation reforms to be predicated on the same principles for all Members, and would provide the sustained political commitment that was instrumental in successful administration. Whereas the Core Group believed that the present autonomous efforts undertaken by many countries in the area of trade facilitation would stimulate an equal amount of political commitment, and that these autonomous efforts were generally on the basis of models that would ensure that countries were moving in the same direction. They thought that a focus on creating rules on trade facilitation was inappropriate at that time.[14]

In practice, the Colorado Group was a party of steadfast proponents of starting the negotiations as soon as possible; on the contrary, the Core Group were opposed to tabling trade facilitation for negotiation and insisted the work be maintained only to the exploratory and analytical extent, for they were not sufficiently prepared – many Members in the Core Group argued that they were still grappling with the implementation of certain commitments from the Uruguay Round, and that these implementation issues needed to be addressed before consideration could be given to additional rules.[15] The 'to negotiate or not to negotiate' debate remained the keynote over the earliest years of talks on trade facilitation.

Table 5.1 Debate between the Colorado Group and the Core Group

The Colorado Group:	
US	'Our goals are a negotiating agenda which is ambitious [. . .]. If we approve a Ministerial Declaration that meets these tests, we can [. . .] examine the basic questions of trade facilitation and customs, to ensure that trade proceeds as smoothly and easily as it should in today's high-tech world'. (1999)[16]
EC	'In years to come, people will wonder why the world hesitated to start negotiations over investment, competition and trade facilitation. People know our views on these issues, which we consider critical to our work here. But I ask them to consider carefully: if we do not start these negotiations here and now, it could be ten years before we really tackle these vital issues'. (1999)[17]
	'On the so-called Singapore issues, we have shown understanding and indeed flexibility across the board on all four issues in order that the negotiations can be launched at this meeting'. (2003)[18]
Japan	'Japan, together with other like-minded countries, is strongly calling for negotiations to be launched on cover new issues that are commonly referred to as the 'Singapore Issues', such as investment and trade facilitation'. (2003)[19]
Korea	'In order for the WTO to remain relevant in the global economy, the WTO must start negotiations on the Singapore Issues'. (2003)[20]

The Core Group:

Malaysia	'There are proposals by some Members that we should commence negotiations on investment, competition, transparency in government procurement and trade facilitation. Malaysia, like many other Members, is not in a position to support all these proposals. We note that these issues are subjects of discussion in the working groups. [. . .] We cannot undertake negotiations in areas where there has been insufficient preparation'. (1999)[21]
	'Many countries are not ready to discuss negotiations on the new or Singapore issues, but can go along with further work on the educative process'. (2001)[22]
	'The 'New Issues' that is investment, competition, transparency in government procurement and trade facilitation continue to be advocated by several Members for inclusion into the negotiations process. These issues remain contentious and are opposed to by most WTO Members'. (2003)[23]
Philippines	'The same process should apply as well to the case of trade facilitation, where work is directly being done under the auspices of the General Council. The Philippines, however, would wish to caution those Members who tend to be overly ambitious in laying down various elements for future work. It might be more productive to concentrate on the immediate relationship between trade facilitation and rules that already exist in the WTO. We also need to keep in mind that the 'principle of subsidiarity' dictates that we should leave to those international organizations (like the World Customs Organization) subject matters they are more competent in addressing'. (1998)[24]
	'A number of issues – such as those on investment, competition policy and even trade facilitation and electronic commerce – are plainly not ripe for negotiations. We should, however, be able to simply continue useful analytical work on these areas'. (1999)[25]
	'On the new issues, the so-called 'Singapore Issues', the Philippines is uncertain of their substantive implications for our interests and thus remains unconvinced of the need to begin negotiations'. (2003)[26]

Binding vs. non-binding

One of the maces that the WTO system owns is its Dispute Settlement Mechanism that ensures its rules are binding and enforceable to all Members. If a new set of rules are to be fitted to the WTO system, they shall, theoretically, be as binding as the existing WTO rulebook is, and shall be likewise subject to the Dispute Settlement Mechanism.

At the beginning, Members were, however, debating on such a basic question: should the rules on trade facilitation be binding or not? This question is associated with why there is the shortest but special provision that 'all provisions of this Agreement are binding on all Members' (q.v. Article 24:2) in the legal text of the TFA.

Developed country Members, who were proponents of starting the negotiations, mainly contended that the rules should be binding. They argued:

> Regarding other subjects, where initiatives in other organizations had not succeeded in bringing about multilaterally applied disciplines, Members had in the past been able to develop regulatory frameworks in the GATT/WTO that they were willing to respect. This apparent strength of the organization could also be used for the development of a multilaterally binding set of rules on trade facilitation.[27]

But many developing country and LDC Members were against this argument and expressed their serious concerns:

> The current state of development of many developing countries and their resource constraints would not allow them to engage in new commitments on an equal level as developed country Members. A 'one-size-fits-all' approach would not work.[28]

> The problems that the developing countries were facing in this area [of trade facilitation] could not be solved by the introduction of binding commitments subject to the WTO Dispute Settlement Mechanism.[29]

While concurring with the benefits that trade facilitation would bring about, they negated the usefulness and necessity of developing binding trade facilitation rules,[30] and suggested instead that the development of best practice or non-binding recommendations, built on work carried out in other organizations (e.g., the Revised Kyoto Convention administered by the WCO), should be considered.[31]

More specifically, the LDCs Group made reference again to Footnote 1 of the Modalities for Negotiations on Trade Facilitation, which stated that 'it was understood that [the aim of clarifying and improving relevant aspects of GATT Articles V, VIII and X] was without prejudice to the possible format of the final result of the negotiations and would allow consideration of various forms of outcomes'. The LDCs Group stressed:

> The nature and scope of possible commitments accordingly were yet to be determined, including the applicability or otherwise of the Dispute Settlement Understanding. Thus, negotiations at this stage should be without prejudice to the final outcomes of the negotiations.[32]

Insisting on the principle of being binding, the US proposed 'creative' but frothy solutions:

> GATT Articles V, VIII and X already impose binding obligations on Members. It follows, therefore, that any further agreement on trade facilitation

would enhance existing rights and obligations. Nevertheless, a number of Members have raised concerns regarding the application of dispute settlement provisions to any new agreement. The United States places great importance upon bringing the results of the negotiations on trade facilitation into the sphere of WTO rights and obligations. However, the WTO's undertaking into this area also presents its own exceptional challenges that may require some creative thinking as we proceed into the negotiations, including giving consideration to approaches that would address concerns without otherwise diminishing the fundamental role of dispute settlement proceedings.[33]

Meanwhile, some Members followed eclecticism with regard to this question. For example, Korea stated that 'an agreement promoting trade facilitation within the framework of the WTO could embody either obligations with a legal binding force or simple recommendations with no such binding power, depending on the issues concerned'.[34]

'Chicken' first vs. 'egg' first

It had already been agreed in the Modalities for Negotiations on Trade Facilitation, as a prerequisite of launching the negotiations, that: if it was determined to impose binding trade facilitation rules on the developing country Members and LDC Members, there should be concomitant rules that would bind the developed country Members to the commitments of providing technical assistance and capacity building (TACB) and leaving special and differential treatment (S&DT) to the developing country Members and LDC Members. But the Members' stances again diverged greatly on a question: who (the developed country Members, or the developing country Members and LDC Members) were to be bound first; in other words, should the developed country Members undertake their commitments in terms of TACB first, or should the developing country Members and LDC Members undertake their commitments of implementing the trade facilitation rules first? Negotiators compared this situation to the 'chicken and egg' problem: the chicken or the egg, which comes first? The 'chicken and egg' problem ran through the entire course of the negotiations.

The developed country Members once promised their TACB offers to the developing country Members and LDC Members, covering their participation in the negotiations and implementation of the rules in the future. The European Communities (EC) declared in 2005 that 'the EC is prepared to consider positively requests from developing countries for assistance linked to the implementation of future trade facilitation commitments, once known'.[35] In 2007, the US stated 'what [the US] was proposing was a concrete undertaking that lent itself well to technical assistance and the development of a path to implementation reflecting whatever special situation existed for a developing country Member'.[36] In the meantime, the EC and the US emphasized that the TACB should be predicated on the condition that the developing country Members and LDC Members were committed to binding trade facilitation rules. Former EC Trade Commissioner, Peter Mandelson, said:

> On Trade Facilitation [. . .] So I hope that the African Union will today come out with a strong statement in support of these negotiations, one that recognizes that we need both strong rules and strong aid commitments to go hand in hand – to the end of the Round and beyond. A positive message from you will enable me to secure more aid on this.[37]

Similarly, the US stressed in a NGTF meeting that 'success is highly dependent on local commitment and intense collaboration with our developing country partners'.[38] But the statements were not sufficient to make sure that the provision of TACB would be 'legally binding, precise, effective and operational' in the African Group's view.[39] The developing country Members and LDC Members collectively insisted on their proposition:

> The Modalities for Negotiations on Trade Facilitation contain a strong commitment by Members, in particular developed countries to provide technical assistance and support for capacity building to enable developing and least-developed countries to participate in and benefit from the negotiations. It is also clear from the modalities on trade facilitation that developing or least-developed countries shall not be required to implement commitments if they lack implementation capacities and have not received the required technical assistance. The success or otherwise of trade facilitation negotiations is therefore dependent on the provision of adequate and sustained technical assistance and capacity building for developing and least-developed countries.[40]

Two communications, namely the TN/TF/W/137 (2006) and the TN/TF/W/147 (2007), were circulated, carrying the antithetical views held by the two camps and presenting a *catch-22*. Although further documents came up later in other forms (e.g., non-papers), the two communications underlay the 'chicken and egg' debate. The TN/TF/W/137 was submitted by a group of developed country Members (including the European Communities, Switzerland and Japan) and developing country Members (including China, Ecuador, Mexico, Sri Lanka, etc.). The TN/TF/W/147 was jointly communicated from the Core Group, the ACP Group, the African Group and the LDCs Group – almost the broadest representation of the southern countries, conveying a consolidated stance on the basis of their previous communications.

Table 5.2 Comparison between the two communications

Issue	TN/TF/W/137	TN/TF/W/147
When to implement the commitments	'The obligations set forth in this agreement apply from the date of its entry into force, except for those contained in the Notification, which shall apply for each Member as from the end of the implementation period set out therein and from the Notifications of the capacity acquisition'.	'Developing countries should not be required to implement TF commitments for which TACB is needed if such TACB is absent'.
Full implementation or partial implementation	'Members shall ensure full implementation of the obligations contained in the Agreement'.	'New TF commitments should therefore be approached in a way that would enable developing Members to commit to a specified minimal level or standard of implementation of commitments, with appropriate flexibility for least-developed Members, and subject to the provision of TACB where needed'. 'There should be two categories of commitments to be implemented by developing Members, subject to the provision of TACB where needed'.
Who determines capacity acquisition	'The implementing developing and least-developed Member and, if so agreed, the other parties involved, shall assess whether TACB has been effectively provided according to the mutually agreed terms and conditions and whether capacity has been acquired'.	'The developing Member who is a TACB recipient should be the one to determine to its satisfaction when such implementation capacity has been acquired, or it may also choose to work out a mutual arrangement with the donor concerned for joint determination of the acquisition of implementation capacity. The determination of acquisition of implementation capacity should be at the discretion of the individual LDC concerned'.
Discretions in implementing the commitments	'Each developing and least-developed Member shall notify all other Members, through the WTO Secretariat for which obligations it needs additional time which shall not exceed [N] years, to implement'.	'For each specific obligation, developing Members could also indicate the limitations or restrictions that they wish to place on their commitment to implement such obligation'.

Issue	TN/TF/W/137	TN/TF/W/147
Early warning	'Any request for modification of a Member's Notification needs to be brought to the Committee on Trade Facilitation for decision as soon as an implementation problem has been identified'.	'Consideration could be given to an early warning mechanism under which developing and LDC Members can inform the WTO that there is going to be a delay in implementing a commitment'.
Exceptions	Not mentioned	'GATT Articles XX and XXI will apply to any TF agreement'.
Dispute settlement	'Other chapters of the agreement will also have to deal with enforcement matters. So far, this communication refers implicitly to enforcement issues'.	'Finally, no developing or least-developed Member should be brought by any other Member to dispute settlement proceedings under the Dispute Settlement Understanding in order to enforce compliance with commitments that such developing or least-developed Member is not yet implementing'.

In point of fact, the 'chicken and egg' dilemma mirrored the lack of trust between the two camps since the 'to negotiate or not to negotiate' divergence. Further, this dilemma had its roots in the well-entrenched rift between the North and the South since the 1960s. Proverbially, North-South cooperation kept gaining ground. For instance, United Nations Declaration on the Establishment of a New International Economic Order (1974)[41] proclaimed the principles of extending 'active assistance to developing countries by the whole international community' and providing 'preferential and non-reciprocal treatment for developing countries, wherever feasible, in all fields of international economic cooperation whenever possible';[42] the Lomé Conventions[43] 'channeled a significant amount of development aid [of the European Economic Community (EEC)/ European Union (EU) countries] into the ACP countries'[44] and set a highly innovative model of North-South cooperation.[45] However, the developing country Members and LDC Members were still worried about 'benign neglect of the poor nations' predicament'.[46] The full trust between the North and the South will not be earned in one day. 'Neither anger nor despair nor resignation nor bluff nor confrontation will bring the needed coherent solutions. Only a dialog can'.[47] Hopefully, the WTO can serve as one of the places where the dialog will go on.

Back to the NGTF, regarding the 'chicken and egg' dilemma, Chairperson's remark in 2005 was pertinent:

The balancing formula was contained in the modalities for negotiations in Annex D of the July package. Any proposal that disregarded the cost factor, the need for substantive and operative S&DT within the meaning of the Doha Ministerial Declaration, and technical and financial assistance and capacity-building on the basis of binding provisions, would be in breach of the compromise solution that enabled those negotiations to be launched.[48]

The 'balance between the contributions of developed country and developing country Members in terms of mutually beneficial commitments'[49] fortunately resulted in the Section II of the TFA at last.

The principles for organizing and managing the negotiations

The GATT/WTO system has drawn from its 70-year history a set of rules of thumb for multilateral trade negotiations (e.g., political will, participation of Members, process transparency, consideration for developing country and LDC Members). The Doha Ministerial Declaration reinforced these rules of thumb and turned them into the principles for organizing and managing the negotiations.[50] On trade facilitation, the principles of single undertaking, inclusiveness, transparency and member-driven, particularly, steered the negotiation process and enabled the groupings to compromise on their well-entrenched stances and to reach the hard-won consensus.[51]

Single undertaking

Single undertaking – the proverbial 'nothing is agreed until everything is agreed' discipline – puts the 20-odd negotiated subjects under the Doha Round into one package so that the final result of negotiations only entails a single signature by each Member and any option to pick between the subjects is ruled out. Single undertaking makes it the case that every negotiated subject cannot be agreed separately.

However, single undertaking allows for tradeoffs between the subjects that are otherwise unrelated at all. Taken as a conventional wisdom stemming from the Uruguay Round, single undertaking (other than sector-by-sector negotiations) 'facilitates side-payments'[52] among the subjects by placing them in one basket, where 'more potential *quids* are available for the *quo*'.[53] A Member can trade with its negotiating rivals off one subject on which it is ready to compromise for another subject in which it has strong interests. After all, negotiations in nature mean reciprocal compromises; it can seldom be the case that all participants see themselves as winners in the negotiations on every subject. This exactly invokes the 'to negotiate or not to negotiate' question for trade facilitation. Once trade facilitation was determined to be put on the Doha Development Agenda, it was destined to be a bargaining chip for other more difficult subjects. In reality, India staked its public stockholding programme on postponing the insertion of the TFA into the WTO. Because of the tradeoff between the US and India, the TFA was able to break out of stalemate.

Single undertaking, nevertheless, has the problem of being complex and time-consuming, since each subject, of which the state of play clearly differs, has to wait for another. Negotiators, ever since the Uruguay Round,[54] had come up with a complementary solution: *early harvest*. This means reaping the benefits of any subject as it ripens; viz. some agreements might be reached in some negotiations without other agreements being reached in other negotiations under the Doha Round.[55] The Doha Ministerial Declaration permitted the case of early harvest, stressing that '[h]owever, agreements reached at an early stage may be implemented on a provisional or a definitive basis; [e]arly agreements shall be taken into account in assessing the overall balance of the negotiations'.[56] William J. Clinton, former US President, used to be an advocate of this solution. He stated that 'we should explore whether there is a way to tear down barriers without waiting for every issue in every sector to be resolved before any issue in any sector is resolved'.[57]

Though trade facilitation was the last item added into the Doha Development Agenda, it ran much faster than any other subject. Early harvest set the scene for the possibility of concluding the negotiations on trade facilitation ahead of other Doha talks.

Inclusiveness

The Agreement Establishing the World Trade Organization has stringently obliged the WTO system to 'continue the practice of decision-making by consensus followed under GATT 1947'.[58] A decision on the negotiated subject can be taken by the relevant WTO body only without formal objection from any Member present at the meetings, even if the Member has the smallest share in the global trade. According to Roberto Azevêdo, Director-General of the WTO, 'Reaching consensus is certainly a lot more complex than simply counting ballots. It requires that all delegations participate constructively and in good faith in consultations'.[59] That means all WTO Members shall be included in the negotiations on an equal footing. The WTO, with its 'one Member, one vote' regime, rests largely on the principle of the sovereign equality of states.[60] As stipulated in the Doha Ministerial Declaration, the negotiations shall be open to all WTO Members and to observers who are negotiating or intending to negotiate their membership (but decisions on the outcomes of the negotiations shall be taken only by WTO Members); and shall be 'conducted with a view to ensuring benefits to all participants and to achieving an overall balance in the outcome of the negotiations'.[61] Thus, each Member is fully within its rights to, at least, participate in the negotiating meetings, be aware of the happenings in Geneva, feel free to fight its corner and so on.

'Consensus among all Members for the adoption of decisions ensures legitimacy'.[62] On the other hand, consensus is also responsible for certain sluggishness in the negotiations.[63] Much different from what the situation was with only 23 signatories to the GATT in 1947, it is more cumbersome today to make for a consensus by the 164 Members of the WTO. Usually, efficiency and inclusiveness seem to be the two sides of one coin (as only one side can be the upside). However, WTO Members took determined efforts around the year of 2000 to enable the two incompatible things to go hand in hand. The *open-ended informal* mode of consultations as a result was applied to the process of reaching consensus.[64] This mode ensured that (i) 'Members were advised of the intention to hold such consultations; (ii) 'those Members with an interest in the specific issue under consideration were given the opportunity to make their views known; (iii) 'no assumption should be made that one Member represented any other Members except where the Members concerned had agreed on such an arrangement; and (iv) 'the outcome of such consultations was reported back to the full membership expeditiously for consideration'.[65] The NGTF, therefore, conducted its consultation meetings (for the most part) in open-ended informal mode. As seen from the minutes of the last NGTF meeting in November 2013 (TN/TF/M/53), for example, it was recorded that '[t]his part of the meeting [on reports by facilitators, consideration of new/revised texts for inclusion into the draft consolidated negotiating text and decision on next steps] was conducted in *informal* mode'. Any multilateral trade deal cannot be reached without concessions on reciprocal basis. However, negotiators are afraid of being observed by their domestic stakeholders in the act of making concessions. The informal mode of consultations serves as an approach to protect the negotiators and conceal their flexibilities in pursuit of consensus.[66]

Transparency

Transparency is entirely in tune with inclusiveness. The two questions of transparency and inclusiveness were once addressed together under the topic of 'internal transparency and effective participation of Members'. The WTO, which claims itself a transparency-pursuing system, affirmed in the Doha Ministerial Declaration that 'the negotiations shall be conducted in a transparent manner among participants'.[67]

Instead of being a frothy slogan, the principle of transparency aims to ensure that the negotiation-related information flows to every Member (especially the smaller ones) adequately and expeditiously. The WTO, like other multilateral fora, is inevitably a field where power plays. Smaller Members normally lack the access to first-hand information; they often rebuke the WTO system for the small-scale consultation activities (such as 'green room' meetings) where they hardly have the power to squeeze into. Albeit the WTO explains that 'decisions to be taken by the entire membership need first to be prepared in smaller formats, like committees in a parliament',[68] this institution still takes technical steps (also as requested by Members)[69] to make the negotiations be conducted more transparently. For instance, the TNC keeps the calendar of meetings under surveillance and, as far as possible, schedules only one negotiating body to meet at a certain time, in view of the constraints of smaller delegations; a Member's proposal for discussion is to be submitted in writing before the meeting so that others can formulate their positions by reading the hard copy in advance; minutes of meetings of the TNC and of negotiating bodies are requested to be circulated expeditiously in all three WTO official languages; reports of panels, working documents, minutes of meetings in all cases are circulated to the Members as unrestricted documents and therefore made publicly available, unless exceptions apply; the WTO Secretariat is urged to take all possible steps to ensure the prompt and efficient dissemination of information relating to negotiations to non-resident and smaller missions in particular; the WTO Secretariat contributes to greater openness to and interaction with the civil society, who might be business communities, trade unions, consumer groups and non-governmental organizations (NGOs) with interests in trade policies, through dialog, symposia or access to information.[70]

The manner in which the NGTF organized and managed the negotiations should, at any rate, be in keeping with the matter – transparency – which it was negotiating on. In practice, most of the documents for negotiations (e.g., Members' communications, communications from other international organizations, minutes of the NGTF meetings, proposed agendas of the Council for Trade in Goods) are publicized on the WTO website.

Member-driven

'The WTO is a member-driven organization; the agenda is member-driven; the process is member-driven; and so success must also by definition be member-driven'.[71] Member-driven, together with inclusiveness and transparency, builds up the democracy that the WTO takes on in establishing new rules for the world trading system. Member-driven sets up the situation that each Member is equally entitled to drive any initiative into the negotiations through, for example, submitting its proposals or co-sponsoring other Members' proposals (though its power matters in respect of how far the drive can go).

Member-driven requires not only Chairpersons of the TNC and relevant negotiating bodies but also the WTO Secretariat to be neutral and objective; viz. Chairpersons and the Secretariat shall not be biased either in favor of or against any Member. Chairpersons shall aim to head for consensus among Members. In their regular reports to the overseeing WTO bodies, Chairpersons shall reflect consensus, or, where this is not possible, different positions on issues.[72] The WTO Secretariat plays a facilitative role in organizing and managing the negotiations. The multitudinous NGTF documents, including Chairperson's reports (TN/TF/*), minutes of meetings (TN/TF/M/*), working documents (TN/TF/W/*), told that the WTO Secretariat had not intervened in or exerted influences over the negotiation process. Instead, the WTO Secretariat compiled and consolidated the negotiating texts for negotiators' reference on the basis of their own contributions.

The negotiations are driven by Members – not only by their governments but also in many cases by their parliaments. The WTO agreements 'must be agreed and ratified by Members' [governments] and parliaments'.[73] Albeit trade ministers concluded the Agreement on Trade Facilitation at the ninth Ministerial Conference in 2013 and the trade diplomats nailed down the legal text of the Agreement at the WTO General Council in 2014, the Agreement still needed sufficient ratifications by Members' parliaments for its entry into force. However, a Member's parliament ought to cast an 'up or down' vote on the TFA, without modifying any contents of the Agreement. After all, it is the government, rather than the parliament, that fills the post of negotiator. On the other hand, the parliament may define the government's negotiating objectives and priorities from the outset, or oversee and guide the government's negotiating work in the interim. For that matter, the Trade Promotion Authority (also called 'Fast Track Negotiating Authority') enacted by the US Congress provides an example of the parliament's counterweight to the government: trade agreements are negotiated in a time-bound – but extendable – period of 'fast track' by the executive branch while congressional bills to implement the agreements are simultaneously taken into consideration.

The growth of an article

As a famous adage says 'Rome was not built in a day', it took years for each article of the TFA to come into being from a Member-driven proposal to an internationally binding rule – from an 'egg' to a 'swan'. The 'egg to swan' growth of an article was painstaking, given that it had to pass muster under Members' consensus. Before the Agreement was unanimously adopted, most of its articles underwent three generations: (i) general ideas; (ii) textual proposals; and (iii) draft consolidated negotiating text. The evolution of post-clearance audit (PCA) texts, for example, could illustrate the grueling course of shaping a TFA article.

The first generation: general ideas

The norms of trade facilitation, as basically defined in the Modalities for Negotiations on Trade Facilitation, were more of 'a bare and harsh outline' than of 'light and graceful foliage'[74] at the beginning of negotiations. Fleshing out the norms of trade facilitation became the primary task of the negotiators at that time. Like putting eggs in a basket, negotiators generally proposed ideas that might constitute trade-facilitative measures, which were synchronously compiled by the WTO Secretariat in the working document of TN/TF/W/43 and its subsequent revisions. Most of the proposed ideas were indeed those measures that the proponents were successfully practicing – the negotiations were also a golden opportunity for Members to 'sell' their home-made trade policies abroad.

   Customs, as well-known, is one of the border agencies that control the international movement of goods. As the Revised Kyoto Convention requires, 'the customs control systems shall include the audit-based controls'.[75] The audit-based controls then include post-clearance audit (PCA) and traders' systems audit.[76] PCA 'can be defined as the structured examination of a business' relevant commercial systems, sales contracts, financial and non-financial records, physical stock and other assets as a means to measure and improve compliance'.[77] PCA shifts the focus of customs control from the scattered documents and consignments to the traders who are responsible for legal compliance. In applying PCA, customs administrations 'are able to target their resources more effectively and work in partnership with the business community to improve compliance levels and facilitate trade'.[78] Prior to the negotiations, some Members had already developed their regimes of PCA and proved that it was a useful trade-facilitative measure.

The WTO negotiations, however, were conducted in a Member-driven manner, so PCA should be proposed by one Member or a group of Members to the NGTF. There were three proposals, which explained a general idea that PCA was able to facilitate trade, in the first-generation phase:

(i)   Under the post-clearance audit system, customs may first release most of the consignments, and then conduct a thorough review of the documents of selected consignments after release. (Chinese Taipei, TN/TF/W/10)
(ii) Post-clearance audits will facilitate the expeditious movement of goods at the customs because the clearance processing time will be shortened by allowing the controls to be carried out at a later stage. Post-clearance audits also reduce the need for expensive storage space at ports and the risk of theft and spoilage, so they should also reduce the cost of insurance. (Korea, TN/TF/W/18)
(iii) Establishment of disciplines on the application of [. . .] post-clearance control of goods. Members will be required to grant sufficient authority to customs administration support institutions to safeguard the audit function and effective post-clearance control of goods. (Peru, TN/TF/W/30)

The second generation: textual proposals

The WTO language is mainly about obligations for the Members. Notably, most of the WTO articles opt for 'shall' and against 'may', so obligations are universally imposed on the WTO membership. As the proposals on the general idea of PCA were still raw (as no obligations were explicitly mentioned), they needed to be immediately transformed by the proponents or other interested Members into textual proposals that were in conformity with the WTO language. Otherwise, the general idea would have gone bad. Indeed, some of the general ideas (e.g., 'uniform administration of trade regulations')[79] failed to hatch out and become TFA articles. For the most part, the proponents followed up the general ideas with their textual proposals. In that sense, it seemed that the proponent(s) held the ownership of a general idea (trade-facilitative measure) and the advancement of that idea should be at the hands of its proponent(s). In fact, any Member other than the proponent(s) of the general idea might submit a pertinent textual proposal under the Member-driven negotiating mechanism.

In the case of PCA, China, Korea (one of the original proponents of the general idea in the first generation) and Indonesia, as cosponsors, came forward with a textual proposal in the WTO language:[80]

1   Members shall carry out necessary PCA on the account books, vouchers, commercial documents, customs declaration forms and other trade-related information maintained by enterprises involved directly or indirectly in the transaction of international trade upon the risk analysis results.

2   Members shall conduct PCA through methods of regular audit and targeted audit to identify the risk and assess the compliance of traders.
3   The outcome of PCA shall be fed back timely to relevant Customs officers involved in clearance procedures to take further action. The most compliant traders or low-risk commodities shall be granted simplest and fastest clearance treatment by Customs.
4   Members shall adopt the relevant international standards and instruments as a basis for PCA, where such standards and instruments exist.

This textual proposal provided a 'demo' which was open to other Members' comments. Any Member may comment on, for example, the rationale, the wording and even the punctuations within the textual proposal. In the first rounds of consultations, the proponents defended their initial textual proposal, and, in the meanwhile, revised the text in compromise in order to satisfy, as far as possible, the entire membership. The truth was that other Members' comments had to be absorbed if the textual proposal was aimed at the endorsement by the NGTF, where consensus matters. In that phase, it seemed as if the proponents were negotiating against the rest of the NGTF. After several rounds of consultations, the proponents of PCA submitted a revised version of text:[81]

1   Members shall, where possible, adopt customs audit, especially post-clearance audit, with a view to expediting the release of goods at borders.
2   If a Member adopts customs audit, it shall ensure that the customs audit does not infringe upon the legal interests of the persons concerned.
3   The customs audit shall be implemented in a transparent manner. Members shall notify the persons concerned of the relevant initiation and result of the case, the rights and obligations it has, and the evidences and reasons for the result. The person shall be provided the right to appeal against any specific customs audit case it is involved in.
4   Members may use the result of customs audit as a legal basis for further actions, including investigations into the specific cases, dealing with the persons or goods concerned, etc.
5   Members shall, wherever practicable, use the result of customs audit for reference in applying risk management and identifying authorized trader status.

It can be seen from the revision that: (i) the proponents substituted Customs Audit for PCA, because some Members wanted a distinction between the audit done by the customs administration and the audit done by the third party (e.g., auditing firms); (ii) the focus shifted from the manner in which PCA should be conducted to the disciplines that the conduct of Customs Audit should obey, given that the WTO articles are of disciplinary principles rather than of operational guidance; and (iii) the use of results of PCA/Customs Audit diametrically turned from a 'shall' provision to a 'may' provision, because the use of PCA results was essentially a discretionary power of a Member. Nevertheless, this had not brought the debate on this trade-facilitative measure of PCA/Customs Audit to an end. Consultations went on and more comments from Members sprang up every time this issue was discussed in the NGTF – the negotiations at the technical level would be everlasting, if there was no political will for reaching a deal.

The third generation: draft consolidated negotiating text

The textual proposals were growing increasingly mature after rounds of consultations. Meanwhile, they were always underway to be revised, mostly by the proponents. The proponents lost their 'ownership' of the textual proposals when they were compiled by the WTO Secretariat in the draft consolidated negotiating text. At that stage, the PCA text was drafted as:[82]

1   Members [[may][shall]] [[carry out necessary][adopt or maintain the necessary legislative provisions]] for PCA on [[the accounts, [books], vouchers, commercial documents, customs declaration forms and other trade-related information][the import and export transaction accounts and commercial records][based on accounting records]] maintained by [enterprises] involved directly or indirectly in the transaction of international trade upon the risk [[analysis][management]] results.

[2   Members [[shall][may]] conduct PCA through methods of regular audit and targeted audit to [[identify][verify]] the risk and assess the compliance of traders.]

[3   The outcome of PCA shall be [[[[timely fed back] [communicated]] to relevant Customs officers involved in clearance procedures to take further action] [[provided, where appropriate, timely to other relevant officers and taken into account for further] [or] risk analysis]]. [The most compliant traders or low-risk commodities shall be granted simplest and fastest clearance treatment by Customs.]]

[4   [To the extent possible] Members shall adopt the relevant international standards and instruments as a basis for PCA, where such standards and instruments exist.]

In the draft consolidated negotiating text, all comments from Members were incorporated into a single text. There were hundreds of square brackets within the text. One square bracket represented one point at issue. The negotiations then turned out to be a job of choosing between the bracketed contents, which made the consultations easier and more effective. Each Member – no matter whether it was the proponent or not – was then on equal terms to have its say in adding, removing or maintaining a square bracket. Removing a square bracket signified that consensus was reached at one point. The process, however, was floundering because it might take the NGTF a whole morning to deal with only three square brackets.

With a view to expediting the negotiations, the NGTF once intensified the consultations in an unusual way: a consultation meeting might take a half day – when the plenary meetings adjourned – to focus only on an individual article; a facilitator, in some cases other than the original proponent, was designated to take the place of the NGTF's Chairperson to moderate the discussion on that article. The intensified consultations decentralized the normal but ponderous plenary mechanism for negotiations and provided more flexibilities and convenience to the negotiators in terms of timing and venues (sometimes in the places provided by Member delegations). When chairing the intensified consultations, the facilitators were not as uncompromising as the proponents, but the facilitators on the other hand were apt to add their own 'trimmings' to the draft consolidated negotiating text, which should have been irreversibly slimmed down. If negotiations were done in an irreversible manner, there should have been less back-and-forth and more fruitions in the Doha Round.

Final text in the TFA

Fortunately, consultations on PCA, together with other more than 50 articles in the draft consolidated negotiating text, eventually reached consensus at the last moment of the ninth WTO Ministerial Conference in December 2013. The Article on PCA in the TFA was finalized as:

5 Post-clearance audit

5.1 With a view to expediting the release of goods, each Member shall adopt or maintain post-clearance audit to ensure compliance with customs and other related laws and regulations.

5.2 Each Member shall select a person or a consignment for post-clearance audit in a risk-based manner, which may include appropriate selectivity criteria. Each Member shall conduct post-clearance audits in a transparent manner. Where the person is involved in the audit process and conclusive results have been achieved the Member shall, without delay, notify the person whose record is audited of the results, the person's rights and obligations and the reasons for the results.

5.3 The information obtained in post-clearance audit may be used in further administrative or judicial proceedings.

5.4 Members shall, wherever practicable, use the result of post-clearance audit in applying risk management.

The three generations of transformation finally enabled most of the general ideas, which could be instrumental in facilitating trade, to come true and become articles of the Agreement on Trade Facilitation. With all the square brackets erased from the draft consolidated negotiating text, the clean version of the Agreement came out.

The brand-new WTO Agreement on Trade Facilitation has been in place. A number of trade-facilitative measures (e.g., single window, advance rulings) at the cutting edge of international trade trends have come within the WTO's orbit. The Agreement also encompasses those trade-facilitative measures (e.g., transit, preshipment inspection) which had already been discussed during the times of the League of Nations and the GATT. At the same time, the WTO trade facilitation negotiations regrettably abandoned some conventional trade-facilitative measures. For example, 'abolition of consular invoices' could be found in the 1923 International Convention relating to the Simplification of Customs Formalities and the 1949 International Chamber of Commerce Resolution on Invisible Barriers to Trade and Travel (ICC Brochure 130); it was also subsequently put on the agenda of the GATT meetings;[83] 'prohibition of consular transaction requirement' was once brought forward by some Members (mainly Uganda and the US) to the WTO NGTF.[84] However, this issue faded out from the trade facilitation negotiations and eventually strayed from the WTO system.

Notes

1 WTO, WT/MIN(01)/DEC/1 (2001), para. 46.
2 WTO, WT/MIN(13)/36 (2013).
3 WTO, WT/MIN(01)/DEC/1 (2001), para. 46.
4 For some Doha topics, there are also other types of mechanisms, e.g., subcommittee on cotton under the special session of committee on agriculture for 'cotton'; working group under the General Council for 'trade and transfer of technology'.
5 Nora Neufeld, 'The Long and Winding Road: How WTO Members Finally Reached a Trade Facilitation Agreement', WTO Staff Working Paper, ERSD-2014–06 (2014), p. 3.
6 WTO, WT/MIN(96)/DEC (1996), para. 21.
7 WTO, TN/TF/M/1 (2004).
8 WTO, *WTO Public Forum 2007: How Can the WTO Help Harness Globalization?* (WTO, 2008), p. 6.
9 William Shakespeare, *The Tragedy of Hamlet, Prince of Denmark*, Act III, Scene I.
10 The Colorado Group was formed only for the sake of trade facilitation.
11 The Core Group was formed because of not only trade facilitation but also other subjects.
12 Regular participants were Bangladesh, Botswana, Cuba, Egypt, India, Indonesia, Jamaica, Kenya, Malaysia, Mauritius, Namibia, Nepal, Nigeria, the Philippines, Rwanda, Tanzania, Trinidad & Tobago, Uganda, Venezuela, Zambia and Zimbabwe. See WTO, TN/TF/W/142 (2006).
13 WTO, G/C/W/156 (1999), para. 55.
14 WTO, G/C/W/156 (1999).
15 Ibid.
16 Statement of US in the 3rd WTO Ministerial Conference, see WTO, WT/MIN(99)/ST/12 (1999).
17 Statement of the European Communities in the 3rd WTO Ministerial Conference, see WTO, WT/MIN(99)/ST/3 (1999).
18 Statement of the European Communities in the 5th WTO Ministerial Conference, see WTO, WT/MIN(03)/ST/5 (2003).
19 Statement of Japan in the 5th WTO Ministerial Conference, see WTO, WT/MIN(03)/ST/22 (2003).
20 Statement of Korea in the 5th WTO Ministerial Conference, see WTO, WT/MIN(03)/ST/15 (2003).
21 Statement of Malaysia in the 3rd WTO Ministerial Conference, see WTO, WT/MIN(99)/ST/28 (1999).

22 Statement of Malaysia in the 4th WTO Ministerial Conference, see WTO, WT/MIN(01)/ST/54 (2001).
23 Statement of Malaysia in the 5th WTO Ministerial Conference, see WTO, WT/MIN(03)/ST/30 (2003).
24 Statement of the Philippines in the 2nd WTO Ministerial Conference, see WTO, WT/MIN(98)/ST/11 (1998).
25 Statement of the Philippines in the 3rd WTO Ministerial Conference, see WTO, WT/MIN(99)/ST/6 (1999).
26 Statement of the Philippines in the 5th WTO Ministerial Conference, see WTO, WT/MIN(03)/ST/63 (2003).
27 WTO, G/C/W/156 (1999), para. 32.
28 WTO, G/L/665 (2003), p. 6.
29 WTO, G/C/W/156 (1999), para. 33.
30 WTO, G/L/665 (2003).
31 WTO, G/C/W/156 (1999).
32 WTO, TN/TF/M/5 (2005).
33 WTO, G/C/W/451 (2003).
34 WTO, G/C/W/150 (1999).
35 WTO, TN/TF/W/37 (2005).
36 WTO, TN/TF/M/18 (2007).
37 Peter Mandelson, 'Doha Development Agenda: The Round for Africa', statement to the third African Union Conference of Ministers of Trade in Cairo on June 8, 2005, http://trade.ec.europa.eu/doclib/html/123747.htm.
38 WTO, TN/TF/W/71 (2005).
39 WTO, TN/TF/M/5 (2005).
40 WTO, TN/TF/W/56 (2005).
41 UN, A/RES/S-6/3201 (1974). The Declaration was for the preparation of the Charter of Economic Rights and Duties of States (1974), which was adopted by the 29th UN General Assembly in 1974.
42 UN, A/RES/S-6/3201 (1974), para. 4 (k) and (n).
43 The Lomé Conventions were signed between the EEC/EU and the ACP countries. The first convention (Lomé I) was signed in 1975. Then Lomé II, III and IV were respectively signed in 1979, 1984 and 1989.
44 Kalle Laaksonen, Petri Mäki-Fränti and Meri Virolainen, 'Lomé Convention, Agriculture and Trade Relations Between the EU and the ACP Countries in 1975–2000', EU TRADEAG Working Paper 06/20–2007, p. 1.
45 Ibid., p. 7.
46 Jahangir Amuzegar, former Executive Director of IMF, 'The North-South Dialogue: From Conflict to Compromise', *Foreign Affairs*, April 1976.
47 Ibid.
48 WTO, TN/TF/M/5 (2005), para. 172.
49 WTO, TN/TF/W/147 (2007), para. 4.
50 WTO, WT/MIN(01)/DEC/1 (2001), para. 45–52.
51 Other main negotiations under the Doha Round also followed the principles, but seldom reached agreements.
52 Robert Keohane, *After Hegemony: Cooperation and Discord in the World Political Economy* (Princeton University Press, 1984), p. 91.
53 Ibid.
54 At the 'Mid-Term Review' Ministerial Meeting in Montreal in 1988, for example, 'early harvest' referred to results of certain negotiations under the Uruguay Round, on which clear consensus already existed, would enter into force immediately.

55 See Philip I. Levy, 'Do We Need an Undertaker for the Single Undertaking? Considering the Angles of Variable Geometry', in Simon J. Evenett and Bernard M. Hoekman (eds.), *Economic Development and Multilateral Trade Cooperation* (Palgrave Macmillan and World Bank, 2006), p. 418.
56 WTO, WT/MIN(01)/DEC/1 (2001).
57 WTO, WT/FIFTY/H/ST/8 (1998), p. 4.
58 Agreement Establishing the World Trade Organization, Article IX: 1.
59 Roberto Azevêdo, statement at the meeting where the General Council approved the appointment of Ambassador Roberto Carvalho de Azevêdo (Brazil) as the next Director-General of the WTO on May 14, 2013, www.wto.org/english/news e/news13 e/gc 14may13 e.htm.
60 Pascal Lamy, 'The Place of the WTO in the International Legal Order', lecture to the UN Audiovisual Library of International Law on June 15, 2008, www.wto.org/english/news_e/sppl_e/sppl94_e.htm.
61 WTO, WT/MIN(01)/DEC/1 (2001), para. 48–49.
62 Pascal Lamy, 'The WTO Is "a laboratory for harnessing globalization"', speech at Harvard University on November 1, 2006, www.wto.org/english/news_e/sppl_e/sppl47_e.htm.
63 See *supra* note 60.
64 WTO, WT/GC/M/57 (2000), para. 134.
65 Ibid.
66 Kent Jones, *Reconstructing the World Trade Organization for the 21st Century: An Institutional Approach* (Oxford University Press, 2015), pp. 85–86.
67 WTO, WT/MIN(01)/DEC/1 (2001), para. 49.
68 See *supra* note 62.
69 Mainly the US and the European Communities.
70 See US proposal, WTO, WT/GC/W/88 (1998); EC proposal, WTO, WT/GC/W/92 (1998); Statement by the Chairman of the General Council at the first meeting of the Trade Negotiations Committee on February 1, 2002, WTO, TN/C/1 (2002).
71 John Tsang, Chair of the 6th WTO Ministerial Conference, statement on December 2, 2005, www.wto.org/english/news_e/news05_e/stat_tsang_dec05_e.htm.
72 WTO, TN/C/1 (2002).
73 Mike Moore, speech to Legislators Assembly on December 2, 1999, www.wto.org/english/news_e/spmm_e/spmm18_e.htm.
74 Nathaniel Hawthorne, *The Scarlet Letter*, Chapter 13 'Another View of Hester'.
75 See the International Convention on the Simplification and Harmonization of Customs Procedures (the Revised Kyoto Convention), General Annex, Chapter 6: Customs Control, Standard 6.6.
76 WCO, *The Guidelines on Customs Control for the Kyoto Convention* (2010), pp. 23–27.
77 WCO, *Guidelines for Post-clearance Audit (PCA)* (2012), p. 4.
78 Ibid.
79 WTO, TN/TF/W/8 (2005).
80 WTO, TN/TF/W/134 (2006); TN/TF/W/134/Add.1 (2007).
81 WTO, TN/TF/W/134/Rev.1 (2010).
82 WTO, TN/TF/W/165 (2009).
83 See e.g. GATT, L/92 (1953).
84 See WTO, TN/TF/W/22 (2005); TN/TF/W/104 (2006).

6 A commentary on the Agreement on Trade Facilitation

When the Agreement on Trade Facilitation (TFA) was concluded, it did not mean that the Agreement would automatically blend into the family of WTO agreements and come into force. There needs to be an 'investiture' that accords the TFA the legitimacy of being an international agreement. The Ministerial Decision of December 7, 2013 (WT/MIN(13)/36, WT/L/911) and the Protocol Amending the Marrakesh Agreement on Establishing the WTO (WT/L/940) are the instruments for the 'investiture'.

In the Ministerial Decision of December 7, 2013 (WT/MIN(13)/36, WT/L/911), trade ministers decided:

1   We hereby conclude the negotiation of an Agreement on Trade Facilitation (the 'Agreement'), which is annexed hereto, subject to legal review for rectifications of a purely formal character that do not affect the substance of the Agreement.
2   We hereby establish a Preparatory Committee on Trade Facilitation (the 'Preparatory Committee') under the General Council, open to all Members, to perform such functions as may be necessary to ensure the expeditious entry into force of the Agreement and to prepare for the efficient operation of the Agreement upon its entry into force. In particular, the Preparatory Committee shall conduct the legal review of the Agreement referred to in paragraph 1 above, receive notifications of Category A commitments, and draw up a Protocol of Amendment (the 'Protocol') to insert the Agreement into Annex 1A of the WTO Agreement.
3   The General Council shall meet no later than 31 July 2014 to annex to the Agreement notifications of Category A commitments, to adopt the Protocol drawn up by the Preparatory Committee and to open the Protocol for acceptance until 31 July 2015. The Protocol shall enter into force in accordance with Article X:3 of the WTO Agreement.

This simple three-paragraph Ministerial Decision is critical to the TFA in these respects: (i) it declares the conclusion of negotiations on trade facilitation, and affirms that the annex thereto is the final text of the TFA that cannot be substantially changed; (ii) it addresses the 'who-does-what' question in order to prepare for the TFA's entry into force; and (iii) it determines the responsible WTO body and procedures which will finally bring the TFA into effect.

Following those three paragraphs, the Preparatory Committee on Trade Facilitation during the first half year of 2014 reviewed and improved the TFA to 'a purely formal character that does not affect the substance of the Agreement'.[1] On July 15, 2014, the final version of the Agreement on Trade Facilitation (WT/L/931) was nailed down.

On the back of WT/L/931, the Protocol Amending the Marrakesh Agreement on Establishing the WTO of November 27, 2014 (WT/L/940) inserts the TFA into where it is among the WTO legal texts by setting forth that 'Annex 1A to the WTO Agreement shall [. . .] be amended by the insertion of the Agreement on Trade Facilitation [. . .] to be placed after the Agreement on Safeguards'. In the strict sense, the TFA is the annex to WT/L/940.

Notably, WT/L/940 also states that '[t]his Protocol shall be registered in accordance with the provisions of Article 102 of the Charter of the United Nations'. Article 102 of the Charter of the United Nations (UN) provides that:

1   Every treaty and every international agreement entered into by any Member of the United Nations after the present Charter comes into force shall as soon as possible be registered with the Secretariat and published by it.
2   No party to any such treaty or international agreement which has not been registered in accordance with the provisions of paragraph 1 of this Article may invoke that treaty or agreement before any organ of the United Nations.

According to Article 102, the TFA shall be published on UN Treaties Collection (https://treaties.un.org). Registration of the TFA with the United Nations denotes that the TFA forms a part of public international law.

Structure of the Agreement on Trade Facilitation

Trade facilitation ran much faster than the rest part of Doha Round negotiations, as a cheetah runs faster than other cats. The TFA also has a cheetah-like structure: Preamble as the head, Section I as the fore legs, Section II as the hind legs, and Section III as the tail.

The Preamble – as the head of a cheetah tells its status in the cat family – elucidates the mandates and principles that the negotiations on trade facilitation had followed, the aim of the agreement, the recognition of the needs of developing country Members and least developed country (LDC) Members, and the necessity for cooperation between Members.

Section I – as the fore legs steer the cheetah where to go – is all about the trade-facilitative measures, which originate in the mandates of clarifying and improving relevant aspects of GATT Articles V, VIII and X, as well as the mandates of regulating customs cooperation, as prescribed in the Modalities for Negotiations on Trade Facilitation (namely Annex D of the 2004 'July package'). Article 1 to Article 5 in Section I focus on GATT Article X (Publication and Administration of Trade Regulations), Article 6 to Article 10 on GATT Article VIII (Fees and Formalities connected with Importation and Exportation), Article 11 on GATT Article V (Freedom of Transit) and Article 12 on customs cooperation.

Section II – as the hind legs control the cheetah's paces – is intended to resolve the insistent concerns of the developing country Members and LDC Members about acquiring the capacity to implement the TFA. This section also carries out the mandates in Annex D of the 2004 'July package' regarding technical assistance and capacity building (TACB) as well as special and differential treatment (S&DT). This section determines how thoroughly the developing country Members and LDC Members will implement the TFA. Its Article 13 sets forth general principles in accordance with Annex D of the 2004 'July package' and Annex E of the Hong Kong Ministerial Declaration. Article 14 defines the three categories of commitments (Category A, Category B and Category C) for each individual developing country Member and LDC Member. Then Article 15 demarcates Category A, and Articles 16 to 19 demarcate Category B and C. Article 20 is about the application of dispute settlement mechanism. Articles 21 and 22 (including the Annex 1: Format for Notification under Paragraph 1 of Article 22) specify the provision of TACB.

Section III – as the tail maintains balance when the cheetah is running – consists of institutional arrangements and final provisions. Article 23 mandates the WTO to establish the Committee on Trade Facilitation and mandates each Member to establish the National Committee on Trade Facilitation respectively. Article 24, as the final provisions, involves the issues such as interpretative notes, entry into force, exceptions and exemptions, waivers, reservations.

A commentary on Section I

ARTICLE 1: PUBLICATION AND AVAILABILITY OF INFORMATION

Legal Text:

1   Publication

1.1 Each Member shall promptly publish the following information in a non-discriminatory and easily accessible manner in order to enable governments, traders and other interested parties to become acquainted with them:

(a) procedures for importation, exportation and transit (including port, airport and other entry-point procedures), and required forms and documents;

(b) applied rates of duties and taxes of any kind imposed on or in connection with importation or exportation;

(c) fees and charges imposed by or for governmental agencies on or in connection with importation, exportation or transit;

(d) rules for the classification or valuation of products for customs purposes;

(e) laws, regulations and administrative rulings of general application relating to rules of origin;

(f) import, export or transit restrictions or prohibitions;

(g) penalty provisions for breaches of import, export, or transit formalities;

(h) procedures for appeal or review;

(i) agreements or parts thereof with any country or countries relating to importation, exportation, or transit; and

(j) procedures relating to the administration of tariff quotas.

1.2 Nothing in these provisions shall be construed as requiring the publication or provision of information other than in the language of the Member except as stated in paragraph 2.2.

2   Information Available Through Internet

2.1 Each Member shall make available, and update to the extent possible and as appropriate, the following through the internet:

(a) a description[2] of its procedures for importation, exportation and transit, including procedures for appeal or review, that informs governments, traders and other interested parties of the practical steps needed for importation, exportation and transit;

(b) the forms and documents required for importation into, exportation from, or transit through the territory of that Member;

(c) contact information on its enquiry point(s).

2.2 Whenever practicable, the description referred to in subparagraph 2.1(a) shall also be made available in one of the official languages of the WTO.

2.3 Members are encouraged to make available further trade-related information through the internet, including relevant trade-related legislation and other items referred to in paragraph 1.1.

3   Enquiry Points

3.1 Each Member shall, within its available resources, establish or maintain one or more enquiry points to answer reasonable enquiries of governments, traders and other interested parties on matters covered by paragraph 1.1 and to provide the required forms and documents referred to in subparagraph 1.1(a).

3.2 Members of a customs union or involved in regional integration may establish or maintain common enquiry points at the regional level to satisfy the requirement of paragraph 3.1 for common procedures.

3.3 Members are encouraged not to require the payment of a fee for answering enquiries and providing required forms and documents. If any, Members shall limit the amount of their fees and charges to the approximate cost of services rendered.

3.4 The enquiry points shall answer enquiries and provide the forms and documents within a reasonable time period set by each Member, which may vary depending on the nature or complexity of the request.

4   Notification

Each Member shall notify the Committee on Trade Facilitation established under paragraph 1.1 of Article 23 (referred to in this Agreement as the 'Committee') of:

(a) the official place(s) where the items in subparagraphs 1.1(a) to (j) have been published;

(b) the Uniform Resource Locators of website(s) referred to in paragraph 2.1; and

(c) the contact information of the enquiry points referred to in paragraph 3.1.

This article to a high degree rekindles the spirits imbedded in GATT Article X:1 by reiterating the aim to 'enable governments, traders and other interested parties to become acquainted with [the information]'. The new article largely reinforces the disciplines on the publication and availability of information in these respects: scope, means and tangibility.

With respect to the scope of publication, this article numerates the types of information that are subject to publication at a very detailed level (with 10 bullets) (q.v. Article 1:1.1), and, thus, enriches the jurisdiction of GATT Article X:1, which roughly encompasses 'laws, regulations, judicial decisions and administrative rulings of general application'. However, GATT Article X:1, as part of the WTO legal texts, is still valid, and provides for some issues (e.g., disclosure of confidential information) that the new article has ignored. Regarding the substance to be published, the WTO Members are committed to the combination of both GATT Article X:1 and TFA Article 1, which complement (rather than displace) each other.

This *zeitgeist* article introduces internet (q.v. Article 1:2) and enquiry points (q.v. Article 1:3) as means of information publication. In fact, at the time of drafting the GATT, the internet had not emerged and telecommunication had not been so popularized. The website and enquiry point shall function not only to provide the types of information defined by this article but also to physically afford (or allow downloading) forms and documents.

This article accentuates the tangibility of publication; a tangible facility (viz. the official publication places, the website and the enquiry points) should be notified to the WTO Trade Facilitation Committee (q.v. Article 1:1.4).

There are yet some ambiguities (or rather 'loopholes') in this article that would probably cause controversy when it comes to relevant implementation or interpretation: (i) This article requires that 'each Member shall *promptly* publish the information'. It is, however, difficult to judge how 'promptly' the publication shall be conducted. Could one week be considered not prompt yet? Or, otherwise, could three months be regarded as not that delayed? At least, in the *EEC-Restrictions on Imports of Apples*, the Panel found that 'the [European Economic Community] had been in breach of these [prompt publication] requirements since it had given public notice of the quota allocation only about two months after the quota period had begun'.[3] (ii) The new article has added 'other interested parties' to 'governments and traders' (as previously defined in GATT Article X:1) that have already exhaustively made up the audience for publication. Besides the public sector (i.e., domestic and foreign government agencies) and the private sector (i.e., traders in a broad sense), who else could be the 'other interested parties' then? This broad, but notional, group of audience need to be specified in the future interpretation of this article. (iii) This article stipulates that 'the enquiry points shall answer enquiries and provide the forms and documents within a reasonable time period set by each Member'. Therefore, there must be an explicit time limit – which may differ – for each individual Member to respond to the public's enquiries. Moreover, as enquiries would be raised by the public on a case-by-case basis, can we infer that the answers given by Members' governments shall be concrete so as to interpret the applicability of trade regulations and policies to certain trading operations, rather than simply reading the notes scripted in advance? If so, what are the legal effects of these answers, and how to distinguish issuing advance rulings from answering enquiries? Perhaps, these questions are left for the possibly future Panel or Appellate Body on the TFA-related disputes to conclude.

ARTICLE 2: OPPORTUNITY TO COMMENT, INFORMATION BEFORE ENTRY INTO FORCE, AND CONSULTATIONS

Legal Text:

1   Opportunity to Comment and Information before Entry into Force

1.1 Each Member shall, to the extent practicable and in a manner consistent with its domestic law and legal system, provide opportunities and an appropriate time period to traders and other interested parties to comment on the proposed introduction or amendment of laws and regulations of general application related to the movement, release, and clearance of goods, including goods in transit.

1.2 Each Member shall, to the extent practicable and in a manner consistent with its domestic law and legal system, ensure that new or amended laws and regulations of general application related to the movement, release, and clearance of goods, including goods in transit, are published or information on them made otherwise publicly available, as early as possible before their entry into force, in order to enable traders and other interested parties to become acquainted with them.

1.3 Changes to duty rates or tariff rates, measures that have a relieving effect, measures the effectiveness of which would be undermined as a result of compliance with paragraphs 1.1 or 1.2, measures applied in urgent circumstances, or minor changes to domestic law and legal system are each excluded from paragraphs 1.1 and 1.2.

2   Consultations

Each Member shall, as appropriate, provide for regular consultations between its border agencies and traders or other stakeholders located within its territory.

Some Uruguay Round agreements, such as the Sanitary and Phytosanitary (SPS) Agreement (q.v. Annex B:5), have absorbed the idea of furnishing the traders and other interested parties with the opportunities and appropriate time to comment or consult on a proposed regulation. The SPS Agreement, however, only allows 'other Members' to initiate a talk with a Member on its sanitary or phytosanitary regulations. In the context of the WTO's transparency principles, the TFA Article 2 is groundbreaking, because it for the first time accords the private sector (viz. 'traders and other interested parties') not only a channel for dialog with the Member's government agencies but also an opportunity of engaging broadly in 'the proposed introduction or amendment of laws and regulations of general application related to the movement, release and clearance of goods, including goods in transit'. In fact, this practice has been well-tried in many countries' *due process* of lawmaking and can be traced to the 1946 US Administrative Procedure Act (APA), which provided that:

RULE MAKING

SEC. 4. Except to the extent that there is involved (1) any military, naval, or foreign affairs function of the United States or (2) any matter relating to agency management or personnel or to public property, loans, grants, benefits, or contracts –

(a) NOTICE – General notice of proposed rulemaking shall be published in the Federal Register (unless all persons subject thereto are named and either personally served or otherwise have actual notice thereof in accordance with law) and shall include (1) a statement of the time, place, and nature of public rule making proceedings; (2) reference to the authority under which the rule is proposed; and (3) either the terms or substance of the proposed rule or a description of the subjects and issues involved. Except where notice or hearing is required by statute, this subsection shall not apply to interpretative rules, general statements of policy, rules of agency organization, procedure, or practice, or in any situation in which the agency for good cause finds (and incorporates the finding and a brief statement of the reasons therefor in the rules issued) that notice and public procedure thereon are impracticable, unnecessary, or contrary to the public interest.

(b) PROCEDURES – After notice required by this section, the agency shall afford interested persons an opportunity to participate in the rule making through submission of written data, views, or arguments with or without opportunity to present the same orally in any manner; and, after consideration of all relevant matter presented, the agency shall incorporate in any rules adopted a concise general statement of their basis and purpose. Where rules are required by statute to be made on the record after opportunity for an agency hearing, the requirements of sections 7 and 8 shall apply in place of the provisions of this subsection.

(c) EFFECTIVE DATES – The required publication or service of any substantive rule (other than one granting or recognizing exemption or relieving restriction or interpretative rules and statements of policy) shall be made not less than thirty days prior to the effective date thereof except as otherwise provided by the agency upon good cause found and published with the rule.

(d) PETITIONS – Every agency shall accord any interested person the right to petition for the issuance, amendment, or repeal of a rule.[4]

The wording 'in a manner consistent with its domestic law and legal system' (q.v. Article 2:1.1) would, however, weaken the extent of private sector's engagement in the introduction and amendment of laws and regulations. Lack of disciplines on a Member's uptake of the comments and consultations in this article (in contrast to the above APA provisions) would possibly lead to the situation that the private sector's engagement might be vain in the end.

ARTICLE 3: ADVANCE RULINGS

Legal Text:

1   Each Member shall issue an advance ruling in a reasonable, time-bound manner to the applicant that has submitted a written request containing all necessary information. If a Member declines to issue an advance ruling, it shall promptly notify the applicant in writing, setting out the relevant facts and the basis for its decision.

2   A Member may decline to issue an advance ruling to the applicant where the question raised in the application:

(a) is already pending in the applicant's case before any governmental agency, appellate tribunal, or court; or
(b) has already been decided by any appellate tribunal or court.

3   The advance ruling shall be valid for a reasonable period of time after its issuance unless the law, facts, or circumstances supporting that ruling have changed.

4   Where the Member revokes, modifies, or invalidates the advance ruling, it shall provide written notice to the applicant setting out the relevant facts and the basis for its decision. Where a Member revokes, modifies, or invalidates advance rulings with retroactive effect, it may only do so where the ruling was based on incomplete, incorrect, false, or misleading information.

5   An advance ruling issued by a Member shall be binding on that Member in respect of the applicant that sought it. The Member may provide that the advance ruling is binding on the applicant.

6   Each Member shall publish, at a minimum:

(a) the requirements for the application for an advance ruling, including the information to be provided and the format;
(b) the time period by which it will issue an advance ruling; and
(c) the length of time for which the advance ruling is valid.

7   Each Member shall provide, upon written request of an applicant, a review of the advance ruling or the decision to revoke, modify, or invalidate the advance ruling.[5]

8   Each Member shall endeavor to make publicly available any information on advance rulings which it considers to be of significant interest to other interested parties, taking into account the need to protect commercially confidential information.

9   Definitions and scope:

(a) An advance ruling is a written decision provided by a Member to the applicant prior to the importation of a good covered by the application that sets forth the treatment that the Member shall provide to the good at the time of importation with regard to:

(i) the good's tariff classification; and
(ii) the origin of the good.[6]

(b) In addition to the advance rulings defined in subparagraph (a), Members are encouraged to provide advance rulings on:

(i) the appropriate method or criteria, and the application thereof, to be used for determining the customs value under a particular set of facts;

(ii) the applicability of the Member's requirements for relief or exemption from customs duties;

(iii) the application of the Member's requirements for quotas, including tariff quotas; and

(iv) any additional matters for which a Member considers it appropriate to issue an advance ruling.

(c) An applicant is an exporter, importer or any person with a justifiable cause or a representative thereof.

(d) A Member may require that the applicant have legal representation or registration in its territory. To the extent possible, such requirements shall not restrict the categories of persons eligible to apply for advance rulings, with particular consideration for the specific needs of small and medium-sized enterprises. These requirements shall be clear and transparent and not constitute a means of arbitrary or unjustifiable discrimvination.

Although GATT Article X:3 has required Members to 'administer in a uniform, impartial and reasonable manner all its laws, regulations, decisions and rulings', traders are often confronted with inconsistent decisions on customs affairs (e.g., customs valuation, verification of the origin of goods and tariff classification), which cause uncertainty to the entire trade transaction.[7] The concept of advance ruling is therefore introduced into the TFA as a means of uniform and impartial administration of customs affairs.

The benefits of advance ruling are obvious: a trader will be officially notified within a given period of time by a Member's responsible government agency (mostly the customs administration) the treatment to his trading transaction prior to the authentic occurrence of the claimed transaction; both the applicant (trader) and government agency (customs administration), therefore, simply need to follow the advance ruling set forth beforehand without any back-and-forth later on. An advance ruling has the essentials: (i) the ruling, as an administrative decision, is made on the basis of a trading transaction that is taking place expectantly but not at the present time; (ii) the ruling (other than an answer to an enquiry) is binding on the responsible government agency (customs administration) and possibly the applicant (trader) regarding the application ruled on; (iii) the ruling is valid for a reasonable period of time unless the supportive elements have changed; and (iv) the ruling, if published without prejudice to the commercial confidentiality, works as a benchmark that can be referred to by other 'interested parties' in identical or similar cases.

Advance ruling enables the certainty and predictability of the government agency's processing of trading operations. According to OECD, advance ruling is the most significant trade-facilitative measure that would 'lead to the highest increases in trade flows'.[8] However, the TFA article on advance ruling, as a result of compromise in the multilateral trade negotiations, is far less voluminous than the domestic statute of the proponents (e.g., the US). For example, US Title 19-Customs Duties, Code of Federal Regulations, Part 177 (19 C.F.R. 177) provides: 'if the transaction described in the ruling letter and the actual transaction are the same, and any and all conditions set forth in the ruling letter have been satisfied, the ruling will be applied to the transaction'.[9] According to the TFA Article 3:5, in contrast, an advance ruling shall be binding on the Member that issues it, and the Member may provide that the advance ruling is binding on the applicant – it implies that an advance ruling is not necessarily binding on the applicant. If so, the applicant is likely to abuse the ruling that is not binding on him in bad faith: (i) he may sound the responsible government agency out about policy enforcement by fabricating a trading transaction he has no intension to conduct; or (ii) he may retreat from the trading transaction in case the ruling does not satisfy his expectation. Thus, it would be a waste of the governmental resources.

Box 6.1   Application of advance rulings by the US

The US customs service began offering advance rulings as Treasury Decisions and Customs Service Decisions in the late 1960s. US Customs and Border Protection ('CBP') now offers advance rulings for all matters for which CBP has enforcement authority. Those topics include: tariff classification, valuation, country of origin, duty drawback, etc.

The benefits of CBP's advance rulings are numerous and extensive. First, for CBP, it has consolidated its decision-making in one location. Rather than decisions on classification and valuation being made by over 300 ports of entry during the compressed time of the entry of goods, any interested party can ask CBP to make a decision prior to importation. The advance ruling decision makers are located together which brings great consistency and managed outcomes. As advance rulings in the US are published on the Customs Rulings On-line Search System ('CROSS'), they are accessible and easily searchable by all CBP officers at all ports of entry, again allowing for great consistency and certainty in decision-making. Finally, based on the expertise the agency has gained in the subject matters of advance rulings, the consistency in agency positions, transparency in the process and well-developed reasoning, US courts recognize that CBP decisions are entitled to a level of deference by the courts that have jurisdiction over customs matters.

The benefits for traders are predictability, consistency, certainty and efficiency. CBP's advance rulings bring predictability and consistency by allowing a trader to apply for an advance ruling and comfort of knowing that he will be given the treatment set forth in the advance ruling at every US port of entry. The trader finds certainty in the advance ruling because his goods are entitled to the treatment set forth in the advance ruling until, if ever, the ruling is modified or revoked. US advance rulings do not expire. Availability of advance rulings brings efficiency and cost effectiveness to traders by allowing them to make decisions early and make those decisions part of their manufacturing, importing and business plans for all stages of business and contract planning.

A further benefit to both CBP and traders is that advance rulings allow traders to take proactive measures to ensure their compliance with US customs laws. Advance rulings further the goal of shared responsibility and informed compliance on behalf of traders and CBP by giving traders the ability to seek an answer to their questions ahead of engaging in a transaction, and CBP a chance to make these decisions in a thoughtful way and in a managed environment.

Source: Presentation of the US in the Symposium of Practical Experience of Implementing Trade Facilitation Reforms, held on November 8–9, 2011 at the WTO Secretariat, https://www.wto.org/english/tratop_e/tradfa_e/casestudies_reports_e.htm.

ARTICLE 4: PROCEDURES FOR APPEAL OR REVIEW

Legal Text:

1   Each Member shall provide that any person to whom customs issues an administrative decision[10] has the right, within its territory, to:

   (a) an administrative appeal to or review by an administrative authority higher than or independent of the official or office that issued the decision; and/or
   (b) a judicial appeal or review of the decision.

2   The legislation of a Member may require that an administrative appeal or review be initiated prior to a judicial appeal or review.

3   Each Member shall ensure that its procedures for appeal or review are carried out in a nondiscriminatory manner.

4   Each Member shall ensure that, in a case where the decision on appeal or review under subparagraph 1(a) is not given either:

   (a) within set periods as specified in its laws or regulations; or
   (b) without undue delay

   the petitioner has the right to either further appeal to or further review by the administrative authority or the judicial authority or any other recourse to the judicial authority.[11]

5   Each Member shall ensure that the person referred to in paragraph 1 is provided with the reasons for the administrative decision so as to enable such a person to have recourse to procedures for appeal or review where necessary.

6   Each Member is encouraged to make the provisions of this Article applicable to an administrative decision issued by a relevant border agency other than customs.

GATT Article X:3(b) has had a provision concerning 'tribunals or procedures for prompt review and correction of administrative action relating to customs matters', which chimes with the maxim of William Blackstone, a famous English jurist in the eighteenth century, that 'where there is a legal right, there is also a legal remedy, by suit or action at law, whenever that right is invaded'.[12] That said, the TFA Article 4 fills the void GATT Article X leaves: (i) an eligible petitioner could extensively be 'any person to whom customs issues an administrative decision' (q.v. Article 4:1); (ii) the new article establishes – in the form of a *proviso* (viz. 'the legislation of a Member may require that [. . .]') – a principle that administrative appeal/review is prior to judicial appeal/review (q.v. Article 4:2); (iii) the petitioner's right of further having recourse to the judicial authority is therein guaranteed (q.v. Article 4:1), because judicial review is generally a remedy of last resort;[13] and (iv) relevant border agencies other than customs are encouraged to apply this article (q.v. Article 4:6).

There are still some demerits in this article: (i) Article 4:4 implies that the petitioner has the right to further resort to the administrative or judicial authority only if the administrative authority exceeds the time limit (viz. in a case where the decision on appeal or review is not given either within set periods as specified in its laws or regulations or without undue delay). However, can a petitioner turn to the court for other reasons (e.g., he is discontented with the result of the administrative appeal/review)? (ii) According to the provision that '[e]ach Member shall ensure that the person [. . .] is provided with the reasons for the administrative decision so as to enable such a person to have recourse to procedures for appeal or review where necessary' (q.v. Article 4:5), the main obligation for a Member is to provide the reasons for the administrative decision.[14] In fact, this provision is drawn up primarily for the purpose of regulating a Member's administrative decision-making process (in particular discouraging the Member from crudely notifying the administrative decision without providing the reasons and other information at the same time). Furthermore, the aim of enabling 'such a person to have recourse to procedures for appeal or review' has been provided in Article 4:1 and is irrelevant to the provision of the reasons for the administrative decision.

ARTICLE 5: OTHER MEASURES TO ENHANCE IMPARTIALITY, NON-DISCRIMINATION AND TRANSPARENCY

Legal Text:

1   Notifications for Enhanced Controls or Inspections

Where a Member adopts or maintains a system of issuing notifications or guidance to its concerned authorities for enhancing the level of controls or inspections at the border in respect of foods, beverages, or feedstuffs covered under the notification or guidance for protecting human, animal, or plant life or health within its territory, the following disciplines shall apply to the manner of their issuance, termination, or suspension:

(a) the Member may, as appropriate, issue the notification or guidance based on risk;

(b) the Member may issue the notification or guidance so that it applies uniformly only to those points of entry where the sanitary and phytosanitary conditions on which the notification or guidance are based apply;

(c) the Member shall promptly terminate or suspend the notification or guidance when circumstances giving rise to it no longer exist, or if changed circumstances can be addressed in a less trade-restrictive manner; and

(d) when the Member decides to terminate or suspend the notification or guidance, it shall, as appropriate, promptly publish the announcement of its termination or suspension in a non-discriminatory and easily accessible manner, or inform the exporting Member or the importer.

2   Detention

A Member shall promptly inform the carrier or importer in case of detention of goods declared for importation, for inspection by customs or any other competent authority.

3   Test Procedures

3.1 A Member may, upon request, grant an opportunity for a second test in case the first test result of a sample taken upon arrival of goods declared for importation shows an adverse finding.

3.2 A Member shall either publish, in a non-discriminatory and easily accessible manner, the name and address of any laboratory where the test can be carried out or provide this information to the importer when it is granted the opportunity provided under paragraph 3.1.

3.3 A Member shall consider the result of the second test, if any, conducted under paragraph 3.1, for the release and clearance of goods and, if appropriate, may accept the results of such test.

This article is made up of three seemingly unrelated provisions: (i) 'notifications for enhanced controls or inspections' is designed to impose disciplines on the system (originally called 'import alerts/rapid alerts')[15] of issuing notifications or guidance concerning 'the level of controls or inspections at the border in respect of foods, beverages, or feedstuffs' (q.v. Article 5:1), but looks fairly associated with the SPS Agreement Article 5 (assessment of risk and determination of the appropriate level of SPS protection); (ii) 'detention' requires a Member's customs administration or other competent authority to inform the carrier or importer in case of detention of goods declared for importation (q.v. Article 5:2); and (iii) 'test procedures' addresses the importer's (the exporter is excluded as per the provision) need for a second confirmatory test (q.v. Article 5:3).

During the negotiations, a number of negotiators insisted that the issues that this article dealt with should normally fall under the SPS domain. They, therefore, discouraged the TFA's adoption of this article. Nevertheless, 'notifications for enhanced controls or inspections' could be interpreted as a new set of disciplines in addition to the existing SPS measures, while 'detention' and 'test procedures' both contain issues on which the SPS Agreement is silent. The entire TFA Article 5 could thus be seen as SPS-plus provisions,[16] notwithstanding the stipulation that nothing in the TFA shall be construed as diminishing the SPS Agreement (q.v. Article 24: 6).

ARTICLE 6: DISCIPLINES ON FEES AND CHARGES IMPOSED ON OR IN CONNECTION WITH IMPORTATION AND EXPORTATION AND PENALTIES

Legal Text:

1 **General Disciplines on Fees and Charges Imposed on or in Connection with Importation and Exportation**

1.1 The provisions of paragraph 1 shall apply to all fees and charges other than import and export duties and other than taxes within the purview of Article III of GATT 1994 imposed by Members on or in connection with the importation or exportation of goods.

1.2 Information on fees and charges shall be published in accordance with Article 1. This information shall include the fees and charges that will be applied, the reason for such fees and charges, the responsible authority and when and how payment is to be made.

1.3 An adequate time period shall be accorded between the publication of new or amended fees and charges and their entry into force, except in urgent circumstances. Such fees and charges shall not be applied until information on them has been published.

1.4 Each Member shall periodically review its fees and charges with a view to reducing their number and diversity, where practicable.

2 **Specific Disciplines on Fees and Charges for Customs Processing Imposed on or in Connection with Importation and Exportation**

Fees and charges for customs processing:

(i) shall be limited in amount to the approximate cost of the services rendered on or in connection with the specific import or export operation in question; and

(ii) are not required to be linked to a specific import or export operation provided they are levied for services that are closely connected to the customs processing of goods.

3 Penalty Disciplines

3.1 For the purpose of paragraph 3, the term 'penalties' shall mean those imposed by a Member's customs administration for a breach of the Member's customs laws, regulations, or procedural requirements.

3.2 Each Member shall ensure that penalties for a breach of a customs law, regulation, or procedural requirement are imposed only on the person(s) responsible for the breach under its laws.

3.3 The penalty imposed shall depend on the facts and circumstances of the case and shall be commensurate with the degree and severity of the breach.

3.4 Each Member shall ensure that it maintains measures to avoid:

(a) conflicts of interest in the assessment and collection of penalties and duties; and

(b) creating an incentive for the assessment or collection of a penalty that is inconsistent with paragraph 3.3.

3.5 Each Member shall ensure that when a penalty is imposed for a breach of customs laws, regulations, or procedural requirements, an explanation in writing is provided to the person(s) upon whom the penalty is imposed specifying the nature of the breach and the applicable law, regulation or procedure under which the amount or range of penalty for the breach has been prescribed.

3.6 When a person voluntarily discloses to a Member's customs administration the circumstances of a breach of a customs law, regulation, or procedural requirement prior to the discovery of the breach by the customs administration, the Member is encouraged to, where appropriate, consider this fact as a potential mitigating factor when establishing a penalty for that person.

3.7 The provisions of this paragraph shall apply to the penalties on traffic in transit referred to in paragraph 3.1.

This article is largely in keeping with the rules prescribed in GATT Article VIII, and furthermore brings forth reinforced disciplines on fees and charges.

The provision of 'general disciplines on fees and charges imposed on or in connection with importation and exportation' is nothing new but reiteration of the spirits of TFA Article 1:1.1(c) (about adequate disclosure), GATT Article X:2 (about an interval between publication and entry into force), GATT Article VIII:2 (about review of operation of laws and regulations), and GATT Article VIII:1(b) (about reducing the number and diversity of fees and charges).

The provision of 'specific disciplines on fees and charges for customs processing imposed on or in connection with importation and exportation' on the one hand duplicates GATT Article VIII:1(a) that requires a Member to limit 'all fees and charges in amount to the approximate cost of services rendered', and on the other hand gives a Member permission to levy fees and charges for customs processing services regardless of any links to a specific import or export operation. Interpretations of the relevant terms embodied in this provision can be found in the Panel Report on *United States – Customs User Fee* (1988).[17] For example, as regards 'services rendered', the Panel concluded that 'government activities closely enough connected to the processes of customs entry that they might, with no more than the customary artistic license accorded to taxing authorities, be called a 'service' to the importer in question;[18] with respect to 'cost of the services rendered', the Panel agreed that this term 'must be interpreted to refer to the cost of the customs processing for the individual entry in question'.[19]

The provision of 'penalty disciplines' transcends GATT Article VIII:3 (about no substantial penalties for minor breaches of customs regulations or procedural requirements) by forming a more robust set of rules. Penalty clauses, as a means of 'righting a wrong', are common in countries' administrative laws and regulations. No matter for what purpose a penalty is imposed (e.g., restoring the loss already incurred, preventing reoccurrence of a previous violation, incapacitating the violator's ability to conduct further violations or demonstrating to the public corresponding treatment to a bad example), the penalty must be just. In line with this jurisprudence, the TFA Article 6:3 obviates unjust penalties through underlining the norms that: (i) the innocent shall not be penalized (q.v. Article 6:3.2) ; (ii) a penalty shall be judged on the basis of a *fait accompli* (accomplished fact) (q.v. Article 6:3.3); (iii) excessively harsh penalty shall be discouraged (q.v. Article 6:3.3 and 3.4); (iv) the person to be penalized shall be put on notice of the necessary information (especially the legal grounds) as per the procedure for *service of notice* (q.v. Article 6:3.5); and (v) voluntary disclosure is encouraged to be taken as a mitigating factor in determining the penalty (q.v. Article 6:3.6).[20] Despite the norms herein that are already comprehensive for penalty, this article yet lacks a fundamental principle of *nulla poena sine lege* (no penalty without a law). Additionally, according to a normative service of notice, the rights and obligations that the penalized person has pertaining to the penalty shall be explained to him, but this is omitted from Article 6:3.5.

ARTICLE 7: RELEASE AND CLEARANCE OF GOODS

1   Pre-arrival Processing

Legal Text:

> 1.1 Each Member shall adopt or maintain procedures allowing for the submission of import documentation and other required information, including manifests, in order to begin processing prior to the arrival of goods with a view to expediting the release of goods upon arrival.
>
> 1.2 Each Member shall, as appropriate, provide for advance lodging of documents in electronic format for pre-arrival processing of such documents.

The idea of 'advance submission/processing' has been drawn on in a number of areas (e.g., taxation, transportation) for the sake of facilitating doing business or securing the society. For example, the US Internal Revenue Service (IRS) adopts a certain procedure and form (Form 8940) for 'advance approval' of issues (including set-asides, voter registration activities, scholarship procedures, etc.) which a private foundation may demonstrate in its request for tax exemption under 25 U.S.C. 501(c)(3).[21] Moreover, the US Department of Homeland Security (DHS) has launched the Advance Passenger Information System (APIS) since 2009, which allows DHS to review passenger information transmitted by the commercial airline and vessel operators prior to departure in order to identify potential threats caused by the boarding of a person of interest. Pre-arrival processing (as well as advance ruling) in trade facilitation terms follows this idea. Pre-arrival processing ingeniously places the lodging/processing of import documentation and information in advance of the physical arrival of goods so that the goods are given the green light when disembarking.

In reality, there are a variety of agencies (e.g., customs, quarantine inspection, port administration and licensing authorities) that process various import documentation and information (e.g., manifests, customs declaration forms, quarantine certificates and import licenses). It might be too ideal to have all the involved agencies adopt pre-arrival processing procedures for all types of documentation and information. Except for manifests, the TFA Article 7:1 fails to list the specific documentation and information that are subject to pre-arrival processing. This probably results in the situation that some reluctant Members would implement the minimum standard – only allowing for pre-arrival processing of manifests.

2   Electronic Payment

Legal Text:

Each Member shall, to the extent practicable, adopt or maintain procedures allowing the option of electronic payment for duties, taxes, fees, and charges collected by customs incurred upon importation and exportation.

There was a provision in the International Convention relating to the Simplification of Customs Formalities (1923): '[c]onsideration should be given to the possibility of using postal money-orders or cheques, against security of a permanent character, for the payment or guarantee of Customs duties'.[22] In a similar vein, Article 7:2 of the TFA keeps pace with the development in financial industry. However, the TFA Article 7:2 confines the applicability of electronic payment to duties, taxes, fees and charges; guarantees are not required or even encouraged to be paid electronically.

3   Separation of Release from Final Determination of Customs Duties, Taxes, Fees and Charges

Legal Text:

3.1 Each Member shall adopt or maintain procedures allowing the release of goods prior to the final determination of customs duties, taxes, fees and charges, if such a determination is not done prior to, or upon arrival, or as rapidly as possible after arrival and provided that all other regulatory requirements have been met.

    3.2 As a condition for such release, a Member may require:

        (a) payment of customs duties, taxes, fees and charges determined prior to or upon arrival of goods and a guarantee for any amount not yet determined in the form of a surety, a deposit, or another appropriate instrument provided for in its laws and regulations; or

        (b) a guarantee in the form of a surety, a deposit, or another appropriate instrument provided for in its laws and regulations.

    3.3 Such guarantee shall not be greater than the amount the Member requires to ensure payment of customs duties, taxes, fees and charges ultimately due for the goods covered by the guarantee.

    3.4 In cases where an offence requiring imposition of monetary penalties or fines has been detected, a guarantee may be required for the penalties and fines that may be imposed.

    3.5 The guarantee as set out in paragraphs 3.2 and 3.4 shall be discharged when it is no longer required.

    3.6 Nothing in these provisions shall affect the right of a Member to examine, detain, seize or confiscate or deal with the goods in any manner not otherwise inconsistent with the Member's WTO rights and obligations.

The International Convention relating to the Simplification of Customs Formalities (1923) had spoken of the concept of guarantee/security:

> It is desirable that guarantees should be accepted in the form either of properly secured bonds or of payments in cash; It is desirable that the security given should be refunded or released as soon as all the obligations which had been contracted have been fulfilled.[23]

The Agreement on Implementation of Article VII of GATT 1994 (Customs Valuation), concluded in the Uruguay Round, has similarly provided for norms of guarantee in its Article 13:

> If, in the course of determining the customs value of imported goods, it becomes necessary to delay the final determination of such customs value, the importer of the goods shall nevertheless be able to withdraw them from customs if, where so required, the importer provides sufficient guarantee in the form of a surety, a deposit or some other appropriate instrument, covering the ultimate payment of customs duties for which the goods may be liable. The legislation of each Member shall make provisions for such circumstances.

The TFA Article 7:3 improves the previous disciplines on guarantee by linking guarantee to the release of goods. It, as a 'green light' measure, enables the goods to be released before the final determination of customs duties, taxes, fees and charges. This provision also leaves Members the discretion of setting conditions (i.e., actual payment or a guarantee) for such release (q.v. Article 7:3.2). Meanwhile, the amount of guarantee shall be as appropriate as possible to 'ensure payment of customs duties, taxes, fees and charges ultimately due for the goods' (q.v. Article 7:3.3). Besides being required for the customs duties, taxes, fees and charges, a guarantee may also 'be required for the penalties and fines that may be imposed' (q.v. Article 7:3.4) – indeed, this provision has little to do with the theme of this article, which is about release of goods rather than penalty or fine. A guarantee must be discharged if no longer required so that the trader can maintain a fast turnover of money (q.v. Article 7:3.5).

4   Risk Management

Legal Text:

> 4.1 Each Member shall, to the extent possible, adopt or maintain a risk management system for customs control.
>
> 4.2 Each Member shall design and apply risk management in a manner as to avoid arbitrary or unjustifiable discrimination, or a disguised restriction on international trade.
>
> 4.3 Each Member shall concentrate customs control and, to the extent possible other relevant border controls, on high-risk consignments and expedite the release of low-risk consignments. A Member also may select, on a random basis, consignments for such controls as part of its risk management.
>
> 4.4 Each Member shall base risk management on an assessment of risk through appropriate selectivity criteria. Such selectivity criteria may include, inter alia, the Harmonized System code, nature and description of the goods, country of origin, country from which the goods were shipped, value of the goods, compliance record of traders and type of means of transport.

This provision acquiesces in the view that customs control – though it is extremely essential for protecting the society, ensuring revenue collection, monitoring trade flow, etc. – hinders the release of goods. Therefore, risk management is introduced as a solution to alleviate negative effect of customs control on trade facilitation. Risk management distinguishes the low-risk consignments, which shall be more rapidly released, from the high-risk consignments, on which customs control shall be concentrated (q.v. Article 7:4.3). Use of risk management shall also follow certain disciplines. For example, it shall 'avoid arbitrary or unjustifiable discrimination, or a disguised restriction on international trade' (q.v. Article 7:4.2), and shall be assessed 'through appropriate selectivity criteria' (q.v. Article 7:4.4). In fact, each Member's selectivity criteria are discretionary, so it would be highly debatable in future disputes in regard to whether the selectivity criteria are 'appropriate'.

5   Post-clearance Audit

Legal Text:

> 5.1 With a view to expediting the release of goods, each Member shall adopt or maintain post clearance audit to ensure compliance with customs and other related laws and regulations.

5.2 Each Member shall select a person or a consignment for post-clearance audit in a risk-based manner, which may include appropriate selectivity criteria. Each Member shall conduct post clearance audits in a transparent manner. Where the person is involved in the audit process and conclusive results have been achieved the Member shall, without delay, notify the person whose record is audited of the results, the person's rights and obligations and the reasons for the results.

5.3 The information obtained in post-clearance audit may be used in further administrative or judicial proceedings.

5.4 Members shall, wherever practicable, use the result of post-clearance audit in applying risk management.

Post-clearance audit is strongly linked to risk management in these aspects: (i) the targeted person or consignment shall be selected on the basis of risk management (q.v. Article 7:5.2); and (ii) the result of post-clearance audit shall be used for applying risk management (q.v. Article 7:5.4). Post-clearance is also useful for 'further administrative or judicial proceedings' (e.g., seizure, or penalty) (q.v. Article 7:5.3). There shall be some disciplines (e.g., transparency, service of notice) monitoring the conduct of post-clearance audit (q.v. Article 7:5.2).

Box 6.2   Rationales for Articles 7:1–7:5

Traditionally, the release/clearance of goods follows the steps: (i) the goods arrive at the border of an importing country; (ii) the importer submits all the necessary documentation and information to the border agencies (mainly the customs) for processing; and (iii) the border agencies release the goods upon finishing all the formalities and collecting the customs duties, taxes, fees and charges. In this case, the trader has to bide his time at the borders till every formality, documentation, or payment is completed. Release/clearance of goods is much slowed so that trade is not as facilitative as expected.

Articles 7:1–7:5 are a group of 'green light' measures that re-sequence the steps: (i) documentation and information are processed before arrival of goods via 'pre-arrival processing; (ii) goods are released/cleared upon arrival without actual payment of duties, taxes, fees and charges via 'separation of release from final determination of customs duties, taxes, fees and charges; and (iii) the duties, taxes, fees and charges are easily paid via 'electronic payment'. As the goods have been released/cleared through 'green light', 'risk management' and 'post-clearance audit' follow-up to fulfill the due customs control in order to monitor trade flow, ensure revenue collection, protect the society, etc.

6 Establishment and Publication of Average Release Times

Legal Text:

> 6.1 Members are encouraged to measure and publish their average release time of goods periodically and in a consistent manner, using tools such as, inter alia, the Time Release Study of the World Customs Organization (referred to in this Agreement as the 'WCO').[24]
>
> 6.2 Members are encouraged to share with the Committee their experiences in measuring average release times, including methodologies used, bottlenecks identified, and any resulting effects on efficiency.

This soft provision encourages Members to use the WCO's tool of Time Release Study (TRS) 'to measure and publish their average release time of goods', and to share with the WTO Trade Facilitation Committee their relevant experiences. This is a rare provision that thoroughly uses 'are encouraged to' rather than 'shall' in its legal text. This diction, probably, implies that no dispute would be filed regarding this provision.

7 Trade Facilitation Measures for Authorized Operators

Legal Text:

> 7.1 Each Member shall provide additional trade facilitation measures related to import, export, or transit formalities and procedures, pursuant to paragraph 7.3, to operators who meet specified criteria, hereinafter called authorized operators. Alternatively, a Member may offer such trade facilitation measures through customs procedures generally available to all operators and is not required to establish a separate scheme.
>
> 7.2 The specified criteria to qualify as an authorized operator shall be related to compliance, or the risk of non-compliance, with requirements specified in a Member's laws, regulations or procedures.
>
> > (a) Such criteria, which shall be published, may include:
> >
> > > (i) an appropriate record of compliance with customs and other related laws and regulations;
> > > (ii) a system of managing records to allow for necessary internal controls;
> > > (iii) financial solvency, including, where appropriate, provision of a sufficient security or guarantee; and
> > > (iv) supply chain security.
> >
> > (b) Such criteria shall not:
> >
> > > (i) be designed or applied so as to afford or create arbitrary or unjustifiable discrimination between operators where the same conditions prevail; and

(ii) to the extent possible, restrict the participation of small and medium-sized enterprises.

7.3 The trade facilitation measures provided pursuant to paragraph 7.1 shall include at least three of the following measures:[25]

(a) low documentary and data requirements, as appropriate;
(b) low rate of physical inspections and examinations, as appropriate;
(c) rapid release time, as appropriate;
(d) deferred payment of duties, taxes, fees and charges;
(e) use of comprehensive guarantees or reduced guarantees;
(f) a single customs declaration for all imports or exports in a given period; and
(g) clearance of goods at the premises of the authorized operator or another place authorized by customs.

7.4 Members are encouraged to develop authorized operator schemes on the basis of international standards, where such standards exist, except when such standards would be an inappropriate or ineffective means for the fulfilment of the legitimate objectives pursued.

7.5 In order to enhance the trade facilitation measures provided to operators, Members shall afford to other Members the possibility of negotiating mutual recognition of authorized operator schemes.

7.6 Members shall exchange relevant information within the Committee about authorized operator schemes in force.

As this provision requires each Member to take 'additional trade facilitation measures' for certain 'authorized operators', it is a controversial issue whether this is a trade-facilitative or a 'trade-facilitative plus' measure.

There shall be compliance-based criteria (e.g., record of compliance, internal control capability, financial solvency and supply chain management) for an authorized operator (q.v. Article 7:7.2(a)). These criteria entail infrastructure input (e.g., financial solvency, including provision of a sufficient security or guarantee), which some operators cannot necessarily afford. This provision underlines fair play between operators (viz. no 'arbitrary or unjustifiable discrimination between operators where the same conditions prevail') on the one hand, and emphasizes 'the participation of small and medium-sized enterprises' (SMEs) on the other (q.v. Article 7:7.2). However, if factors like financial solvency are taken as criteria to qualify an authorized operator, the SMEs, who are usually the grass roots, would have more difficulties in gaining such a status. Article 7:7.2 per se causes a quandary.

Article 7:7.3 lists seven additional trade-facilitative measures, among which a Member shall choose at least three to treat the authorized operators. It is artful that a basic discipline (viz. implementing at least three measures) is imposed on each Member while considerable flexibility (viz. choosing at random amidst the seven measures) is given to the Member. This squarely tells how the multilateral negotiations can reach a consensus by keeping poised between the discipline for all Members and the liberty of an individual Member.

International standards are advocated to be used in the development of Members' authorized operator schemes (q.v. Article 7:7.4). So far, the WCO, with its 'Authorized Economic Operator' (AEO) programme, has been a veteran in this field. Members could turn to the WCO for relevant international standards.

'Mutual recognition of authorized operator schemes' would enable a trader to enjoy the treatment not only in his own country but reciprocally in another country where he does trade. In this regard, Article 7:7.5 wants Members to afford others the opportunity of negotiations on this issue.

8   Expedited Shipments[26]

Legal Text:

8.1 Each Member shall adopt or maintain procedures allowing for the expedited release of at least those goods entered through air cargo facilities to persons who apply for such treatment, while maintaining customs control.[27] If a Member employs criteria[28] limiting who may apply, the Member may, in published criteria, require that the applicant shall, as conditions for qualifying for the application of the treatment described in paragraph 8.2 to its expedited shipments:

(a) provide adequate infrastructure and payment of customs expenses related to processing of expedited shipments in cases where the applicant fulfils the Member's requirements for such processing to be performed at a dedicated facility;

(b) submit in advance of the arrival of an expedited shipment the information necessary for the release;

(c) be assessed fees limited in amount to the approximate cost of services rendered in providing the treatment described in paragraph 8.2;

(d) maintain a high degree of control over expedited shipments through the use of internal security, logistics, and tracking technology from pick-up to delivery;

(e) provide expedited shipment from pick-up to delivery;

(f) assume liability for payment of all customs duties, taxes, fees, and charges to the customs authority for the goods;

(g) have a good record of compliance with customs and other related laws and regulations;

(h) comply with other conditions directly related to the effective enforcement of the Member's laws, regulations, and procedural requirements, that specifically relate to providing the treatment described in paragraph 8.2.

8.2 Subject to paragraphs 8.1 and 8.3, Members shall:

(a) minimize the documentation required for the release of expedited shipments in accordance with paragraph 1 of Article 10 and, to the extent possible, provide for release based on a single submission of information on certain shipments;

(b) provide for expedited shipments to be released under normal circumstances as rapidly as possible after arrival, provided the information required for release has been submitted;

(c) endeavour to apply the treatment in subparagraphs (a) and (b) to shipments of any weight or value recognizing that a Member is permitted to require additional entry procedures, including declarations and supporting documentation and payment of duties and taxes, and to limit such treatment based on the type of good, provided the treatment is not limited to low value goods such as documents; and

(d) provide, to the extent possible, for a de minimis shipment value or dutiable amount for which customs duties and taxes will not be collected, aside from certain prescribed goods. Internal taxes, such as value added taxes and excise taxes, applied to imports consistently with Article III of the GATT 1994 are not subject to this provision.

8.3 Nothing in paragraphs 8.1 and 8.2 shall affect the right of a Member to examine, detain, seize, confiscate or refuse entry of goods, or to carry out post-clearance audits, including in connection with the use of risk management systems. Further, nothing in paragraphs 8.1 and 8.2 shall prevent a Member from requiring, as a condition for release, the submission of additional information and the fulfilment of non-automatic licensing requirements.

Express shipments, rather than *expedited shipments*, is the jargon more customarily used by trading practitioners. The express shipments might be carried by means of air, railway, road or waterway. The TFA, however, narrows the shipments down to 'those goods entered through air cargo facilities' (q.v. Article 7:8.1); in other words, an express shipment conveyed through the supply chains without any air transport (e.g., purely through railway or road) cannot be regarded as an expedited shipment and shall not be applicable to this article.

According to the Central Product Classification (CPC) of the United Nations (Version 2.1), the delivery of expedited shipments may be classified as *air and space transport services of freight* (CPC code: 6531), but it mainly falls under the classes of *postal services* (CPC code: 6801) and *courier services* (CPC code: 6802). The distinction between postal services and courier services is clear: postal services are provided under a universal service obligation (viz. postal services are universal) while courier services are not. As defined by the Universal Postal Union

(UPU), *universal postal service* refers to 'the permanent provision of quality basic postal services at all points in a member country's territory, for all customers, at affordable prices'.[29] In many countries, the postal services are usually provided by the *designated operator(s)*.[30] The monopolistic regimes of universal postal service and designated operator (mostly the national postal service) exclude the private sector from postal services (though some countries are privatizing their postal services).[31] Then, the class of courier services encompasses the services provided by the private express shipment companies (e.g., UPS, FedEx, DHL). Thus, an expedited shipment operator might be a national postal service or a private express shipment company, only if it is able to carry the shipments by air.

The two-tiered structure of this provision makes it look like a contract between the expedited shipment operator and a Member's government: (i) Article 7:8.1 prescribes the obligations of an expedited shipment operator applying for treatment of 'expedited release of at least those goods entered through air cargo facilities'. Their obligations include providing infrastructure, assuming liability of payment, ensuring trade and customs compliance and so on, which are indeed 'games for the rich; and (ii) Article 7:8.2 contains substantive treatments that a Member is committed to providing to that expedited shipment operator (e.g., minimizing the documentation requirements, releasing expedited shipments rapidly, applying treatment for expedited shipments irrespective of their weight and value, allowing for a *de minimis* threshold of shipment value or dutiable amount for which customs duties and taxes will not be collected). The relation between Article 7:8.1 and Article 7:8.2 is obvious: as long as an expedited shipment operator satisfies the requirements in Article 7:8.1, the Member's government is obliged to provide the treatments in Article 7:8.2. Although Article 7:8.3, as a *proviso*, reserves the necessary rights that a Member may exercise for customs control purpose, it shall not enable a Member to shirk its responsibilities of implementing Article 7:8.2 basically.

This provision is also dubiously an 'authorized operator plus' measure. Some negotiators used to regard that expedited shipment operators could be accredited as 'authorized operators' and thereby enjoy the already trade-facilitative treatments as per Article 7:7. These negotiators, therefore, were not in favor of designing a separate regime for expedited shipments. An expedited shipment operator can certainly apply for the status of authorized operator, but 'at least three of' the seven candidate trade-facilitative measures in Article 7:7 do not necessarily match the expedited shipment operator's needs (e.g., simplified documentation requirements, rapid release and *de minimis* threshold, as provided for in Article 7:8.2).

Before the TFA, Article 60 (De Minimis Imports) of the Agreement on Trade-Related Aspects of Intellectual Property Rights (TRIPS) had introduced the notion of *de minimis* into the WTO legal texts: 'Members may exclude from the application of the above provisions small quantities of goods of a non-commercial nature contained in travelers' personal luggage or sent in small consignments'. *De minimis* literally means a defined threshold based on the fact that one thing is so insignificant as to be unworthy of attention. In jurisprudential terms, there used to be a Latin adage: *de minimis non curat lex,* which means 'the law does not take account of trifles, and will not award damages for a trifling nuisance'.[32] This jurisprudence assumes the nitty-gritty of GATT Article VIII:3:

> No contracting party shall impose substantial penalties for minor breaches of customs regulations or procedural requirements. In particular, no penalty in respect of any omission or mistake in customs documentation which is easily rectifiable and obviously made without fraudulent intent or gross negligence shall be greater than necessary to serve merely as a warning.

Introduction of *de minimis* into the rules on expedited shipments once again carries that maxim of common law forward. With regard to drawing the *de minimis* threshold, Article 7:8.2 (d) is rather flexible: (i) it leaves enough leeway to each Member in determining how high the threshold would be; and (ii) it paves two tracks (the shipment value, and the dutiable amount) for determining the threshold.

9   Perishable Goods[33]

Legal Text:

9.1 With a view to preventing avoidable loss or deterioration of perishable goods, and provided that all regulatory requirements have been met, each Member shall provide for the release of perishable goods:

(a) under normal circumstances within the shortest possible time; and

(b) in exceptional circumstances where it would be appropriate to do so, outside the business hours of customs and other relevant authorities.

9.2 Each Member shall give appropriate priority to perishable goods when scheduling any examinations that may be required.

9.3 Each Member shall either arrange or allow an importer to arrange for the proper storage of perishable goods pending their release. The Member may require that any storage facilities arranged by the importer have been approved or designated by its relevant authorities. The movement of the goods to those storage facilities, including authorizations for the operator moving the goods, may be subject to the approval, where required, of the relevant authorities. The Member shall, where practicable and consistent with domestic legislation, upon the request of the importer, provide for any procedures necessary for release to take place at those storage facilities.

9.4 In cases of significant delay in the release of perishable goods, and upon written request, the importing Member shall, to the extent practicable, provide a communication on the reasons for the delay.

This provision 'gives appropriate priority to perishable goods' that indeed deserve 'proper storage' and rapid release. Five obligations are exerted on a Member: (i) releasing the perishable goods 'under normal circumstances within the shortest possible time'; (ii) working overtime, if possible, for the release of perishable goods; (iii) prioritizing perishable goods in scheduling any examinations; (iv) releasing perishable goods at the storage facilities, if possible; and (v) communicating reasons for significant delay in the release of perishable goods.

This provision is specific to a certain type of goods, which is akin to 'rejected goods' (Article 10:8) and 'temporary admission of goods and inward and outward processing' (Article 10:9), and therefore is irrelevant to other provisions in Article 7. It might be more appropriate, if those three measures (namely, 'perishable goods', 'rejected goods', and 'temporary admission of goods and inward and outward processing') would have been combined into a single article.

ARTICLE 8: BORDER AGENCY COOPERATION

Legal Text:

1   Each Member shall ensure that its authorities and agencies responsible for border controls and procedures dealing with the importation, exportation, and transit of goods cooperate with one another and coordinate their activities in order to facilitate trade.

2   Each Member shall, to the extent possible and practicable, cooperate on mutually agreed terms with other Members with whom it shares a common border with a view to coordinating procedures at border crossings to facilitate cross-border trade. Such cooperation and coordination may include:

   (a) alignment of working days and hours;
   (b) alignment of procedures and formalities;
   (c) development and sharing of common facilities;
   (d) joint controls;
   (e) establishment of one stop border post control.

This article involves two levels of cooperation between border agencies – nationally and internationally. At the national level, 'authorities and agencies responsible for border controls and procedures dealing with the importation, exportation and transit of goods' shall cooperate and coordinate to facilitate trade (q.v. Article 8:1). At the international level, neighboring Members are obliged to (as the legal text uses 'shall') cooperate and coordinate 'on mutually agreed terms' to 'facilitate cross-border trade'. However, the contents of such cooperation and coordination (e.g., alignment of working days and hours, alignment of procedures and formalities, development and sharing of common facilities, joint controls and establishment of one-stop border post control) are discretionary (as the legal text uses 'may') (q.v. Article 8:2). Thus, this article generates the paradox that neighboring Members have the obligations to cooperate and coordinate, but they are not obliged to fulfill the contents as listed in Article 8:2 (a) to (e) amidst their cooperation and coordination.

Operationally, the domestic border agency cooperation and coordination could take place within a Member's National Committee on Trade Facilitation. Though the neighboring Members' cooperation and coordination is done on a bilateral basis, it would in any case benefit 'the current high intensity of intra-regional trade'[34] and would thence speed up the strides of regional integration.

ARTICLE 9: MOVEMENT OF GOODS INTENDED FOR IMPORT UNDER CUSTOMS CONTROL

Legal Text:

Each Member shall, to the extent practicable, and provided all regulatory requirements are met, allow goods intended for import to be moved within its territory under customs control from a customs office of entry to another customs office in its territory from where the goods would be released or cleared.

This one-sentence article simply requires each Member to allow for the movement of imported goods under customs control from the point of entry to another place where the goods are released or cleared so that the inland customs offices can equally release or clear the goods, which would otherwise be stacked up at borders for the processing by frontier customs offices. This idea could also be found in the International Convention relating to the Simplification of Customs Formalities (1923), which provided:

> it is desirable that the formalities in connection both with declaration and verification should be carried out not only in the frontier offices, but also in any offices situated in the interior of the country concerned which possess the necessary authority.[35]

ARTICLE 10: FORMALITIES CONNECTED WITH IMPORTATION, EXPORTATION AND TRANSIT

1 Formalities and Documentation Requirements

Legal Text:

1.1 With a view to minimizing the incidence and complexity of import, export, and transit formalities and to decreasing and simplifying import, export, and transit documentation requirements and taking into account the legitimate policy objectives and other factors such as changed circumstances, relevant new information, business practices, availability of techniques and technology, international best practices, and inputs from interested parties, each Member shall review such formalities and documentation requirements and, based on the results of the review, ensure, as appropriate, that such formalities and documentation requirements are:

(a) adopted and/or applied with a view to a rapid release and clearance of goods, particularly perishable goods;

(b) adopted and/or applied in a manner that aims at reducing the time and cost of compliance for traders and operators;

(c) the least trade restrictive measure chosen where two or more alternative measures are reasonably available for fulfilling the policy objective or objectives in question; and

(d) not maintained, including parts thereof, if no longer required.

1.2 The Committee shall develop procedures for the sharing by Members of relevant information and best practices, as appropriate.

This provision echoes GATT Article VIII: 1(c) which had already laid down the requirement of 'minimizing the incidence and complexity of import and export formalities' and of 'decreasing and simplifying import and export documentation requirements'. GATT Article VIII only speaks about 'the need' for doing so, but the TFA Article 10:1 presents a concrete approach to this end, namely reviewing such formalities and documentation requirements from the practical aspects of: (i) rapid release and clearance of goods (particularly perishable goods); (ii) reducing the time and costs of compliance for traders and operators; (iii) alternative measures being reasonably available; and (iv) not being maintained, including parts thereof, if no longer required (q.v. Article 10:1.1). Article 10:1.2 authorizes the WTO Committee on Trade Facilitation to develop procedures for Members to share relevant information and best practices. Could the WTO trade policy review on trade facilitation in the future refer to outcomes of this sharing? If so, how would those Members which are normally prudent in providing information under TPRM react to the sharing under the WTO Committee on Trade Facilitation?

2 Acceptance of Copies

Legal Text:

2.1 Each Member shall, where appropriate, endeavor to accept paper or electronic copies of supporting documents required for import, export, or transit formalities.

2.2 Where a government agency of a Member already holds the original of such a document, any other agency of that Member shall accept a paper or electronic copy, where applicable, from the agency holding the original in lieu of the original document.

2.3 A Member shall not require an original or copy of export declarations submitted to the customs authorities of the exporting Member as a requirement for importation.[36]

Supporting documents (e.g., commercial invoices, bills of lading) are essential to authenticate a trader's declaration submitted to the government agencies. There is, however, usually one original piece for each supporting document, which is probably in the hands of another government agency other than the one that needs it immediately. The acceptance of copies (paper copies or electronic copies) helps break through this predicament by enabling different agencies to simultaneously handle the same document (q.v. Article 10:2.1 and 2.2). In practice, if a government agency accepts a copy in lieu of the original document held by another one, it might be necessary for the holder to issue an authentication (e.g., with signatures or stamps) to make the copies credible. Article 10:2.3 prohibits the importing Member from asking for an original or copy of export declarations submitted to the exporting Member's customs as a requirement for importation, because the delivery of export declarations (either original documents or copies) from the exporting Member to the importing Member normally falls under another subject – customs cooperation.

3   Use of International Standards

Legal Text:

> 3.1 Members are encouraged to use relevant international standards or parts thereof as a basis for their import, export, or transit formalities and procedures, except as otherwise provided for in this Agreement.
> 3.2 Members are encouraged to take part, within the limits of their resources, in the preparation and periodic review of relevant international standards by appropriate international organizations.
> 3.3 The Committee shall develop procedures for the sharing by Members of relevant information, and best practices, on the implementation of international standards, as appropriate.
>
> The Committee may also invite relevant international organizations to discuss their work on international standards. As appropriate, the Committee may identify specific standards that are of particular value to Members.

This is a sheer 'best endeavor' clause, in which Members are only 'encouraged' to use relevant international standards or parts thereof and take part in the preparation or review of the international standards (q.v. Article 10:3.1 and 3.2). Without drawing up a list of specific international standards, this provision associates the TFA with the work done by other international organizations. When it comes to using international standards, there rise a series of questions: for example, (i) how a WTO Member, which is not a member of a certain international organization, is entitled to use the standards developed by that organization; (ii) how the WTO membership chooses between some analogous standards created by competing international organizations; and (iii) how an international standard could generally apply to the entire WTO membership. Therefore, recognition of the international standards and relevant discussions should be held on the platform of the WTO Committee on Trade Facilitation (q.v. Article 10:3.3).

4 Single Window

Legal Text:

4.1 Members shall endeavor to establish or maintain a single window, enabling traders to submit documentation and/or data requirements for importation, exportation, or transit of goods through a single entry point to the participating authorities or agencies. After the examination by the participating authorities or agencies of the documentation and/or data, the results shall be notified to the applicants through the single window in a timely manner.

4.2 In cases where documentation and/or data requirements have already been received through the single window, the same documentation and/or data requirements shall not be requested by participating authorities or agencies except in urgent circumstances and other limited exceptions which are made public.

4.3 Members shall notify the Committee of the details of operation of the single window.

4.4 Members shall, to the extent possible and practicable, use information technology to support the single window.

The core of single window is 'one window, one submission'. In front of a single window, a trader only needs to face one entry point that is connected to several participating agencies working backstage, and does not need to, under normal circumstances, submit the same documentation and data again (q.v. Article 10:4.1 and 4.2). A single window could be physically a window or an online portal so long as it enables submission of documentation or data and feedback of the examination results. The biggest benefit a single window brings forth is that a trader saves his time and labor on going to separate agencies and handing in the documentation repeatedly. From the government's perspective, establishing a single window entails political will, infrastructure building, reform of existing regimes and resources mobilization, etc. Additionally, in a Member that has many ports, 'single windows', other than a single window, need to be established.

5 Preshipment Inspection

Legal Text:

5.1 Members shall not require the use of preshipment inspections in relation to tariff classification and customs valuation.

5.2 Without prejudice to the rights of Members to use other types of preshipment inspection not covered by paragraph 5.1, Members are encouraged not to introduce or apply new requirements regarding their use.[37]

For about a century, it has been customary for companies to arrange for some categories of goods to be inspected prior to shipment in the exporting country, with a view to determining whether they conform to the terms of the contract.[38]

Over the decades, governments of some developing countries depend on the services of specialized agencies (or 'independent entities') to systematically inspect their imports at the port of shipment for the sake of safeguarding national financial interests (e.g., preventing capital flight, commercial fraud and customs duty evasion) and compensating for inadequacy in administrative resources.

During the Uruguay Round, Preshipment Inspection (PSI) was discussed, at the initiative of the US, under the Committee on Customs Valuation.[39] The discussions led to the Agreement on Preshipment Inspection, which covers all PSI activities 'relating to the verification of the quality, the quantity, the price, including currency exchange rate and financial terms, and/or the customs classification of goods to be exported to the territory of the user Member'.

The TFA precludes 'preshipment inspections in relation to tariff classification and customs valuation' (q.v. Article 10:5.1), and adjusts the original applicability of the Agreement on Preshipment Inspection. Except for tariff classification and customs valuation, the Agreement on Preshipment Inspection still applies to 'other types of PSI', to which any new requirements, however, shall not be appended (q.v. Article 10:5.2).

6   Use of Customs Brokers

Legal Text:

6.1 Without prejudice to the important policy concerns of some Members that currently maintain a special role for customs brokers, from the entry into force of this Agreement Members shall not introduce the mandatory use of customs brokers.

6.2 Each Member shall notify the Committee and publish its measures on the use of customs brokers. Any subsequent modifications thereof shall be notified and published promptly.

6.3 With regard to the licensing of customs brokers, Members shall apply rules that are transparent and objective.

This provision discourages Members from introducing the mandatory use of customs brokers, while taking account of 'the important policy concerns of some Members that currently maintain a special role for customs brokers' (q.v. Article 10:6.1). 'Introduce' means 'bring something new', so this provision implies that a Member is not allowed to bring new mandatory use of customs brokers but can maintain its *modus operandi* that already exists. Moreover, Members shall publish its measures on the use of customs brokers and the modifications thereof, and shall apply transparent and objective rules in terms of licensing customs brokers (q.v. Article 10:6.2 and 6.3).

7   Common Border Procedures and Uniform Documentation Requirements

Legal Text:

7.1 Each Member shall, subject to paragraph 7.2, apply common customs procedures and uniform documentation requirements for release and clearance of goods throughout its territory.

7.2 Nothing in this Article shall prevent a Member from:

(a) differentiating its procedures and documentation requirements based on the nature and type of goods, or their means of transport;

(b) differentiating its procedures and documentation requirements for goods based on risk management;

(c) differentiating its procedures and documentation requirements to provide total or partial exemption from import duties or taxes;

(d) applying electronic filing or processing; or

(e) differentiating its procedures and documentation requirements in a manner consistent with the Agreement on the Application of Sanitary and Phytosanitary Measures.

GATT Article VIII:3(a) has stipulated that 'each contracting party shall administer in a uniform, impartial and reasonable manner all its laws, regulations, decisions and rulings'. The TFA Article 10:7.1, focusing on 'common customs procedures and uniform documentation requirements for release and clearance of goods', consolidated that discipline. Whereas, the TFA Article 10:7.2 reserves a Member's flexibilities pursuant to the given circumstances (e.g., the nature and type of goods, or their means of transport; risk management; exemption from import duties or taxes; electronic filing or processing; SPS measures) therein.

8 Rejected Goods

Legal Text:

8.1 Where goods presented for import are rejected by the competent authority of a Member on account of their failure to meet prescribed sanitary or phytosanitary regulations or technical regulations, the Member shall, subject to and consistent with its laws and regulations, allow the importer to re-consign or to return the rejected goods to the exporter or another person designated by the exporter.

8.2 When such an option under paragraph 8.1 is given and the importer fails to exercise it within a reasonable period of time, the competent authority may take a different course of action to deal with such non-compliant goods.

This provision entrusts the importer of a Member with the right to 're-consign or to return the rejected goods to the exporter or another person designated by the exporter' 'within a reasonable period of time' in case of failure to meet SPS or technical regulations. However, the competent authority of the Member maintains the right to 'take a different course of action'.

9 Temporary Admission of Goods and Inward and Outward Processing

Legal Text:

9.1 Temporary Admission of Goods

Each Member shall allow, as provided for in its laws and regulations, goods to be brought into its customs territory conditionally relieved, totally or partially, from payment of import duties and taxes if such goods are brought into its customs territory for a specific purpose, are intended for re-exportation within a specific period, and have not undergone any change except normal depreciation and wastage due to the use made of them.

9.2 Inward and Outward Processing

(a) Each Member shall allow, as provided for in its laws and regulations, inward and outward processing of goods. Goods allowed for outward processing may be reimported with total or partial exemption from import duties and taxes in accordance with the Member's laws and regulations.

(b) For the purposes of this Article, the term 'inward processing' means the customs procedure under which certain goods can be brought into a Member's customs territory conditionally relieved, totally or partially, from payment of import duties and taxes, or eligible for duty drawback, on the basis that such goods are intended for manufacturing, processing, or repair and subsequent exportation.

(c) For the purposes of this Article, the term 'outward processing' means the customs procedure under which goods which are in free circulation in a Member's customs territory may be temporarily exported for manufacturing, processing, or repair abroad and then re-imported.

Members' obligation prescribed in this provision is quite simple: allowing 'temporary admission of goods' and 'inward and outward processing'. Interestingly, the definitions of 'temporary admission of goods', 'inward processing' and outward processing' occupy the most part of this provision.

There was a like article on 'temporary admission of goods' in the International Convention relating to the Simplification of Customs Formalities (1923):

It is desirable that an adequate time-limit should be allowed for the execution of undertakings which involve temporary importation or exportation, and that due consideration should be given to any unforeseen circumstances which may delay their execution, and the time-limit prolonged in case of need.[40]

Nowadays, the most influential international agreements governing the temporary admission of goods are Customs Convention on the ATA Carnet for the

Temporary Admission of Goods (as known as the 'ATA Convention') and Convention on Temporary Admission (as known as the 'Istanbul Convention'), as administered by the WCO.

ARTICLE 11: FREEDOM OF TRANSIT

Legal Text:

1   Any regulations or formalities in connection with traffic in transit imposed by a Member shall not be:

  (a)   maintained if the circumstances or objectives giving rise to their adoption no longer exist or if the changed circumstances or objectives can be addressed in a reasonably available less trade-restrictive manner;

  (b)   applied in a manner that would constitute a disguised restriction on traffic in transit.

2   Traffic in transit shall not be conditioned upon collection of any fees or charges imposed in respect of transit, except the charges for transportation or those commensurate with administrative expenses entailed by transit or with the cost of services rendered.

3   Members shall not seek, take, or maintain any voluntary restraints or any other similar measures on traffic in transit. This is without prejudice to existing and future national regulations, bilateral or multilateral arrangements related to regulating transport, consistent with WTO rules.

4   Each Member shall accord to products which will be in transit through the territory of any other Member treatment no less favorable than that which would be accorded to such products if they were being transported from their place of origin to their destination without going through the territory of such other Member.

5   Members are encouraged to make available, where practicable, physically separate infrastructure (such as lanes, berths and similar) for traffic in transit.

6   Formalities, documentation requirements, and customs controls in connection with traffic in transit shall not be more burdensome than necessary to:

  (a)   identify the goods; and

  (b)   ensure fulfilment of transit requirements.

7   Once goods have been put under a transit procedure and have been authorized to proceed from the point of origination in a Member's territory, they will not be subject to any customs charges nor unnecessary delays or restrictions until they conclude their transit at the point of destination within the Member's territory.

8   Members shall not apply technical regulations and conformity assessment procedures within the meaning of the Agreement on Technical Barriers to Trade to goods in transit.

9 Members shall allow and provide for advance filing and processing of transit documentation and data prior to the arrival of goods.

10 Once traffic in transit has reached the customs office where it exits the territory of a Member, that office shall promptly terminate the transit operation if transit requirements have been met.

11 Where a Member requires a guarantee in the form of a surety, deposit or other appropriate monetary or non-monetary[41] instrument for traffic in transit, such guarantee shall be limited to ensuring that requirements arising from such traffic in transit are fulfilled.

12 Once the Member has determined that its transit requirements have been satisfied, the guarantee shall be discharged without delay.

13 Each Member shall, in a manner consistent with its laws and regulations, allow comprehensive guarantees which include multiple transactions for same operators or renewal of guarantees without discharge for subsequent consignments.

14 Each Member shall make publicly available the relevant information it uses to set the guarantee, including single transaction and, where applicable, multiple transaction guarantee.

15 Each Member may require the use of customs convoys or customs escorts for traffic in transit only in circumstances presenting high risks or when compliance with customs laws and regulations cannot be ensured through the use of guarantees. General rules applicable to customs convoys or customs escorts shall be published in accordance with Article 1.

16 Members shall endeavor to cooperate and coordinate with one another with a view to enhancing freedom of transit. Such cooperation and coordination may include, but is not limited to, an understanding on:

(a) charges;
(b) formalities and legal requirements; and
(c) the practical operation of transit regimes.

17 Each Member shall endeavor to appoint a national transit coordinator to which all enquiries and proposals by other Members relating to the good functioning of transit operations can be addressed.

The erstwhile international rules on transit could be found in the Paris Convention between the Holy Roman Empire and France (1804),[42] the Treaty of Paris (1814)[43] and the Final Act of the Congress of Vienna (1815),[44] which laid down the principle of freedom of transit on the major transnational rivers of Europe (e.g., the Rhine river, the Stecknitz canal). For instance, Article XIV of the Final Act of the Congress of Vienna stipulated that:

> The principles established for the free navigation of rivers and canals, in the whole extent of ancient Poland, as well as for the trade to the ports, for the circulation of articles the growth and produce of the different Polish provinces, and for the commerce, relative to goods in transit, such as they are specified in the 24th, 25th, 26th, 28th and 29th Articles of the Treaty

between Austria and Russia, and in the 22nd, 23rd, 24th, 25th, 28th and 29th Articles of the Treaty between Russia and Prussia, shall be invariably maintained.

At the end of World War I, the Treaty of Peace with Germany (also known as the 'Treaty of Versailles') signed at Versailles on June 28, 1919, further elaborated the principle of freedom of transit. The Covenant of the League of Nations, by which the League of Nations was founded, was Part I of the Treaty of Versailles. The Covenant provided in its Article 23 (e) that:

> The Members of the League will make provision to secure and maintain freedom of communications and of transit and equitable treatment for the commerce of all Members of the League.

In the meantime, other parts of the Treaty of Versailles specified some countries' undertakings regarding freedom of transit. For example,

ARTICLE 89[45]

Poland undertakes to accord freedom of transit to persons, goods, vessels, carriages, wagons and mails in transit between East Prussia and the rest of Germany over Polish territory, including territorial waters, and to treat them at least as favorably as the persons, goods, vessels, carriages, wagons and mails respectively of Polish or of any other more favored nationality, origin, importation, starting point, or ownership as regards facilities, restrictions and all other matters.

ARTICLE 321[46]

Germany undertakes to grant freedom of transit through her territories on the routes most convenient for international transit, either by rail, navigable waterway, or canal, to persons, goods, vessels, carriages, wagons and mails coming from or going to the territories of any of the Allied and Associated Powers (whether contiguous or not); for this purpose the crossing of territorial waters shall be allowed. Such persons, goods, vessels, carriages, wagons and mails shall not be subjected to any transit duty or to any undue delays or restrictions, and shall be entitled in Germany to national treatment as regards charges, facilities, and all other matters.

To realize the purpose of Article 23 (e) of the Covenant,[47] a number of states held a conference in Barcelona on April 14, 1921, and accepted the Convention and Statute on Freedom of Transit.[48] This accord, which is still in effect today,[49] laid the foundation for international rules on transit. In this accord, transit is defined as

> the passage across such territory, with or without trans-shipment, warehousing, breaking bulk, or change in the mode of transport, is only a portion of

a complete journey, beginning and terminating beyond the frontier of the State across whose territory the transit takes place.[50]

Traffic of this nature is termed *traffic in transit*.[51] This definition was repeated in the ensuing international accords (e.g., Article V of the GATT, Article 124 of United Nations Convention on the Law of the Sea (UNCLOS)).

The Convention and Statute on Freedom of Transit set forth several basic disciplines for traffic in transit: (i) contracting parties should facilitate free transit by rail or waterway on routes in use convenient for international transit;[52] (ii) no distinction should be made on the basis of the nationality of persons, the flag of vessels, the place of origin, departure, entry, exit or destination or on any circumstances relating to the ownership of goods or of vessels, coaching or goods stock or other means of transport;[53] (iii) traffic in transit should not be subject to any special dues;[54] and (iv) tariffs on traffic in transit should be fixed at reasonable rates and applied by reasonable methods.[55]

The Convention and Statute on Freedom of Transit, however, was drawn up at a time when transport by road and air had not become prevalent but rail and waterway[56] took a considerable part in carrying traffic in transit. The Convention and Statute on the Regime of Navigable Waterways of International Concern,[57] which was also concluded in Barcelona in 1921, associated itself with the Convention and Statute on Freedom of Transit:

> The transit of vessels and of passengers and goods on navigable waterways of international concern shall, so far as customs formalities are concerned, be governed by the conditions laid down in the Statute of Barcelona on Freedom of Transit.[58]

In building up the post-war multilateral trading system, the Havana Charter for an International Trade Organization (the 'Havana Charter'), in its Article 33, renewed the disciplines for traffic in transit. Some of the new disciplines inherited the spirits reflected in the Convention and Statute on Freedom of Transit (e.g., definition of transit, the principle of non-discrimination), but there were also amendments to the Convention and Statute on Freedom of Transit (e.g., the Havana Charter provided that transit in traffic 'shall be exempt from customs duties and from all transit duties or other charges imposed in respect of transit').[59] As the Havana Charter failed to enter into force, GATT Article V took over Article 33 of the Havana Charter.

In the wake of the GATT, the first United Nations Conference on Trade and Development held in 1964, most notably, adopted the principles relating to the transit trade of landlocked countries:

Principle I: The recognition of the right of each landlocked State of free access to the sea is an essential principle for the expansion of international trade and economic development.

Principle II: In territorial and on internal waters, vessels flying the flag of landlocked countries should have identical rights, and enjoy treatment identical to that enjoyed by vessels flying the flag of coastal States other than the territorial State.

Principle III: In order to enjoy the freedom of the seas on equal terms with coastal States, States having no sea coast should have free access to the sea. To this end, States situated between the sea and a State having no sea coast shall, by common agreement with the latter, and in conformity with existing international conventions, accord to ships flying the flag of that State treatment equal to that accorded to their own ships or to the ships of any other State as regards access to sea ports and the use of such ports.

Principle IV: In order to promote fully the economic development of the land-locked countries, the said countries should be afforded by all States, on the basis of reciprocity, free and unrestricted transit, in such a manner that they have free access to regional and international trade in all circumstances and for every type of goods.

> Goods in transit should not be subject to any customs duty.
> Means of transport in transit should not be subject to special taxes or charges higher than those levied for the use of means of transport of the transit country.

Principle V: The State of transit, while maintaining full sovereignty over its territory, shall have the right to take all indispensable measures to ensure that the exercise of the right of free and unrestricted transit shall in no way infringe its legitimate interests of any kind.

Principle VI: In order to accelerate the evolution of a universal approach to the solution of the special and particular problems of trade and development of landlocked countries in the different geographical areas, the conclusion of regional and other international agreements in this regard should be encouraged by all States.

Principle VII: The facilities and special rights accorded to landlocked countries in view of their special geographical position are excluded from the operation of the most-favored- nation clause.

Principle VIII: The principles which govern the right of free access to the sea of the landlocked State shall in no way abrogate existing agreements between two or more contracting parties concerning the problems, nor shall they raise an obstacle as regards the conclusion of such agreements in the future, provided that the latter do not establish a regime which is less favorable than or opposed to the above-mentioned provisions.[60]

The said principles set the tone for other UN conventions relating to transit – e.g., the Convention on Transit Trade of Land-locked States (1965), Customs Convention on the International Transport of Goods Under Cover of TIR Carnets (1975) and the United Nations Convention on International Multimodal Transport of Goods (1980). In the context of the WTO, which is also a specialized agency of the United Nations, the negotiations on trade facilitation afforded a significant chance to ameliorate GATT Article V, and thereby brought forth the TFA Article 11.

GATT Article V:7 has already provided that this article 'shall not apply to the operation of aircraft in transit, but shall apply to air transit of goods (including baggage)'. Without any special notes that indicate changes to the scope of transit, the operation of aircraft in transit shall be excluded from the TFA's governance.

Article 11:1 stresses the disciplines for the regulations or formalities in connection with traffic in transit: (i) updating the formalities commensurate with the changed circumstances or objectives; (ii) being less trade-restrictive; and (iii) avoiding disguised restriction. In fact, these disciplines also generally apply to regulations or formalities relating to import and export.

Article 11:2 unravels the relation between traffic in transit and collection of fees or charges. 'Collection of fees or charges imposed in respect of transit' shall only be the effect of administrative expenses entailed or cost of services rendered, rather than be the cause (or condition) of traffic in transit.

Article 11:3 discourages Members from seeking, taking or maintaining any voluntary restraints or any other similar measures on traffic in transit, but, at the same time, allows for exceptions or exemptions due to a Member's 'existing and future national regulations, bilateral or multilateral arrangements related to regulating transport'. This provision, however, is a paradox: 'existing and future national regulations, bilateral or multilateral arrangements' trace out the all-inclusive circumstances; the logic of this provision, therefore, sounds like 'any voluntary restraints is prohibited unless any possible circumstances permit'. Moreover, 'national regulations' can be generally deemed as 'voluntary' behaviors of a Member. Thus, the extremely broad *proviso* shatters the binding force of this provision.

Article 11:4 is fairly a reiteration of GATT Article V:6, the purpose of which is to prevent discrimination either against traffic in transit or in favor of direct consignment.

Article 11:5, as a 'best endeavor' clause, encourages Members to make physically separate infrastructure (such as lanes, berths and similar) available for traffic in transit. This endeavor shall entail input to infrastructure. The developing country and LDC Members conceivably need technical assistance in this respect.

Article 11:6 requires each Member to maintain its formalities, documentation requirements and customs controls on transit only to the limit as necessary as to identify the goods and ensure fulfillment of transit requirements

Article 11:7 aims at a proceeding of goods under a transit procedure, immune from the interferences (e.g., customs charges, unnecessary delays or restriction), within a Member's territory.

Article 11:8 prevent Members from applying technical regulations and conformity assessment procedures within the meaning of the Agreement on Technical Barriers to Trade (TBT) to goods in transit.

Article 11:9 is exactly a graft of pre-arrival processing onto traffic in transit.

Article 11:10 demands efficient performance of the customs office that is responsible for transit operation.

Article 11:11 introduces guarantee to traffic in transit and sets up the ceiling for guarantee, which is limited to ensuring that requirements arising from such traffic in transit are fulfilled. Article 11:12, which is similar to Article 7:3, requires Members to discharge the guarantee without delay. Article 11:13 takes consideration of the circumstance of multiple transactions done by the same operators, and thus allows comprehensive guarantees or renewal of guarantees without discharge for subsequent consignments. Article 11:14 emphasizes the principle of transparency on guarantee for transit.

Article 11:15 gives Members the right to use customs convoys or customs escorts for traffic in transit in case of high risks and inefficacy of guarantee to ensure compliance.

Article 11:16 is another 'best endeavor' clause that encourages Members to cooperate and coordinate with each other in terms of charges, formalities and legal requirements, the practical operation of transit regimes and so on.

Article 11:17 comes up with an institutional arrangement where a national transit coordinator will be appointed to address all enquiries and proposals by other Members relating to the good functioning of transit operations.

ARTICLE 12: CUSTOMS COOPERATION

Legal Text:

1   Measures Promoting Compliance and Cooperation

1.1 Members agree on the importance of ensuring that traders are aware of their compliance obligations, encouraging voluntary compliance to allow importers to self-correct without penalty in appropriate circumstances, and applying compliance measures to initiate stronger measures for non-compliant traders.[61]

1.2 Members are encouraged to share information on best practices in managing customs compliance, including through the Committee. Members are encouraged to cooperate in technical guidance or assistance and support for capacity building for the purposes of administering compliance measures and enhancing their effectiveness.

2   Exchange of Information

2.1 Upon request and subject to the provisions of this Article, Members shall exchange the information set out in subparagraphs 6.1(b) and/or (c) for the purpose of verifying an import or export declaration in identified cases where there are reasonable grounds to doubt the truth or accuracy of the declaration.

2.2 Each Member shall notify the Committee of the details of its contact point for the exchange of this information.

3   Verification

A Member shall make a request for information only after it has conducted appropriate verification procedures of an import or export declaration and after it has inspected the available relevant documentation.

4   Request

4.1 The requesting Member shall provide the requested Member with a written request, through paper or electronic means in a mutually agreed official language of the WTO or other mutually agreed language, including:

  (a) the matter at issue including, where appropriate and available, the number identifying the export declaration corresponding to the import declaration in question;

  (b) the purpose for which the requesting Member is seeking the information or documents, along with the names and contact details of the persons to whom the request relates, if known;

  (c) where required by the requested Member, confirmation[62] of the verification where appropriate;

  (d) the specific information or documents requested;

  (e) the identity of the originating office making the request;

  (f) reference to provisions of the requesting Member's domestic law and legal system that govern the collection, protection, use, disclosure, retention, and disposal of confidential information and personal data.

4.2 If the requesting Member is not in a position to comply with any of the subparagraphs of paragraph 4.1, it shall specify this in the request.

5   Protection and Confidentiality

5.1 The requesting Member shall, subject to paragraph 5.2:

  (a) hold all information or documents provided by the requested Member strictly in confidence and grant at least the same level of such protection and confidentiality as that provided under the domestic law and legal system of the requested Member as described by it under subparagraphs 6.1(b) or (c);

  (b) provide information or documents only to the customs authorities dealing with the matter at issue and use the information or documents solely for the purpose stated in the request unless the requested Member agrees otherwise in writing;

  (c) not disclose the information or documents without the specific written permission of the requested Member;

(d) not use any unverified information or documents from the requested Member as the deciding factor towards alleviating the doubt in any given circumstance;

(e) respect any case-specific conditions set out by the requested Member regarding retention and disposal of confidential information or documents and personal data; and

(f) upon request, inform the requested Member of any decisions and actions taken on the matter as a result of the information or documents provided.

5.2 A requesting Member may be unable under its domestic law and legal system to comply with any of the subparagraphs of paragraph 5.1. If so, the requesting Member shall specify this in the request.

5.3 The requested Member shall treat any request and verification information received under paragraph 4 with at least the same level of protection and confidentiality accorded by the requested Member to its own similar information.

6   Provision of Information

6.1 Subject to the provisions of this Article, the requested Member shall promptly:

(a) respond in writing, through paper or electronic means;

(b) provide the specific information as set out in the import or export declaration, or the declaration, to the extent it is available, along with a description of the level of protection and confidentiality required of the requesting Member;

(c) if requested, provide the specific information as set out in the following documents, or the documents, submitted in support of the import or export declaration, to the extent it is available: commercial invoice, packing list, certificate of origin and bill of lading, in the form in which these were filed, whether paper or electronic, along with a description of the level of protection and confidentiality required of the requesting Member;

(d) confirm that the documents provided are true copies;

(e) provide the information or otherwise respond to the request, to the extent possible, within 90 days from the date of the request.

6.2 The requested Member may require, under its domestic law and legal system, an assurance prior to the provision of information that the specific information will not be used as evidence in criminal investigations, judicial proceedings, or in non-customs proceedings without the specific written permission of the requested Member. If the requesting Member is not in a position to comply with this requirement, it should specify this to the requested Member.

7   Postponement or Refusal of a Request

7.1 A requested Member may postpone or refuse part or all of a request to provide information, and shall inform the requesting Member of the reasons for doing so, where:

(a) it would be contrary to the public interest as reflected in the domestic law and legal system of the requested Member;

(b) its domestic law and legal system prevents the release of the information. In such a case it shall provide the requesting Member with a copy of the relevant, specific reference;

(c) the provision of the information would impede law enforcement or otherwise interfere with an on-going administrative or judicial investigation, prosecution or proceeding;

(d) the consent of the importer or exporter is required by its domestic law and legal system that govern the collection, protection, use, disclosure, retention, and disposal of confidential information or personal data and that consent is not given; or

(e) the request for information is received after the expiration of the legal requirement of the requested Member for the retention of documents.

7.2 In the circumstances of paragraphs 4.2, 5.2, or 6.2, execution of such a request shall be at the discretion of the requested Member.

8   Reciprocity

If the requesting Member is of the opinion that it would be unable to comply with a similar request if it was made by the requested Member, or if it has not yet implemented this Article, it shall state that fact in its request. Execution of such a request shall be at the discretion of the requested Member.

9   Administrative Burden

9.1 The requesting Member shall take into account the associated resource and cost implications for the requested Member in responding to requests for information. The requesting Member shall consider the proportionality between its fiscal interest in pursuing its request and the efforts to be made by the requested Member in providing the information.

9.2 If a requested Member receives an unmanageable number of requests for information or a request for information of unmanageable scope from one or more requesting Member(s) and is unable to meet such requests within a reasonable time, it may request one or more of the requesting Member(s) to prioritize with a view to agreeing on a practical limit within its resource constraints. In the absence of a mutually-agreed approach, the execution of such requests shall be at the discretion of the requested Member based on the results of its own prioritization.

10 Limitations

A requested Member shall not be required to:

(a) modify the format of its import or export declarations or procedures;

(b) call for documents other than those submitted with the import or export declaration as specified in subparagraph 6.1(c);

(c) initiate enquiries to obtain the information;

(d) modify the period of retention of such information;

(e) introduce paper documentation where electronic format has already been introduced;

(f) translate the information;

(g) verify the accuracy of the information; or

(h) provide information that would prejudice the legitimate commercial interests of particular enterprises, public or private.

11 Unauthorized Use or Disclosure

11.1 In the event of any breach of the conditions of use or disclosure of information exchanged under this Article, the requesting Member that received the information shall promptly communicate the details of such unauthorized use or disclosure to the requested Member that provided the information and:

(a) take necessary measures to remedy the breach;

(b) take necessary measures to prevent any future breach; and

(c) notify the requested Member of the measures taken under subparagraphs (a) and (b).

11.2 The requested Member may suspend its obligations to the requesting Member under this Article until the measures set out in paragraph 11.1 have been taken.

12 Bilateral and Regional Agreements

12.1 Nothing in this Article shall prevent a Member from entering into or maintaining a bilateral, plurilateral, or regional agreement for sharing or exchange of customs information and data, including on a secure and rapid basis such as on an automatic basis or in advance of the arrival of the consignment.

> 12.2   Nothing in this Article shall be construed as altering or affecting a Member's rights or obligations under such bilateral, plurilateral, or regional agreements, or as governing the exchange of customs information and data under such other agreements.

Customs cooperation in the WTO context is mainly inscribed in the TRIPS Agreement, the Decision regarding Cases where Customs Administrations Have Reasons to Doubt the Truth or Accuracy of the Declared Value,[63] the Agreement on the Implementation of Article VII of the General Agreement on Tariffs and Trade 1994[64] and the Agreement on Trade Facilitation, and, therefore, falls under three dimensions: TRIPS, customs valuation and trade facilitation.[65] In the TRIPS dimension, customs cooperation is for the purpose of eliminating international trade in goods infringing intellectual property rights, in particular trade in counterfeit trademark goods and pirated copyright goods.[66] Under customs valuation, a customs administration may seek cooperation from a foreign counterpart when it has reasonable grounds to doubt the truth or accuracy of the declared value.[67] Customs cooperation under trade facilitation springs from the relevant discussions under the Committee on Customs Valuation.

In response to the concern raised by Belize about the effects of false invoicing at the special meeting of GATT Committee on Customs Valuation in May 1985, the Committee requested the Technical Committee on Customs Valuation of the Customs Cooperation Council (CCC) to examine this issue.[68] In its report to the Committee, the Technical Committee concluded that 'attention should be drawn to the resources and instruments for mutual administrative assistance which exists at international level'.[69] During the Uruguay Round, India, as well as other developing countries, put forward proposals regarding the 'burden of proof' (a general concern that the GATT Valuation Code, which was signed by a limited number of countries as a result of the Tokyo Round negotiations, 'placed too great a burden on customs to prove that a declared price was false before it could reject the transaction value, particularly in cases where importers and their suppliers acted in collusion to hide the fraud'.)[70] 'Recognizing that the customs administration may have to address cases where it has reason to doubt the truth or accuracy of the particulars or of documents produced by traders in support of a declared value', the Ministerial Decision Regarding Cases Where Customs Administrations Have Reasons to Doubt the Truth or Accuracy of the Declared Value (1995) stated that 'it is entirely appropriate in applying the Agreement [on Implementation of Article VII of GATT 1994] for one Member to assist another Member on mutually agreed terms'. This Decision, however, was rather exhortatory than mandatory; the mechanism for a Member to assist another was unclear. As commented by some Members (e.g., India), 'it proved of little help, as evidence was needed to establish fraud in judicial proceedings'.[71]

The Doha Ministerial Decision Regarding Implementation-related Issues and Concerns (2001)[72] at last took the issue of customs cooperation (including exchange of information) on board by affirming:

> Underlines the importance of strengthening cooperation between the customs administrations of members in the prevention of customs fraud. In this regard, it is agreed that, further to the 1994 Ministerial Decision Regarding Cases Where Customs Administrations Have Reasons to Doubt the Truth or Accuracy of the Declared Value, when the customs administration of an importing member has reasonable grounds to doubt the truth or accuracy of the declared value, it may seek assistance from the customs administration of an exporting member on the value of the good concerned. In such cases, the exporting member shall offer cooperation and assistance, consistent with its domestic laws and procedures, including furnishing information on the export value of the good concerned. Any information provided in this context shall be treated in accordance with Article 10 of the Customs Valuation Agreement. Furthermore, recognizing the legitimate concerns expressed by the customs administrations of several importing members on the accuracy of the declared value, the Committee on Customs Valuation is directed to identify and assess practical means to address such concerns, including the exchange of information on export values and to report to the General Council by the end of 2002 at the latest.[73]

The Modalities for Negotiations on Trade Facilitation (Annex D of the 2004 'July package') defined customs cooperation as one of the pursuits of trade facilitation negotiations, stipulating that '[t]he negotiations shall further aim at provisions for effective cooperation between customs or any other appropriate authorities on trade facilitation and customs compliance issues'. The Negotiating Group on Trade Facilitation (NGTF) eventually brought the relevant GATT and WTO talks on customs cooperation to the TFA Article 12.

The TFA article on customs cooperation is for the purpose of 'ensuring that traders are aware of their compliance obligations, encouraging voluntary compliance to allow importers to self-correct without penalty in appropriate circumstances and applying compliance measures to initiate stronger measures for non-compliant traders' (q.v. Article 12:1.1). When a Member has 'reasonable grounds to doubt the truth or accuracy' of 'an import or export declaration in identified cases' (q.v. Article 12:2.1), it has the right to 'make a request for information' in writing to another Member involved (q.v. Article 12:3). There are, however, conditions for raising such a request: (i) the requesting Member has, as per the principle of *due diligence*, 'conducted appropriate verification procedures' of the declaration and 'inspected the available relevant documentation' (q.v. Article 12:3); (ii) the request shall be written, through paper or electronic means, 'in a mutually agreed official language of the WTO or other mutually agreed language' (q.v. Article 12:4.1); (iii) the request shall include the information such as the matter at issue, the purpose for requesting, confirmation of the verification, the specific information or documents requested, the identity of the originating office making the request, reference to related provisions of the requesting Member's domestic law and legal system, etc. (q.v. Article 12:4.1); and (iv) the requesting Member shall be strictly responsible for protection and confidentiality of the exchanged information (q.v. Article 12:5.1),[74] while the requested Member shall also 'treat any request and verification information received with at least the same level of protection and confidentiality accorded by the requested Member to its own similar information' (q.v. Article 12:5.3). In the event of any breach of the conditions of use or disclosure of information exchanged, the requesting Member shall take necessary measures to remedy the breach and prevent any future breach, and promptly communicate to the requested Member (q.v. Article 12:11.1), whereas the requested Member may suspend its obligations to the requesting Member (q.v. Article 12:11.2).

The requested Member shall (i) provide the information; or otherwise (ii) respond to the request in writing, through paper or electronic means, within 90 days from the date of the request. If the requested Member decides to provide the information as requested, it shall (i) provide the specific information as set out in the import or export declaration, along with a description of the level of protection and confidentiality required of the requesting Member; (ii) provide the documents in support of the declaration, to the extent available; and (iii) confirm that the documents provided are true copies (q.v. Article 12:6.1). The requested Member reserves the right of prohibiting using the exchanged information as evidence in criminal investigations, judicial proceedings or in non-customs proceedings without its specific written permission (q.v. Article 12:6.2).

There are, however, circumstances where a requested Member 'may postpone or refuse part or all of a request to provide information' (q.v. Article 12:7.1).[75] In doing so, the requested Member shall inform the requesting Member of the reasons (q.v. Article 12:7.1).

Provision of information to the foreign counterparts should not run counter to a customs administration's day-to-day job. For this reason, the three principles – *reciprocity, good faith* and *convenience* – are underlined by this article: (i) as per the principle of reciprocity, the requested Member can execute the request at its discretion if the requesting Member states its inability to reciprocally offer *quid pro quo* (q.v. Article 12:8); (ii) as per the principle of good faith, the requesting Member shall not impose administrative burden on the requested Member and shall 'consider the proportionality between its fiscal interest in pursuing its request and the efforts to be made by the requested Member in providing the information' (q.v. Article 12:9.1) – when the number or scope of requests is unmanageable, the requested Member may ask the requesting Member to prioritize its requests 'with a view to agreeing on a practical limit within its resource constraints' (q.v. Article 12:9.2); and (iii) as per the principle of convenience, the requested Member shall not be required to modify the format of its import or export declarations or procedures, call for documents other than those submitted with the import or export declaration, initiate enquiries to obtain the information, modify the period of retention of such information, introduce paper documentation where electronic format has already been introduced, translate the information, verify the accuracy of the information or provide information that would prejudice the legitimate commercial interests of particular enterprises, public or private (q.v. Article 12:10).

Customs cooperation has been long-running on various platforms. This article does not prejudice any bilateral, plurilateral or regional agreement for sharing or exchange of customs information and data (q.v. Article 12:12). The customs community normally uses the jargon of *mutual administrative assistance in customs matters* ('CMA' for short) to refer to their cooperation. Many WTO Members have signed bilateral agreements on CMA. For example, among the European Union (EU), China, Japan, Korea and the US, any pair within the five parties have an agreement on CMA in between. There are also regional/plurilateral agreements on CMA (e.g., the Multilateral Agreement on Mutual Assistance between Customs Administrations of Latin America, Spain and Portugal (COMALEP), the Agreement among the Governments of the Shanghai Cooperation Organization Member States on Cooperation and Mutual Assistance in Customs Affairs). In global terms, the International Convention on Mutual Administrative Assistance for the Prevention, Investigation and Repression of Customs Offences (as known as the 'Nairobi Convention'), administered by the WCO, is the main multilateral agreement on CMA. Besides, the WCO has developed another multilateral agreement on CMA – International Convention on Mutual Administrative Assistance in Customs Matters (as known as the 'Johannesburg Convention'). However, the Johannesburg Convention has not yet entered into force.

A commentary on Section II

'For the first time in WTO history, implementation of an agreement is directly linked to the capacity of the country to do so. [. . .] This has never happened before and it did not happen by accident'.[76] All these are predicated on Section II, which makes 'one reason why the TFA is so significant'.[77]

ARTICLE 13: GENERAL PRINCIPLES

Legal Text:

1   The provisions contained in Articles 1 to 12 of this Agreement shall be implemented by developing and least-developed country Members in accordance with this Section, which is based on the modalities agreed in Annex D of the July 2004 Framework Agreement (WT/L/579) and in paragraph 33 of and Annex E to the Hong Kong Ministerial Declaration (WT/MIN(05)/DEC).

2   Assistance and support for capacity building[78] should be provided to help developing and least-developed country Members implement the provisions of this Agreement, in accordance with their nature and scope.

The extent and the timing of implementation of the provisions of this Agreement shall be related to the implementation capacities of developing and least-developed country Members. Where a developing or least-developed country Member continues to lack the necessary capacity, implementation of the provision(s) concerned will not be required until implementation capacity has been acquired.

3   Least-developed country Members will only be required to undertake commitments to the extent consistent with their individual development, financial and trade needs or their administrative and institutional capabilities.

4   These principles shall be applied through the provisions set out in Section II.

Regarding 'special and differential treatment' (S&DT) and 'technical assistance and support for capacity building' (TACB) (q.v. Article 13:1), Section II largely dovetails with the Modalities for Negotiations on Trade Facilitation and the Hong Kong Ministerial Declaration.[79]

'Special and differential treatment has been a defining feature of the multilateral trading system for most of the post-war period'.[80] The talks on S&DT in the GATT/WTO system have gone through four phases: the first phase from creation of the GATT[81] to the beginning of the Tokyo Round (1947–1973); the second throughout the Tokyo Round[82] (1973–1979); the third from the end of the Tokyo Round[83] to the end of the Uruguay Round[84] (1979–1995); and the fourth from the end of the Uruguay Round until now (since 1995). Under the current Doha Round, S&DT takes on a new meaning:

We reaffirm that provisions for special and differential treatment are an integral part of the WTO Agreements. We note the concerns expressed regarding their operation in addressing specific constraints faced by developing countries, particularly least-developed countries. In that connection, we also note that some members have proposed a Framework Agreement on Special and Differential Treatment (WT/GC/W/442). We therefore agree that all special and differential treatment provisions shall be reviewed with a view to strengthening them and making them more precise, effective and operational. In this connection, we endorse the work programme on special and differential treatment set out in the Decision on Implementation-Related Issues and Concerns.[85]

S&DT, as 'an acquired political right',[86] allows developing country Members and LDC Members a certain degree of flexibility in implementing the WTO rules. The flexibility ordinarily takes the form of 'transitional period of time' – a type of postponement in the WTO terms. A developing country Member or LDC Member is not obliged to fulfill the rules in a WTO agreement within the transitional period of time that privileges the Member, even if this agreement has entered into force.

The ultimate goal of a WTO agreement is that all Members, with capability fully acquired, shall completely and accurately implement the agreement at the end of the day. Transitional period of time is not enough to ensure the acquisition of capability. Technical assistance and capacity building (viz. 'assistance and support for capacity building' in the TFA legal text) augments the efforts to reach that ultimate goal.

Technical Assistance (TA) and Capacity Building (CB) used to be two independent concepts. TA was relevant to the erstwhile Technical Cooperation, which was discussed under the Committee on Trade and Development. Notably, the Committee adopted Guidelines for WTO Technical Cooperation[87] in 1996, which prescribed the objectives and principles for WTO technical assistance. The 2001 Doha Ministerial Declaration merged TA and CB, and affirmed that 'technical assistance and capacity building are core elements of the development dimension of the multilateral trading system'.[88] The New Strategy for WTO Technical Cooperation for Capacity Building, Growth and Integration was also endorsed by the Doha Ministerial.[89] Thenceforth, TA and CB have been basically bound together. For example, the 2004 'July package' stated that:

> [Developing countries and low-income countries in transition], and in particular least-developed countries, should be provided with enhanced trade-related *technical assistance and capacity building*, to increase their effective participation in the negotiations, to facilitate their implementation of WTO rules, and to enable them to adjust and diversify their economies.[90]

'Critically, TACB in the WTO system has a deeply political and legal context'.[91] The implementation of TFA cannot go without the faith that: (i) the extent and the timing of implementing the provisions of TFA shall be related to the implementing capacities of developing country Members and LDC Members (q.v. Article 13:2);[92] (ii) TACB shall be provided to developing country Members and LDC Members to help them acquire the capacity of implementing the TFA provisions (q.v. Article 13:2); and (iii) LDC Members shall only be required to undertake commitments to the extent commensurate with their individual development, financial and trade needs or their administrative and institutional capabilities (q.v. Article 13:3).

ARTICLE 14 – ARTICLE 16

ARTICLE 14: CATEGORIES OF PROVISIONS

Legal Text:

1   There are three categories of provisions:

(a) Category A contains provisions that a developing country Member or a least-developed country Member designates for implementation upon entry into force of this Agreement, or in the case of a least-developed country Member within one year after entry into force, as provided in Article 15.

(b) Category B contains provisions that a developing country Member or a least-developed country Member designates for implementation on a date after a transitional period of time following the entry into force of this Agreement, as provided in Article 16.

(c) Category C contains provisions that a developing country Member or a least developed country Member designates for implementation on a date after a transitional period of time following the entry into force of this Agreement and requiring the acquisition of implementation capacity through the provision of assistance and support for capacity building, as provided for in Article 16.

2 Each developing country and least-developed country Member shall self-designate, on an individual basis, the provisions it is including under each of the Categories A, B and C.

ARTICLE 15: NOTIFICATION AND IMPLEMENTATION OF CATEGORY A

Legal Text:

1 Upon entry into force of this Agreement, each developing country Member shall implement its Category A commitments. Those commitments designated under Category A will thereby be made an integral part of this Agreement.

2 A least-developed country Member may notify the Committee of the provisions it has designated in Category A for up to one year after entry into force of this Agreement. Each least-developed country Member's commitments designated under Category A will thereby be made an integral part of this Agreement.

ARTICLE 16: NOTIFICATION OF DEFINITIVE DATES FOR IMPLEMENTATION OF CATEGORY B AND CATEGORY C

Legal Text:

1 With respect to the provisions that a developing country Member has not designated in Category A, the Member may delay implementation in accordance with the process set out in this Article.

Developing Country Member Category B

(a) Upon entry into force of this Agreement, each developing country Member shall notify the Committee of the provisions that it has designated in Category B and their corresponding indicative dates for implementation.[93]

(b) No later than one year after entry into force of this Agreement, each developing country Member shall notify the Committee of its definitive dates for implementation of the provisions it has designated in Category B. If a developing country Member, before this deadline, believes it requires additional time to notify its definitive dates, the Member may request that the Committee extend the period sufficient to notify its dates.

Developing Country Member Category C

(c) Upon entry into force of this Agreement, each developing country Member shall notify the Committee of the provisions that it has designated in Category C and their corresponding indicative dates for implementation. For transparency purposes, notifications submitted shall include information on the assistance and support for capacity building that the Member requires in order to implement.[94]

(d) Within one year after entry into force of this Agreement, developing country Members and relevant donor Members, taking into account any existing arrangements already in place, notifications pursuant to paragraph 1 of Article 22 and information submitted pursuant to subparagraph (c) above, shall provide information to the Committee on the arrangements maintained or entered into that are necessary to provide assistance and support for capacity building to enable implementation of Category C.[95] The participating developing country Member shall promptly inform the Committee of such arrangements. The Committee shall also invite non-Member donors to provide information on existing or concluded arrangements.

(e) Within 18 months from the date of the provision of the information stipulated in subparagraph (d), donor Members and respective developing country Members shall inform the Committee of the progress in the provision of assistance and support for capacity building. Each developing country Member shall, at the same time, notify its list of definitive dates for implementation.

2   With respect to those provisions that a least-developed country Member has not designated under Category A, least-developed country Members may delay implementation in accordance with the process set forth in this Article.

Least-Developed Country Member Category B

(a) No later than one year after entry into force of this Agreement, a least-developed country Member shall notify the Committee of its Category B provisions and may notify their corresponding indicative dates for implementation of these provisions, taking into account maximum flexibilities for least-developed country Members.

(b) No later than two years after the notification date stipulated under subparagraph (a) above, each least-developed country Member shall notify the Committee to confirm designations of provisions and notify its dates for implementation. If a least-developed country Member, before this deadline, believes it requires additional time to notify its definitive dates, the Member may request that the Committee extend the period sufficiently to notify its dates.

Least-Developed Country Member Category C

(c) For transparency purposes and to facilitate arrangements with donors, one year after entry into force of this Agreement, each least-developed country Member shall notify the Committee of the provisions it has designated in Category C, taking into account maximum flexibilities for least-developed country Members.

(d) One year after the date stipulated in subparagraph (c) above, least-developed country Members shall notify information on assistance and support for capacity building that the Member requires in order to implement.[96]

(e) No later than two years after the notification under subparagraph (d) above, least-developed country Members and relevant donor Members, taking into account information submitted pursuant to subparagraph (d) above, shall provide information to the Committee on the arrangements maintained or entered into that are necessary to provide assistance and support for capacity building to enable implementation of Category C.[97] The participating least-developed country Member shall promptly inform the Committee of such arrangements. The least-developed country Member shall, at the same time, notify indicative dates for implementation of corresponding Category C commitments covered by the assistance and support arrangements. The Committee shall also invite non-Member donors to provide information on existing and concluded arrangements.

(f) No later than 18 months from the date of the provision of the information stipulated in subparagraph (e), relevant donor Members and respective least-developed country Members shall inform the Committee of the progress in the provision of assistance and support for capacity building. Each least-developed country Member shall, at the same time, notify the Committee of its list of definitive dates for implementation.

3 Developing country Members and least-developed country Members experiencing difficulties in submitting definitive dates for implementation within the deadlines set out in paragraphs 1 and 2 because of

the lack of donor support or lack of progress in the provision of assistance and support for capacity building should notify the Committee as early as possible prior to the expiration of those deadlines. Members agree to cooperate to assist in addressing such difficulties, taking into account the particular circumstances and special problems facing the Member concerned. The Committee shall, as appropriate, take action to address the difficulties including, where necessary, by extending the deadlines for the Member concerned to notify its definitive dates.

4 Three months before the deadline stipulated in subparagraphs 1(b) or (e), or in the case of a least-developed country Member, subparagraphs 2(b) or (f), the Secretariat shall remind a Member if that Member has not notified a definitive date for implementation of provisions that it has designated in Category B or C. If the Member does not invoke paragraph 3, or in the case of a developing country Member subparagraph 1(b), or in the case of a least-developed country Member subparagraph 2(b), to extend the deadline and still does not notify a definitive date for implementation, the Member shall implement the provisions within one year after the deadline stipulated in subparagraphs 1(b) or (e), or in the case of a least-developed country Member, subparagraphs 2(b) or (f), or extended by paragraph 3.

5 No later than 60 days after the dates for notification of definitive dates for implementation of Category B and Category C provisions in accordance with paragraphs 1, 2, or 3, the Committee shall take note of the annexes containing each Member's definitive dates for implementation of Category B and Category C provisions, including any dates set under paragraph 4, thereby making these annexes an integral part of this Agreement.

The TFA defines three categories (namely, Category A, B and C) for each developing country Member and LDC Member, who shall designate by itself the Section I provisions individually to any of the categories (q.v. Article 14:2). In brief, Category A contains provisions to be implemented upon entry into force of the TFA (except for the circumstance that a least-developed country Member notifies the provisions it has designated in Category A within one year after entry into force of the TFA); Category B contains provisions that need a transitional period of time; Category C contains provisions that need both a transitional period of time and TACB (q.v. Article 14:1).

The TFA, however, distinguishes between developing country Members and LDC Members, and therefore draws different schedules of implementing the Agreement for each of the groups. The arrangements for S&DT and TACB are built into the schedules (q.v. Article 15 and 16).

Table 6.1 The schedule for Developing Country Members

Category A	Implement		
Category B	Notify the Category B provisions and their indicative implementation dates.	Notify definitive implementation dates.	
Category C	Notify the Category C provisions and their indicative implementation dates.	Notify (together with donors) of TACB arrangements.	Update on TACB provision; notify definitive implementation dates.
	Entry into Force	1 Year	2.5 Years

Table 6.2 The schedule for Least-Developed Country Members

Category A	Notify Category A provisions.				
Category B	Notify Category B provisions and their indicative implementation dates.		Confirm Category B provisions; notify definitive implementation dates; request extension of time.		
Category C	Notify Category C provisions.	Notify information on TACB required.		Notify (together with donors) of TACB arrangements; notify indicative implementation dates.	Update on TACB provision; notify definitive implementation dates.
	1 Year	2 Years	3 Years	4 Years	5.5 Years

ARTICLE 17: EARLY WARNING MECHANISM: EXTENSION OF IMPLEMENTATION DATES FOR PROVISIONS IN CATEGORIES B AND C

Legal Text:

1 (a) A developing country Member or least-developed country Member that considers itself to be experiencing difficulty in implementing a provision that it has designated in Category B or Category C by the definitive date established under subparagraphs 1(b) or (e) of Article

16, or in the case of a least-developed country Member subparagraphs 2(b) or (f) of Article 16, should notify the Committee. Developing country Members shall notify the Committee no later than 120 days before the expiration of the implementation date. Least-developed country Members shall notify the Committee no later than 90 days before such date.

(b) The notification to the Committee shall indicate the new date by which the developing country Member or least-developed country Member expects to be able to implement the provision concerned. The notification shall also indicate the reasons for the expected delay in implementation. Such reasons may include the need for assistance and support for capacity building not earlier anticipated or additional assistance and support to help build capacity.

2   Where a developing country Member's request for additional time for implementation does not exceed 18 months or a least-developed country Member's request for additional time does not exceed 3 years, the requesting Member is entitled to such additional time without any further action by the Committee.

3   Where a developing country or least-developed country Member considers that it requires a first extension longer than that provided for in paragraph 2 or a second or any subsequent extension, it shall submit to the Committee a request for an extension containing the information described in subparagraph 1(b) no later than 120 days in respect of a developing country Member and 90 days in respect of a least-developed country Member before the expiration of the original definitive implementation date or that date as subsequently extended.

4   The Committee shall give sympathetic consideration to granting requests for extension taking into account the specific circumstances of the Member submitting the request. These circumstances may include difficulties and delays in obtaining assistance and support for capacity building.

In case a developing country Member or LDC Member feels the difficulty in implementing a Category B or Category C provision by the definitive date it has notified, it may resort to the early warning mechanism that enables the extension of implementation date. In this regard, the early warning mechanism is essentially a 'transitional period of time plus'. A developing country Member shall inform the Committee on Trade Facilitation at least 120 days before the expiration of the implementation date (q.v. Article 17:1a). If this Member's request for additional time for implementation does not exceed 18 months, it is entitled to such additional time without any further action by the Committee (q.v. Article 17:2); otherwise, this Member shall indicate the new date by which it would be able to implement the provision concerned, as well as reasons for the expected delay in implementation (e.g., unforeseen or additional need for TACB) (q.v. Article 17:3 and 1b). A LDC Member shall inform the Committee on Trade Facilitation at least 90 days before the expiration of the implementation date (q.v. Article 17:1a). If this Member's request for additional time for implementation does not exceed 3 years, it is entitled to such additional time without any further action by the Committee (q.v. Article 17:2); otherwise, this Member shall indicate the new date by which it would be able to implement the provision concerned, as well as reasons for the expected delay in implementation (q.v. Article 17:3 and 1b). The Committee shall give sympathetic consideration to granting requests for extension, taking into account the specific circumstances of the Member submitting the request (q.v. Article 17:4).

ARTICLE 18: IMPLEMENTATION OF CATEGORY B AND CATEGORY C

Legal Text:

1 In accordance with paragraph 2 of Article 13, if a developing country Member or a least-developed country Member, having fulfilled the procedures set forth in paragraphs 1 or 2 of Article 16 and in Article 17, and where an extension requested has not been granted or where the developing country Member or least-developed country Member otherwise experiences unforeseen circumstances that prevent an extension being granted under Article 17, self-assesses that its capacity to implement a provision under Category C continues to be lacking, that Member shall notify the Committee of its inability to implement the relevant provision.

2 The Committee shall establish an Expert Group immediately, and in any case no later than 60 days after the Committee receives the notification from the relevant developing country Member or least-developed country Member. The Expert Group will examine the issue and make a recommendation to the Committee within 120 days of its composition.

3 The Expert Group shall be composed of five independent persons that are highly qualified in the fields of trade facilitation and assistance and support for capacity building. The composition of the Expert Group shall ensure balance between nationals from developing and developed country Members. Where a least-developed country Member is involved, the Expert Group shall include at least one national from a least-developed country Member. If the Committee cannot agree on the composition of the Expert Group within 20 days of its establishment, the Director-General, in consultation with the chair of the Committee, shall determine the composition of the Expert Group in accordance with the terms of this paragraph.

4 The Expert Group shall consider the Member's self-assessment of lack of capacity and shall make a recommendation to the Committee. When considering the Expert Group's recommendation concerning a least-developed country Member, the Committee shall, as appropriate, take

action that will facilitate the acquisition of sustainable implementation capacity.

5   The Member shall not be subject to proceedings under the Dispute Settlement Understanding on this issue from the time the developing country Member notifies the Committee of its inability to implement the relevant provision until the first meeting of the Committee after it receives the recommendation of the Expert Group. At that meeting, the Committee shall consider the recommendation of the Expert Group. For a least-developed country Member, the proceedings under the Dispute Settlement Understanding shall not apply to the respective provision from the date of notification to the Committee of its inability to implement the provision until the Committee makes a decision on the issue, or within 24 months after the date of the first Committee meeting set out above, whichever is earlier.

6   Where a least-developed country Member loses its ability to implement a Category C commitment, it may inform the Committee and follow the procedures set out in this Article.

Ideally, a developing country Member or LDC Member shall implement its Category B and Category C commitments in accordance with the definitive dates for implementation; or shall have recourse to the early warning mechanism to extend its implementation date, if necessary. However, what if (i) 'an extension requested has not been granted'; or (ii) the developing country Member or LDC Member 'otherwise experiences unforeseen circumstances that prevent an extension', and 'self-assesses that its capacity to implement a provision under Category C continues to be lacking?' (q.v. Article 18:1). In such a case, the Committee shall 'establish an Expert Group immediately' upon that Member's notification within 60 days (q.v. Article 18:2). The Expert Group, composed of five independent experts,[98] 'will examine the issue and make a recommendation to the Committee within 120 days' (q.v. Article 18:2). Considering the Expert Group's recommendation, the Committee shall take appropriate action that facilitates the Member's acquisition of sustainable implementation capacity (q.v. Article 18:4). Before the Expert Group submits its recommendation, a developing country Member shall not be subject to the Dispute Settlement Understanding (DSU); before the Committee makes a decision on the relevant issue, or within 24 months after the date of the first Committee meeting after it receives the recommendation of the Expert Group, a LDC Member shall not be subject to the DSU (q.v. Article 18:5).

ARTICLE 19: SHIFTING BETWEEN CATEGORIES B AND C

Legal Text:

1   Developing country Members and least-developed country Members who have notified provisions under Categories B and C may shift provisions between such categories through the submission of a notification to the Committee. Where a Member proposes to shift a provision from

Category B to Category C, the Member shall provide information on the assistance and support required to build capacity.

2   In the event that additional time is required to implement a provision shifted from Category B to Category C, the Member may:

  (a) use the provisions of Article 17, including the opportunity for an automatic extension; or
  (b) request an examination by the Committee of the Member's request for extra time to implement the provision and, if necessary, for assistance and support for capacity building, including the possibility of a review and recommendation by the Expert Group under Article 18; or
  (c) in the case of a least-developed country Member, any new implementation date of more than four years after the original date notified under Category B shall require approval by the Committee. In addition, a least-developed country Member shall continue to have recourse to Article 17. It is understood that assistance and support for capacity building is required for a least-developed country Member so shifting.

Category C signifies that there are needs for TACB; provision of TACB, however, is time-consuming. Therefore, Category C means possibly longer transitional period of time than Category B. In case a Member changes its mind of categorizing certain provisions, it may request a shift between Category B and C (normally from B to C rather than from C to B). If a Member wants such a shift, (i) in respect of TACB, it shall notify to the Committee the information on required TACB (q.v. Article 19:1); and (ii) in respect of more transitional period of time, it may turn to early warning mechanism, or the Committee (because an extension of more than 4 years after the original date under Category B needs to be approved by the Committee) (q.v. Article 19:2).

ARTICLE 20: GRACE PERIOD FOR THE APPLICATION OF THE UNDERSTANDING ON RULES AND PROCEDURES GOVERNING THE SETTLEMENT OF DISPUTES

Legal Text:

1   For a period of two years after entry into force of this Agreement, the provisions of Articles XXII and XXIII of GATT 1994 as elaborated and applied by the Understanding on Rules and Procedures Governing the Settlement of Disputes shall not apply to the settlement of disputes against a developing country Member concerning any provision that the Member has designated in Category A.

2   For a period of six years after entry into force of this Agreement, the provisions of Articles XXII and XXIII of GATT 1994 as elaborated and applied by the Understanding on Rules and Procedures Governing the

Settlement of Disputes shall not apply to the settlement of disputes against a least-developed country Member concerning any provision that the Member has designated in Category A.

3   For a period of eight years after implementation of a provision under Category B or C by a least-developed country Member, the provisions of Articles XXII and XXIII of GATT 1994 as elaborated and applied by the Understanding on Rules and Procedures Governing the Settlement of Disputes shall not apply to the settlement of disputes against that least-developed country Member concerning that provision.

4   Notwithstanding the grace period for the application of the Understanding on Rules and Procedures Governing the Settlement of Disputes, before making a request for consultations pursuant to Articles XXII or XXIII of GATT 1994, and at all stages of dispute settlement procedures with regard to a measure of a least-developed country Member, a Member shall give particular consideration to the special situation of least-developed country Members. In this regard, Members shall exercise due restraint in raising matters under the Understanding on Rules and Procedures Governing the Settlement of Disputes involving least-developed country Members.

5   Each Member shall, upon request, during the grace period allowed under this Article, provide adequate opportunity to other Members for discussion with respect to any issue relating to the implementation of this Agreement.

A very special S&DT granted to the developing country Members and LDC Members in the TFA is the grace period for the application of DSU. In the WTO's DSU terms, a grace period normally means a reasonable period of time, during which a Member may continue to apply WTO-inconsistent measures before it brings the measures into conformity with the recommendations or rulings of the Dispute Settlement Body (DSB) and its WTO obligations.[99] The TFA goes much beyond in the way that a developing country Member or LDC Member is given a grace period when the WTO rules regarding dispute settlement (viz. Articles XXII and XXIII of GATT 1994 and Understanding on Rules and Procedures Governing the Settlement of Disputes) shall not be applicable to them at all.

Table 6.3 Grace period for each Category

Member	Category	Grace Period
Developing country Member	A	2 years since entry into force
	B	Not given
	C	Not given
Least-developed country Member	A	6 years since entry into force
	B	8 years since implementation of provision
	C	8 years since implementation of provision

There might be a loophole that the grace periods for developing country Members' Category B and Category C are not defined in the TFA. It is reasonable to infer that (i) Category B and C of the developing country Members are not eligible for grace period; or (ii) the developing country Members automatically own the grace period lasting 2 to 8 years since implementation of the relevant provisions. This loophole needs a clarification in the future.

ARTICLE 21: PROVISION OF ASSISTANCE AND SUPPORT FOR CAPACITY BUILDING

Legal Text:

1   Donor Members agree to facilitate the provision of assistance and support for capacity building to developing country and least-developed country Members on mutually agreed terms either bilaterally or through the appropriate international organizations. The objective is to assist developing country and least-developed country Members to implement the provisions of Section I of this Agreement.

2   Given the special needs of least-developed country Members, targeted assistance and support should be provided to the least-developed country Members so as to help them build sustainable capacity to implement their commitments. Through the relevant development cooperation mechanisms and consistent with the principles of technical assistance and support for capacity building as referred to in paragraph 3, development partners shall endeavour to provide assistance and support for capacity building in this area in a way that does not compromise existing development priorities.

3   Members shall endeavour to apply the following principles for providing assistance and support for capacity building with regard to the implementation of this Agreement:

(a) take account of the overall developmental framework of recipient countries and regions and, where relevant and appropriate, ongoing reform and technical assistance programs;

(b) include, where relevant and appropriate, activities to address regional and subregional challenges and promote regional and subregional integration;

(c) ensure that ongoing trade facilitation reform activities of the private sector are factored into assistance activities;

(d) promote coordination between and among Members and other relevant institutions, including regional economic communities, to ensure maximum effectiveness of and results from this assistance. To this end:

(i) coordination, primarily in the country or region where the assistance is to be provided, between partner Members and donors and among bilateral and multilateral donors should aim to avoid overlap and duplication in assistance programs and inconsistencies in reform activities through close coordination of technical assistance and capacity building interventions;

(ii) for least-developed country Members, the Enhanced Integrated Framework for trade-related assistance for the least-developed countries should be a part of this coordination process; and

(iii) Members should also promote internal coordination between their trade and development officials, both in capitals and in Geneva, in the implementation of this Agreement and technical assistance.

(e) encourage use of existing in-country and regional coordination structures such as roundtables and consultative groups to coordinate and monitor implementation activities; and

(f) encourage developing country Members to provide capacity building to other developing and least-developed country Members and consider supporting such activities, where possible.

4   The Committee shall hold at least one dedicated session per year to:

(a) discuss any problems regarding implementation of provisions or sub-parts of provisions of this Agreement;

(b) review progress in the provision of assistance and support for capacity building to support the implementation of the Agreement, including any developing or least-developed country Members not receiving adequate assistance and support for capacity building;

(c) share experiences and information on ongoing assistance and support for capacity building and implementation programs, including challenges and successes;

(d) review donor notifications as set forth in Article 22; and

(e) review the operation of paragraph 2.

According to Paragraph 5 of the Modalities for Negotiations on Trade Facilitation, providing TACB appropriately to the developing country Members and LDC Members commensurate with their notifications of Category C commitments shall be the obligation of the donor Members. However, this article does not explicitly demonstrate which certain Members shall be the donor Members. In fact, only when a Member has provided TACB, it could be called, *post hoc*, a donor. Thus, providing TACB seems like a voluntary behavior of some 'generous' Members rather than an obligation imposed on a definite scope of Members. In light of the 'chicken-and-egg' debate during the negotiations, donor Members shall at least include those proponents (mostly developed countries) of putting trade facilitation on the WTO negotiating agenda. Moreover, the donor

Members are not limited to developed country Members; developing country Members are also encouraged to provide TACB (though they are not obliged to do so) (q.v. Article 21:3f).

TACB can be provided via two channels: (i) bilaterally between the recipient Member and the donor Member; or (ii) through the appropriate international organizations (q.v. Article 21:1). Clearly, the TFA articles are not binding on any international organizations. Even if a donor Member provides TACB through the international organizations, it shall notify the relevant information to the WTO Committee on Trade Facilitation.

Another concept – development partner – appears in Article 21:2. In TACB's terms, a development partner usually refers to an institution that delivers development programmes to a recipient Member (which shall be a developing country Member or a LDC Member). A development partner might be an international development agency of a country (e.g., Department for International Development of UK, Swedish International Development Cooperation Agency), an international organization, or any other institution with such a function. A development partner, which is responsible for implementing development and aid policies, is not necessarily equivalent to a donor Member, though they are tightly associated.

Article 21:3 follows up the general principle specified in Article 13:2. The principles underlined by Article 21:3 take comprehensive account of the circumstances that both the donor Members and the recipient Members might face when dealing with the provision of TACB operationally. The purpose of the principles is to make sure that the provision of TACB exactly satisfies the authentic needs and priorities of the recipient Members.

The Committee on Trade Facilitation shall play a central role in the discussions on problems regarding implementing the TFA provisions, reviewing process of TACB provision, sharing experiences and information on TACB, reviewing donor notifications and reviewing operation of targeted TACB to LDC Members (q.v. Article 21:4).

ARTICLE 22: INFORMATION ON ASSISTANCE AND SUPPORT FOR CAPACITY BUILDING TO BE SUBMITTED TO THE COMMITTEE

Legal Text:

1   To provide transparency to developing country Members and least-developed country Members on the provision of assistance and support for capacity building for implementation of Section I, each donor Member assisting developing country Members and least-developed country Members with the implementation of this Agreement shall submit to the Committee, at entry into force of this Agreement and annually thereafter, the following information on its assistance and support for

capacity building that was disbursed in the preceding 12 months and, where available, that is committed in the next 12 months:[100]

(a) a description of the assistance and support for capacity building;
(b) the status and amount committed/disbursed;
(c) procedures for disbursement of the assistance and support;
(d) the beneficiary Member or, where necessary, the region; and
(e) the implementing agency in the Member providing assistance and support.

The information shall be provided in the format specified in Annex 1. In the case of Organization for Economic Cooperation and Development (referred to in this Agreement as the OECD) Members, the information submitted can be based on relevant information from the OECD Creditor Reporting System. Developing country Members declaring themselves in a position to provide assistance and support for capacity building are encouraged to provide the information above.

2   Donor Members assisting developing country Members and least-developed country Members shall submit to the Committee:

(a) contact points of their agencies responsible for providing assistance and support for capacity building related to the implementation of Section I of this Agreement including, where practicable, information on such contact points within the country or region where the assistance and support is to be provided; and
(b) information on the process and mechanisms for requesting assistance and support for capacity building.

Developing country Members declaring themselves in a position to provide assistance and support are encouraged to provide the information above.

3   Developing country Members and least-developed country Members intending to avail themselves of trade facilitation-related assistance and support for capacity building shall submit to the Committee information on contact point(s) of the office(s) responsible for coordinating and prioritizing such assistance and support.

4   Members may provide the information referred to in paragraphs 2 and 3 through internet references and shall update the information as necessary. The Secretariat shall make all such information publicly available.

5   The Committee shall invite relevant international and regional organizations (such as the International Monetary Fund, the OECD, the United Nations Conference on Trade and Development, the WCO, United Nations Regional Commissions, the World Bank, or their subsidiary bodies, and regional development banks) and other agencies of cooperation to provide information referred to in paragraphs 1, 2, and 4.

Table 6.4 Information on TACB to be submitted to the Committee

Donor Members	Recipient Members
• contact points of agencies responsible for TACB • the process and mechanisms for requesting TACB • TACB disbursed in the preceding 12 months and committed in the next 12 months	• contact point(s) of the office(s) responsible for coordinating and prioritizing TACB

A developing country Member or LDC Member can acquire the capacity of implementing the TFA only if TACB is provided in place. There needs to be a transparent mechanism where the donor Members and recipient Members can be well matched. In doing so, both the donor Members and the recipient Members shall submit relevant information to the Committee (q.v. Article 22:1,2,3). Relevant international organizations are also invited by the Committee to provide information as such (q.v. Article 22:5).

A commentary on Section III

There was no Section III in the TFA text (WT/MIN(13)/36, WT/L/911), when the Agreement was concluded at the 2013 Bali Ministerial Conference. In the primary text of the TFA, the Article on Institutional Arrangements belonged to Section I. Because institutional arrangements and the final provisions both deal with cross-cutting issues, the legal text of the TFA (WT/L/931), which was finally endorsed by the Preparatory Committee on Trade Facilitation in July 2014, rearranged the Article on Institutional Arrangements and the Article on Final Provisions together into Section III.

ARTICLE 23: INSTITUTIONAL ARRANGEMENTS

Legal Text:

1   Committee on Trade Facilitation

    1.1 A Committee on Trade Facilitation is hereby established.

    1.2 The Committee shall be open for participation by all Members and shall elect its own Chairperson. The Committee shall meet as needed and envisaged by the relevant provisions of this Agreement, but no less than once a year, for the purpose of affording Members the opportunity to consult on any matters related to the operation of this Agreement or the furtherance of its objectives. The Committee shall carry out such responsibilities as assigned to it under this Agreement or by the Members. The Committee shall establish its own rules of procedure.

1.3 The Committee may establish such subsidiary bodies as may be required. All such bodies shall report to the Committee.

1.4 The Committee shall develop procedures for the sharing by Members of relevant information and best practices as appropriate.

1.5 The Committee shall maintain close contact with other international organizations in the field of trade facilitation, such as the WCO, with the objective of securing the best available advice for the implementation and administration of this Agreement and in order to ensure that unnecessary duplication of effort is avoided. To this end, the Committee may invite representatives of such organizations or their subsidiary bodies to:

(a) attend meetings of the Committee; and

(b) discuss specific matters related to the implementation of this Agreement.

1.6 The Committee shall review the operation and implementation of this Agreement four years from its entry into force, and periodically thereafter.

1.7 Members are encouraged to raise before the Committee questions relating to issues on the implementation and application of this Agreement.

1.8 The Committee shall encourage and facilitate ad hoc discussions among Members on specific issues under this Agreement with a view to reaching a mutually satisfactory solution promptly.

2 National Committee on Trade Facilitation

Each Member shall establish and/or maintain a national committee on trade facilitation or designate an existing mechanism to facilitate both domestic coordination and implementation of the provisions of this Agreement.

An administrative body for the TFA – the Committee on Trade Facilitation – will be established. Functions of the Committee are: (i) developing procedures for sharing relevant information and best practices (q.v. Article 23:1.4), in particular on the implementation of international standards (q.v. Article 10:3.3); (ii) maintaining close contact with other international organizations to secure the best available advice for the implementation and administration of the TFA and avoid unnecessary duplication of effort (q.v. Article 23:1.5); (iii) reviewing the operation and implementation of the TFA (q.v. Article 23:1.6); (iv) encouraging and facilitating *ad hoc* discussions among Members on specific issues with a view to reaching a mutually satisfactory solution promptly (q.v. Article 23:1.8); and (v) managing and facilitating TACB and S&DT for developing country Members and LDC Members. It follows from Article IX of Agreement of Establishing the WTO that the Committee shall 'continue the practice of decision-making by consensus'. From the Negotiating Group on Trade Facilitation (NGTF) to the

Preparatory Committee on Trade Facilitation, consensus enabled the TFA to come true; under the Committee on Trade Facilitation, consensus will continue to make the TFA come right.

Additionally, a National Committee on Trade Facilitation (NCTF) is required by the TFA to be established or maintained for domestic coordination and implementation of this agreement (q.v. Article 23:2). However, the links between the NCTFs and the WTO Committee on Trade Facilitation are undefined. It is desirable that the links be specified (e.g., the NCTFs could act as Members' contact points for the WTO Committee on Trade Facilitation; each Member would better notify the information of its NCTF to the WTO Committee on Trade Facilitation). Indeed, there are already such stipulations in other WTO agreements. For example, Article 69 of the TRIPS Agreement stipulates that Members shall establish and notify contact points in their administrations for exchanging information on trade in infringing goods.

ARTICLE 24: FINAL PROVISIONS

Legal Text:

1 For the purpose of this Agreement, the term 'Member' is deemed to include the competent authority of that Member.
2 All provisions of this Agreement are binding on all Members.
3 Members shall implement this Agreement from the date of its entry into force. Developing country Members and least-developed country Members that choose to use the provisions of Section II shall implement this Agreement in accordance with Section II.
4 A Member which accepts this Agreement after its entry into force shall implement its Category B and C commitments counting the relevant periods from the date this Agreement enters into force.
5 Members of a customs union or a regional economic arrangement may adopt regional approaches to assist in the implementation of their obligations under this Agreement including through the establishment and use of regional bodies.
6 Notwithstanding the general interpretative note to Annex 1A to the Marrakesh Agreement Establishing the World Trade Organization, nothing in this Agreement shall be construed as diminishing the obligations of Members under the GATT 1994. In addition, nothing in this Agreement shall be construed as diminishing the rights and obligations of Members under the Agreement on Technical Barriers to Trade and the Agreement on the Application of Sanitary and Phytosanitary Measures.
7 All exceptions and exemptions[101] under the GATT 1994 shall apply to the provisions of this Agreement. Waivers applicable to the GATT 1994 or any part thereof, granted according to Article IX:3 and Article IX:4 of the Marrakesh Agreement Establishing the World Trade Organization

and any amendments thereto as of the date of entry into force of this Agreement, shall apply to the provisions of this Agreement.

8 The provisions of Articles XXII and XXIII of GATT 1994 as elaborated and applied by the Dispute Settlement Understanding shall apply to consultations and the settlement of disputes under this Agreement, except as otherwise specifically provided for in this Agreement.

9 Reservations may not be entered in respect of any of the provisions of this Agreement without the consent of the other Members.

10 The Category A commitments of developing country Members and least-developed country Members annexed to this Agreement in accordance with paragraphs 1 and 2 of Article 15 shall constitute an integral part of this Agreement.

11 The Category B and C commitments of developing country Members and least-developed country Members taken note of by the Committee and annexed to this Agreement pursuant to paragraph 5 of Article 16 shall constitute an integral part of this Agreement.

The simplest provision in the TFA – 'all provisions of this Agreement are binding on all Members' (q.v. Article 24:2) – evokes the debate on 'binding or not' at the beginning of the trade facilitation negotiations. In the sense of *pacta sunt servanda* (treaties should be observed),[102] Article 26 of Vienna Convention on the Law of Treaties has already stipulated that 'every treaty in force is binding upon the parties to it and must be performed by them in good faith'. The WTO, with its unique dispute settlement system, brings this norm of international law onto an enforceable level. If trade measures of a Member 'are found to be inconsistent with the provisions of any of the covered agreements', actions – in the form of (i) withdrawal of the measures, (ii) provision of compensation, or (iii) suspension of concessions or other obligations under the covered agreements on a discriminatory basis vis-à-vis the Member concerned – would be possibly incurred under the WTO dispute settlement system.[103]

In jurisprudential terms, implementing each of the TFA provisions is a *must* for each Member. However, the widespread 'best endeavor' wordings (e.g., 'may', 'shall endeavor', 'to the extent possible', 'whenever practicable', 'are encouraged' and 'as appropriate') sharply weaken the binding force of the provision concerned. With regard to the 'best endeavor' provisions, there are several unanswered questions. For instance, (i) can a Member use an airy-fairy trade facilitation strategy or blueprint to justify that it has 'endeavored', albeit the strategy or blueprint has not started or has failed? and (ii) in case of a dispute on a Member's non-compliance of a 'best endeavor' provision, is it the complainant that bears the burden of proof that the respondent has not reached 'the extent possible', or is it the respondent that proves itself has reached 'the extent possible?' The answers would most likely ride on the reports of the future Panel or Appellate Body.

At last, it is still necessary to distinguish between the confusingly similar concepts: exception, exemption and waiver (q.v. Article 24:7). In the WTO context, *exception* means a Member owns the right to adopt or enforce measures for given purposes or under given circumstances, which are mainly provided for in GATT Article XX and XXI; *exemption* is associated with the conditions (e.g., Annex on Article II Exemptions to the General Agreement on Trade in Services), under which a Member is exempt from its obligations under certain articles of an agreement (usually at the entry into force of that agreement);[104] *waiver* is governed by Article IX:3 and IX:4 of the Agreement Establishing the WTO, the Understanding in Respect to Waivers of Obligations under GATT 1994, the Decision-Making Procedures under Articles IX and XII of the WTO Agreement agreed by the General Council,[105] and the Guiding Principles to be Followed in Considering Applications for Waivers Adopted on 1 November 1956,[106] under which the Ministerial Conference or the General Council[107] may decide,[108] in exceptional circumstances, to waive[109] a specific obligation imposed on a Member by the WTO agreements.

Notes

1 WTO, WT/MIN(13)/36, WT/L/911 (2013)
2 Each Member has the discretion to state on its website the legal limitations of this description.
3 GATT, L/6513–36S/135 (1989), paras. 5.20–5.23.
4 US Administrative Procedure Act, SEC. 4, 79TH CONG., 2n SESS.-CHS. 299, 324-JUNE 10, 11, 1946.
5 Under this paragraph: (a) a review may, either before or after the ruling has been acted upon, be provided by the official, office, or authority that issued the ruling, a higher or independent administrative authority, or a judicial authority; and (b) a Member is not required to provide the applicant with recourse to paragraph 1 of Article 4.
6 It is understood that an advance ruling on the origin of a good may be an assessment of origin for the purposes of the Agreement on Rules of Origin where the ruling meets the requirements of this Agreement and the Agreement on Rules of Origin. Likewise, an assessment of origin under the Agreement on Rules of Origin may be an advance ruling on the origin of a good for the purposes of this Agreement where the ruling meets the requirements of both agreements. Members are not required to establish separate arrangements under this provision in addition to those established pursuant to the Agreement on Rules of Origin in relation to the assessment of origin provided that the requirements of this Article are fulfilled.
7 See ITC, *WTO Trade Facilitation Agreement: A Business Guide for Developing Countries* (ITC, 2013), p. 10.
8 OECD, TAD/TC/WP(2011)5/FINAL, p. 5.
9 See 177.9: Effect of ruling letters. See also 19 CFR 181-NAFTA, Subpart I, which also provides for advance ruling procedures.
10 An administrative decision in this Article means a decision with a legal effect that affects the rights and obligations of a specific person in an individual case. It shall be understood that an administrative decision in this Article covers an administrative action within the meaning of Article X of the GATT 1994 or failure to take an administrative action or decision as provided for in a Member's domestic law and legal system. For addressing such failure, Members may maintain an alternative administrative mechanism or judicial recourse to direct the customs

authority to promptly issue an administrative decision in place of the right to appeal or review under subparagraph 1(a).

11 Nothing in this paragraph shall prevent a Member from recognizing administrative silence on appeal or review as a decision in favor of the petitioner in accordance with its laws and regulations.

12 William Blackstone, *Commentaries on the Laws of England: In Four Books with an Analysis of the Work* (1753), Chapter III.

13 David Emmet (ed.), *Remedies* (Oxford University Press, 17th edn, 2014), p. 149.

14 In the first version of the draft consolidated negotiating text, it was drawn up that: 'Members [[shall][may]] ensure that customs and other relevant border agencies afford opportunities for [[traders][interested parties]], upon request, to receive information concerning the administrative decision [such as the reasoning of the decision] including applied laws and regulations'. See WTO, TN/TF/W/165 (2009), p. 10.

15 See WTO, TN/TF/W/122 (2006).

16 WTO, 'The Relationship Between the TFA and the SPS Agreement', March, 2014, www.wto.org/english/tratop_e/tradfa_e/tradfa_e.htm.

17 The case was complained by Canada and the European Economic Community against the 'merchandise processing fee' levied by the United States Customs Service, see GATT, L/6264–35S/245 (1987).

18 GATT, L/6264–35S/245 (1987), para. 77.

19 Ibid., para. 86.

20 Such a principle is also widely reflected in other laws and regulations of the WTO Members. For example, the US INTERNATIONAL TRAFFIC IN ARMS REGULATIONS provides that 'The Department may consider a voluntary disclosure as a mitigating factor in determining the administrative penalties, if any, that should be imposed'. See 22 C.F.R. 127.12 (a).

21 25 U.S.C. 501(c)(3) provides that an organization, which shall be exempt from taxation, includes: corporations, and any community chest, fund, or foundation, organized and operated exclusively for religious, charitable, scientific, testing for public safety, literary, or educational purposes, or to foster national or international amateur sports competition (but only if no part of its activities involve the provision of athletic facilities or equipment), or for the prevention of cruelty to children or animals, no part of the net earnings of which inures to the benefit of any private shareholder or individual, no substantial part of the activities of which is carrying on propaganda, or otherwise attempting, to influence legislation (except as otherwise provided in subsection (h)), and which does not participate in, or intervene in (including the publishing or distributing of statements), any political campaign on behalf of (or in opposition to) any candidate for public office.

22 The International Convention relating to the Simplification of Customs Formalities (1923), Annex to Article 14:7.

23 Ibid., Annex to Article 16.

24 Each Member may determine the scope and methodology of such average release time measurement in accordance with its needs and capacity.

25 A measure listed in subparagraphs 7.3 (a) to (g) will be deemed to be provided to authorized operators if it is generally available to all operators.

26 See, for more details, Hao Wu, "A Commentary on the Article on Expedited Shipments in the WTO Trade Facilitation Agreement", (2017) 12 *Global Trade and Customs Journal* 141, pp. 141–148.

27 In cases where a Member has an existing procedure that provides the treatment in paragraph 8.2, this provision does not require that Member to introduce separate expedited release procedures.

28 Such application criteria, if any, shall be in addition to the Member's requirements for operating with respect to all goods or shipments entered through air cargo facilities.

29 Universal Postal Convention, Article 1.13.

30 Ibid., Article 1.8.

31 Ruosi Zhang, 'The Liberalization of Postal and Courier Services: Ready for Delivery?' in Juan A. Marchetti and Martin Roy (eds.), *Opening Markets for Trade in Services: Countries and Sectors in Bilateral and WTO Negotiations* (Cambridge University Press, 2008), pp. 380–381.

32 *Oxford Dictionary of Law* (Oxford University Press, 8th edn, 2015), p. 183.

33 For the purposes of this provision, perishable goods are goods that rapidly decay due to their natural characteristics, in particular in the absence of appropriate storage conditions.

34 WTO, *World Trade Report 2013: Factors Shaping the Future of World Trade* (WTO, 2013), p. 94.

35 See *supra* note 22, Annex to Article 16.

36 Nothing in this paragraph precludes a Member from requiring documents such as certificates, permits or licenses as a requirement for the importation of controlled or regulated goods.

37 This paragraph refers to preshipment inspections covered by the Agreement on Preshipment Inspection, and does not preclude preshipment inspections for sanitary and phytosanitary purposes.

38 GATT, MTN.GNG/NG2/W/11 (1988).

39 Ibid.

40 See supra note 22, Annex to Article 16.

41 Nothing in this provision shall preclude a Member from maintaining existing procedures whereby the means of transport can be used as a guarantee for traffic in transit.

42 See Lilian del Castillo-Laborde, 'Case Law on International Watercourses', in Joseph W. Dellapenna and Joyeeta Gupta (eds.), *The Evolution of the Law and Politics of Water* (Springer, 2009), p. 330.

43 See its Article 5.

44 See its Article XIV, Article XXX; see also The Treaty between Russia and Austria and The Treaty between Russia and Prussia annexed to the Final Act.

45 See Part III Political Clauses for Europe, Section VIII, Poland.

46 See Part XII Ports, Waterways and Railways, Section I, General Provisions.

47 See the preamble of the Convention and Statute on Freedom of Transit.

48 The Statute on Freedom of Transit is an annex to the Convention and Statute on Freedom of Transit. See League of Nations, Treaty Series (1921), No. 171.

49 The latest contracting party is Armenia, which acceded on May 24, 2013.

50 The Statute on Freedom of Transit, Article 1.

51 Ibid.

52 Ibid., Article 2.

53 Ibid., Article 2.

54 Ibid., Article 3.

55 Ibid., Article 4.

56 The Barcelona Transit Statue mainly focused on transit by rail and waterway. See its Article 2.

57 See League of Nations, *Treaty Series* (1921), No. 172.

58 See the Convention and Statute on the Regime of Navigable Waterways of International Concern, Article 8.

59 See Havana Charter for an International Trade Organization, Article 33:3.

60 United Nations, *Proceedings of the United Nations Conference on Trade and Development*, E/CONF.46/141 Vol. I (1964), pp. 11–12.

61 Such activity has the overall objective of lowering the frequency of non-compliance, and consequently reducing the need for exchange of information in pursuit of enforcement.

62 This may include pertinent information on the verification conducted under paragraph 3. Such information shall be subject to the level of protection and confidentiality specified by the Member conducting the verification.

63 WTO, G/VAL/1 (1995); G/VAL/M/1 (1995), Section F.

64 WT/MIN(01)/17 (2001), para. 8.

65 See Hao Wu, 'Customs Cooperation in the WTO: From Uruguay to Doha', (2017) 51 *Journal of World Trade* 843, pp. 843–857.

66 Agreement on Trade-Related Aspects of Intellectual Property Rights (TRIPS), Article 69.

67 WT/MIN(01)/17 (2001), para. 8.3.

68 See GATT, VAL/W/32 (1985).

69 Ibid.

70 Sheri Rosenow and Brian J. O'Shea, *A Handbook on the WTO Customs Valuation Agreement* (Cambridge University Press, 2010), pp. 15–19.

71 WTO, G/VAL/M/31 (2002), para. 1.7.

72 WTO, WT/MIN(01)/17 (2001).

73 Ibid., para. 8.3.

74 The requirements of protection and confidentiality include: (a) hold all information or documents provided by the requested Member strictly in confidence and grant at least the same level of such protection and confidentiality as that provided under the domestic law and legal system of the requested Member; (b) provide information or documents only to the customs authorities dealing with the matter at issue and use the information or documents solely for the purpose stated in the request unless the requested Member agrees otherwise in writing; (c) not disclose the information or documents without the specific written permission of the requested Member; (d) not use any unverified information or documents from the requested Member as the deciding factor towards alleviating the doubt in any given circumstance; (e) respect any case-specific conditions set out by the requested Member regarding retention and disposal of confidential information or documents and personal data; (f) upon request, inform the requested Member of any decisions and actions taken on the matter as a result of the information or documents provided.

75 These circumstances include: (a) it would be contrary to the public interest as reflected in the domestic law and legal system of the requested Member; (b) its domestic law and legal system prevents the release of the information. In such a case it shall provide the requesting Member with a copy of the relevant, specific reference; (c) the provision of the information would impede law enforcement or otherwise interfere with an ongoing administrative or judicial investigation, prosecution or proceeding; (d) the consent of the importer or exporter is required by its domestic law and legal system that govern the collection, protection, use, disclosure, retention and disposal of confidential information or personal data and that consent is not given; or (e) the request for information is received after the expiration of the legal requirement of the requested Member for the retention of documents.

76 Roberto Azevêdo, speech at the WTO Trade Facilitation Workshop on June 10, 2014, www.wto.org/english/news_e/spra_e/spra23_e.htm.

77 Ibid.

78 For the purposes of this Agreement, 'assistance and support for capacity build-ing' may take the form of technical, financial, or any other mutually agreed form of assistance provided.

79 See its paragraph 33 and Annex E.

80 Alexander Keck and Patrick Low, 'Special and Differential Treatment in the WTO: Why, When and How?' WTO Staff Working Paper ERSD-2004–03, p. 3.

81 See GATT 1947, Part IV: Trade and Development.

82 See the Tokyo Declaration of 14 September 1973, GATT/1134 (1973), para. 6.

83 See the Decision of 28 November 1979 on Differential and More Favoura-ble Treatment, Reciprocity and Fuller Participation of Developing Countries, GATT, L/4903 (1979). It is informally called 'the Enabling Clause'.

84 See the Decision on Measures in Favor of Least-Developed Countries.

85 WTO Doha Ministerial Declaration, WT/MIN(01)/DEC/1 (2001), para. 44.

86 Keck and Low, see *supra* note 80, p. 6.

87 WTO, WT/COMTD/8 (1996).

88 Doha Ministerial Declaration, WT/MIN(01)/DEC/1 (2001), para. 38.

89 Ibid.

90 Decision Adopted by the General Council on 1 August 2004 (the 'July pack-age'), WTO, WT/L/579 (2004).

91 WTO, *WTO Public Forum 2007: How Can the WTO Help Harness Globalization* (WTO, 2008), p. 14.

92 Where a developing-country Member or a least-developed country Member continues to lack the necessary capacity, implementation of the provision(s) concerned will not be required until implementation capacity has been acquired.

93 Notifications submitted may also include such further information as the notify-ing Member deems appropriate. Members are encouraged to provide informa-tion on the domestic agency or entity responsible for implementation.

94 Members may also include information on national trade facilitation implemen-tation plans or projects, the domestic agency or entity responsible for imple-mentation, and the donors with which the Member may have an arrangement in place to provide assistance.

95 Such arrangements will be on mutually agreed terms, either bilaterally or through appropriate international organizations, consistent with paragraph 3 of Article 21.

96 Members may also include information on national trade facilitation implemen-tation plans or projects, the domestic agency or entity responsible for imple-mentation, and the donors with which the Member may have an arrangement in place to provide assistance.

97 Such arrangements will be on mutually agreed terms, either bilaterally or through appropriate international organizations, consistent with paragraph 3 of Article 21.

98 The composition of the Expert Group shall ensure balance between nationals from developing and developed country Members. Where a least-developed country Member is involved, the Expert Group shall include at least one national from a least-developed country Member. If the Committee cannot agree on the composition of the Expert Group within 20 days of its establishment, the Director-General, in consultation with the chair of the Committee, shall deter-mine the composition of the Expert Group (q.v. Article 18:3).

99 See Understanding on Rules and procedures Governing the Settlement of Dis-putes, Article 21:3.

100 The information provided will reflect the demand driven nature of the provision of assistance and support for capacity building.
101 This includes Articles V:7 and X:1 of the GATT 1994 and the Ad note to Article VIII of the GATT 1994.
102 *Oxford Dictionary of Law* (8th edn, 2015), p. 440.
103 See *supra* note 99, Article 3:7.
104 However, Article 24:7 of the TFA only focuses on the exceptions and exemptions embodied in GATT Articles V:7 and X:1, and the ad note to GATT Article VIII, as seen in its footnote.
105 WTO, WT/L/93 (1995).
106 See e.g., the WTO Ministerial Decision of 14 November 2001, WT/MIN(01)/15.
107 The General Council conducts the function of the Ministerial Conference in the interval between meetings, pursuant to paragraph 2 of Article IV of the WTO Agreement. A request for a waiver concerning the Multilateral Trade Agreements in Annexes 1A or 1B or 1C and their annexes shall be submitted initially to the Council for Trade in Goods, the Council for Trade in Services or the Council for TRIPS, respectively, for consideration during a time period which shall not exceed 90 days. At the end of the time period, the relevant Council shall submit a report to the Ministerial Conference.
108 Any such decision shall be taken by three-fourths of the Members, but a decision to grant a waiver in respect of any obligation subject to a transition period or a period for staged implementation that the requesting Member has not performed by the end of the relevant period shall be taken only by consensus.
109 The Ministerial Conference may extend, modify or terminate the waiver.

7   A symphony of trade facilitation

The Modalities for Negotiations on Trade Facilitation (namely, Annex D of the 2004 'July package') mandated that

> in order to make technical assistance and capacity building (TACB) more effective and operational and to ensure better coherence, Members shall invite relevant international organizations, including the IMF, OECD, UNCTAD, WCO and the World Bank to undertake a collaborative effort in this regard.

Since then, the IMF, OECD, UNCTAD, WCO and the World Bank have been collectively called the 'Annex D organizations'. In fact, long before the negotiations on trade facilitation in the WTO, these organizations had been forerunners in this field. During the course from Doha to Bali, they also paid various forms of tributes to the negotiations (e.g., developing negotiating tools, providing assistance to negotiators).

Recitals by the Annex D organizations

International Monetary Fund (IMF)

Articles of Agreement of the International Monetary Fund endow this global monetary institution with the mission 'to facilitate the expansion and balanced growth of international trade'.[1] Thus, the IMF is engaged in trade facilitation in nature. Work of the IMF relating to trade facilitation takes these forms: (i) as part of its regular consultations with countries on their economic policies and developments; (ii) as a component of countries' stabilization programmes supported by the IMF; and (iii) as technical assistance on tariff policy and customs administration provided to the requesting countries.[2]

Trade Integration Mechanism (TIM)[3]

The IMF finds that trade liberalization in multilateral frameworks (e.g., the Doha Development Agenda of the WTO) could generate short-term balance of payment challenges (e.g., a temporary reduction of export revenues due to adjustment pressures coming from more competitive conditions in a country's export markets, or an increase in import bills). With the aim of mitigating the concerns of its Member countries (in particular, developing countries) about financing balance of payments shortfalls resulting from multilateral trade liberalization, the IMF projected the Trade Integration Mechanism (TIM) in 2004. Under the TIM, a country can request consideration of the IMF financing if it expects a net balance of payments shortfall as a result of measures implemented by other countries that lead to more open market access for goods and services. Such measures should typically be introduced either under a WTO agreement or in some other ways that all countries are treated on a non-discriminatory basis. The TIM is not a special lending facility, but rather a policy designed to make resources more predictably available under the IMF existing lending facilities. Bangladesh, the Dominican Republic and the Republic of Madagascar have so far requested and obtained support under the TIM. With the birth of the TFA which is a new WTO agreement, does it imply that a country is eligible for applying for the IMF lending out of its anticipated impact of other countries' implementation of the TFA (if taken as trade adjustment) on its balance of payments?

Organization for Economic Cooperation and Development (OECD)

Convention on the Organization for Economic Cooperation and Development (OECD), which was agreed in Paris in 1960, begins with the articles that

> the aims of the Organization shall be to promote policies designed [. . .] to contribute to the expansion of world trade on a multilateral, non-discriminatory basis in accordance with international obligations', and 'the Members agree that they will, both individually and jointly, [. . .] pursue their efforts to reduce or abolish obstacles to the exchange of goods and services'.[4]

The OECD's involvement in trade facilitation is not as early as other Annex D organizations,[5] but its econometric methodology has earned it a place in this field.

Trade Facilitation Indicators (TFIs)

On the ground of its series of calculations of the impact, costs and benefits of trade-facilitative measures, the OECD published the Trade Facilitation Indicators (TFIs) – a gravity modeling tool – in 2009.[6] The TFIs follow the 12 articles in Section I of the WTO draft consolidated negotiating text of TFA 'in order to maintain the relevance of the resulting indicators for the negotiators, implementing authorities and donors'. Taking into account the similarities, shared components and distinctions amidst the TFA articles, the OECD re-organizes the trade-facilitative measures embodied in those articles and categorize them into 16 indicators.[7] These indicators are composed of 100 variables (e.g., consultations between traders and government, evaluation of fees and charges, percentage of import declarations cleared electronically). The weight of each variable is distributed according to its relative importance (which actually differs). The OECD runs regressions introducing different sets of variables to its gravity equations. Based on data drawn both from the public resources (e.g., the WTO's Trade Policy Reviews, the World Banks' Doing Business and the World Economic Forum's Global Competitiveness Report)[8] and from replies of its Members and some observers to its designed questionnaire (the replies provide more reliable hard data and internal data),[9] the OECD is able to conduct quantitative analysis for targeting sectors (e.g., agriculture, manufacture) or country groupings (e.g., lower middle income country group, Sub-Saharan African country group). When all the TFIs are aggregated, their impact on trade flow and trade costs is estimated. This tool makes more visible which dimensions of trade facilitation lead to higher increases in trade flow and greater reductions in trade costs, and helps provide advice for prioritizing trade facilitation policies.

United Nations Conference on Trade and Development (UNCTAD)

UNCTAD has a rich history of work on trade facilitation. The Final Act and Report of its first Ministerial Conference in 1964 recommended that UNCTAD 'should promote, within the United Nations family, arrangements for [. . .] intergovernmental action for research into [. . .] the simplification of formalities relating to customs procedure, commercial travel, etc.'[10]

In the 1960s, a growing number of Member countries of the United Nations (UN) became aware of the need for coordinating trade facilitation efforts on a worldwide scale. This awareness led to the creation of Interregional Advisory Services on Trade Facilitation within UNCTAD.[11] In 1975, UNCTAD launched a Special Program on Trade Facilitation (FALPRO) whose terms of reference covered the development of trade-facilitative measures, provision of substantive support for technical assistance and cooperation globally with the regional economic commissions and other international organizations.[12]

In 1992, the UNCTAD VIII Cartagena Conference agreed to set up an Expert Working Group on Trade Efficiency that 'would produce guidelines needed to take concrete steps towards trade efficiency at the national and international levels, especially in developing countries',[13] and decided that '[t]he culmination of the work of the Group would be an international symposium on trade efficiency'.[14] In 1994, the United Nations International Symposium on Trade Efficiency was accordingly held at Columbus, Ohio in the US. The Symposium adopted the Columbus Ministerial Declaration on Trade Efficiency, which was instrumental in fitting trade facilitation into the 1996 WTO Singapore Ministerial Conference agenda.[15] Then the FALPRO was incorporated into the Special Program for Trade Efficiency (SPTE). In the 1996 re-organization of UNCTAD, SPTE was transformed into the Division of Services Infrastructure for Development and

Trade Efficiency (SITE).[16] Nowadays, trade facilitation in UNCTAD falls under the Division on Technology and Logistics (DTL). UNCTAD has carried out its trade facilitation mandates in a variety of forms.

For over 50 years, UNCTAD has provided TACB to developing countries in the domain of trade facilitation. UNCTAD's TACB included assisting those countries in assessing their needs and priorities in trade facilitation, developing institutional and technical tools for implementing their trade facilitation reforms and facilitating their participation in regional and global events for setting trade facilitation standards. Since 2004, UNCTAD focused its TACB on supporting developing countries in terms of participating in trade facilitation negotiations in the WTO and drawing up their national implementation plans for the future TFA.

Automated System for Customs Data (ASYCUDA)[17]

Since the 1980s, UNCTAD has developed the Automated System for Customs Data (ASYCUDA). ASYCUDA is a computerized customs management system, which covers mostly customs procedures and provides statistical output. The system handles manifests and customs declarations, accounting procedures, transit and suspense procedures. ASYCUDA takes account of the international codes and standards developed by the International Organization for Standardization (ISO), the World Customs Organization (WCO) and the United Nations (UN). It provides for Electronic Data Interchange (EDI) between traders and customs at national level, applying Electronic Data Interchange for Administration, Commerce and Transport (EDIFACT) rules. Trade data that ASYCUDA generates can be also used for statistical purpose.

ASYCUDA can be configured to suit the national characteristics of countries in terms of customs regimes, tariffs, legislation and so on. ASYCUDA is currently operational in more than 90 developing countries under a technical assistance programme that delivers a comprehensive package, including software, documentation, technical and functional expertise and capacity building.[18] According to UNCTAD, ASYCUDA provides tools for implementing the majority of trade-facilitative measures in the TFA.[19] ASYCUDA World is the latest version of the software which would enable possibilities of using ASYCUDA as a national single window.

Port Training Programme under TrainForTrade

The TrainForTrade Programme was launched in 1989 to address trade-related human and institutional capacity needs of developing and transition countries and to ultimately increase their participation in international trade in an equitable and sustainable manner. As a development-oriented initiative, the TrainForTrade Programme has helped in facilitating South-South and North-South collaboration and improving communication between trade and training experts.[20]

Under the TrainForTrade Programme, the Port Training Programme contributes to consolidating trade facilitation by supporting port communities in developing countries in quest of efficient and competitive port management. In order to increase trade flow and foster economic development, this Programme creates port networks bringing together public, private and international entities with a view to sharing knowledge and expertise between port operators and strengthening talent management and human resources development in port communities.[21] So far, UNCTAD has established four port networks respectively in Portuguese, Spanish, French and English.

National Trade Facilitation Bodies (NTFBs)

In 1974, the UNECE Working Party on Facilitation of International Trade Procedures (WP.4) adopted Recommendation No. 4 – National Trade Facilitation Organs – in order to encourage the establishment of national organizations, or other suitable means, for the facilitation of international trade procedures. In 1999, in view of the political, economic and technological developments in trade and transport, the UN Center for the Facilitation of Procedures and Practices for Administration, Commerce and Transport (UN/CEFACT), which had replaced the WP.4, revamped the Recommendation No. 4 and changed the title to National Trade Facilitation Bodies (NTFBs).[22]

In line with the UNECE/CEFACT Recommendation No.4, UNCTAD, through advisory services as well as technical assistance and training activities, is dedicated to promoting the creation of NTFBs.[23] The NTFBs would serve as a national forum and be able to bring together representatives of both public and private parties in a country to jointly strengthen pushes for trade facilitation. This is precisely what the TFA Article 23 (Institutional Arrangements) requires the WTO Members to do (viz. establishing and/or maintaining a national committee on trade facilitation or designate an existing mechanism to facilitate both domestic coordination and implementation of the provisions of the TFA).

In 2013, UNCTAD created an online repository which provides more than 80 countries' cases from different geographical regions on the establishment and management of NTFBs. It overviews the existing NTFBs around the world from a comparative perspective. In its recent work, UNCTAD highlights the key steps towards effective and strong NTFBs, points out the main obstacles that the NTFBs confront and comes up with solutions taken from successful cases.

In 2018, UNCTAD published its latest study on National Trade Facilitation Committees – *Beyond Compliance with the WTO Trade Facilitation Agreement?* The study provides an overview of good practices for establishing and operating the Committees in over 50 countries.

Assistance in transit

There are 32 landlocked developing countries in the world, more than half of which are classified as LDCs.[24] 'Recognizing that, as a result of the geographic situation of the landlocked developing countries, of the high cost of transportation and of the poor development of their infrastructure in all field, the expansion of their trade and economic development is inhibited', the UN General Assembly Resolution 2971 of December 14, 1972 invited 'all Member States and the competent international organizations to assist the landlocked developing countries in facilitating, within the framework of appropriate agreements, the exercise of their right of freedom of access to and from the sea'.[25] In 1997, the 52nd UN General Assembly adopted a resolution on the issue of Specific Actions Related to the Particular Needs and Problems of Landlocked Developing Countries, which

> Requests the Secretary-General of the United Nations Conference on Trade and Development to seek voluntary contributions to ensure the participation of representatives of landlocked and transit developing countries, donor countries and financial and development institutions;
>
> Notes with appreciation the contribution of the United Nations Conference on Trade and Development to formulating international measures to deal with the special problems of the landlocked developing countries, and urges the Conference, inter alia, to keep under constant review the evolution of transit transport infrastructure facilities, institutions and services, monitor the implementation of agreed measures, including by means of a case study as necessary, collaborate in all relevant initiatives, including those of the private sector and non-governmental organizations, and serve as a focal point for cross-regional issues of landlocked developing countries.[26]

Under this mandate, UNCTAD offers assistance to landlocked developing countries and their transit neighbors, in Africa, Central Asia and other regions, in terms of negotiating or implementing bilateral and regional transit agreements and arrangements, streamlining and harmonizing administrative and customs procedures and documentation, implementing policies and procedures to reduce transit costs, building institution and developing human resource in the transit sector, reducing transit time of goods through the facilitation of traffic flows at border crossings and interchange of rolling stock between networks, simplifying wagon hire compensation formalities, etc.[27] Those efforts of UNCTAD are consistent with its mandate provided for in the Almaty Declaration and the Almaty Program of Action,[28] and the ensuing Vienna Declaration and Vienna Program of Action for Landlocked Developing Countries for the Decade 2014–2024,[29] which reflect the strong commitment of the international community to addressing the special needs and problems of landlocked developing countries in the UN context.

Business Facilitation Program[30]

UNCTAD started the Business Facilitation Program in 2005 to help governments improve the enabling environment for business by streamlining administrative processes and mobilizing technology. The Program is designed to reduce informality and corruption, to empower small entrepreneurs, to remove bureaucratic barriers to trade and investment and to increase government revenue. The eRegulations system, the eSimplifications system and the eRegistrations system are main components of the Program.

The eRegulations system, in particular, is an affordable turn-key solution for governments to clarify and publicize administrative procedures. It shows administrative procedures step by step from the user's point of view. For each step, it provides contact data (e.g., entity, office, person in charge), expected result of the step, required documents, cost, duration, legal justification and ways to complain. Any type of administrative procedure (e.g., company creation, tax payment, activity licenses, construction permit, import and export) can be documented or clarified through an eRegulations portal. The eRegulations system meets the requirements of TFA Article 1:1 (Publication) and Article 1:3 (Inquiry Points). Kenya has set an example of trade facilitation portal based on the UNCTAD eRegulations approach (http://infotradekenya.go.ke/).

World Customs Organization (WCO)

In 1952, 'convinced that it will be in the interest of international trade to promote cooperation between Governments in [harmony and uniformity in their customs systems]',[31] 13 European countries established the Customs Cooperation Council (CCC). After years of membership expansion, the Council adopted 'World Customs Organization' (WCO) as its informal working name in 1994[32] to align with the creation of the World Trade Organization. Today, the WCO has developed to a global intergovernmental institution. The WCO's mission is to 'provide leadership, guidance and support to customs administrations to secure and facilitate legitimate trade, realize revenues, protect society and build capacity'.[33] Thus, trade facilitation is firmly on the agenda of the WCO.

'Noting that the [Bali] Ministerial Decision highlights the role of the WCO in the implementation and administration of the Trade Facilitation Agreement', the WCO stated in its 2013 Dublin Resolution[34] that it would be committed to the efficient implementation of the TFA. Kunio Mikuriya, Secretary General of the WCO, stated:

> With its standards-setting activities for customs at the global level, its ability to cooperate with other border regulatory agencies, international organizations and the private sector, its worldwide network of customs experts, its acknowledged professionalism and its long-standing support for trade facilitation globally, the WCO is certainly well-positioned.[35]

Mercator Program

In 2014, the 123/124 Sessions of the Customs Cooperation Council endorsed 'the WCO Mercator Program – a strategic initiative to support trade facilitation'. The Program is named after Gerardus Mercator, a Flemish cartographer in the sixteenth century, who was the first to refer to a collection of maps as an 'atlas' and created the global map projection that enabled mariners to sail on straight courses in the ocean.

The Program is aimed at assisting governments in implementing the TFA expeditiously and in a harmonized manner by using core WCO instruments and tools. Built upon years of WCO experience in customs reforms and modernization deliveries, the Program offers operational and technical support in response to the requests of WCO Members.[36] The Program consists of dual tracks: (i) an overall track that raises awareness of both the TFA obligations and the WCO's instruments and tools through regional and national events; and (ii) a tailor-made track that develops results-based assistance projects for individual countries on the basis of the WCO's capacity building methodology that simultaneously satisfies the needs of recipient Members and the interests of donors.

According to the WCO, by means of coordinating donor engagement, consolidating the relationship with development partners and taking advantage of the wealthy network of customs experts that spreads over the world, the Program is well equipped to provide technical assistance and capacity building in implementing the TFA. The WCO Working Group on the TFA (WGTFA) serves as the vehicle for supporting and monitoring the Program.

Box 7.1   Core WCO instruments and tools on trade facilitation

- Revised Kyoto Convention
- SAFE Framework of Standards, including Authorized Economic Operators (AEO)
- Time Release Study Guide
- Risk Management Compendium
- Post Clearance Audit Guidelines
- Single Window Compendium
- WCO Data Model
- Coordinated Border Management Compendium
- Transit Handbook
- Customs-Business Partnership/Engagement Guidance
- Capacity Building Strategy, including ownership approach
- Capacity Building Diagnostic Framework
- Performance Contracts Guide
- Leadership and Management Development and other Human Resource Programs

Source: the WCO

Revised Kyoto Convention

In 1973, International Convention on the Simplification and Harmonization of Customs Procedures (also known as the 'Kyoto Convention') was agreed. The Kyoto Convention has two parts. The first part is comprised of 19 articles setting out the general provisions. The second part contains 31 annexes. Each annex is specific to a type of customs procedure, and consists of definitions of customs terms, generally applicable standards, recommended practices and notes, which collectively constitute the approach to simplifying and harmonizing that type of customs procedure. For the sake of accession to the Kyoto Convention, a country may select among the annexes but has to accept at least one annex. Each of the annexes can be accepted individually and it enters into force upon five contracting parties' acceptance of it.

Considering the radical changes in trade environment and customs administrative techniques, the WCO amended the 1973 Kyoto Convention in 1999 for the purpose of drawing 'the blueprint for standard and facilitative customs procedures in the 21st Century'.[37]

The amended Convention (also known as the 'Revised Kyoto Convention' or 'RKC' for short) has a new structure made up of a Body, a General Annex and 10 Specific Annexes. The Body sets forth the scope of the Convention, management of the Convention, general rights and obligations of contracting parties, entry into force and depositary of the Convention, etc. The General Annex deals with issues that are key and common to the dimensions of harmonizing and simplifying customs procedures: clearance and other customs formalities; security; customs control; application of information technology; relationship between the customs and third parties; information, decision and rulings supplied by the customs; appeals in the customs matter. Disciplines embodied in the General Annex take the form of 'standards' or 'transition standards'. Implementation of the 'transition standards' is given a 2-year extension over the 3-year requirement for 'standards'. The Specific Annexes encompass these areas: arrival of goods in a customs territory; importation; exportation; customs warehouses and free zones; transit; processing; temporary admission; offences; special procedures; and origin. The Specific Annexes contain 'standards' and 'recommended practices'. Both of the General Annex and the Specific Annexes are accompanied by 'guidelines', which are not binding on contracting parties.

The Revised Kyoto Convention is featured in the way that the General Annex is obligatory for accession and implementation by contracting parties without any reservations against the 'standards' and 'transition standards' therein; while the Specific Annexes and the Chapters thereof are subject to selection by contracting parties, who are bound by the 'standards' but can notify its reservations against the 'recommended practices; any Specific Annexes or Chapters thereof adopted by a contracting party are construed to be an integral part of the Convention.

A Management Committee is established to administer the Revised Kyoto Convention and is also empowered to extend the period for implementation of the General Annex and Specific Annexes upon requests from contracting parties. Disputes concerning the interpretation or application of the Revised Kyoto Convention shall as far as possible be settled through negotiations or be referred to the Management Committee which will make recommendations for their settlement.

Do the flexibilities given by the Revised Kyoto Convention to the contracting parties (e.g., transitional arrangements, countries' freedom in deciding their commitments, possibility of extending the period for implementation) look similar to the arrangements in the Section II and Section III of the TFA? However, those flexibilities embodied in the two international accords are not identical at all. Different from the Revised Kyoto Convention, in the TFA, for example, (i) all provisions are binding and Members are not allowed to pick up the provisions that they are committed to; (ii) transitional period of time is determined by the Members' own schedule of implementing the Agreement rather than stuck to the individual provisions; and (iii) reservations may not be entered in respect of any provisions without other Members' consent.

As of August 11, 2017, 112 contracting parties, at different levels of accepting the contents, have acceded to the Revised Kyoto Convention. According to the WCO, the Revised Kyoto Convention is at the center of its instruments and tools on trade facilitation.

Nairobi Convention

The mission of the WCO is to provide leadership, guidance and support to customs administrations to secure and facilitate legitimate trade. Therefore, it is necessary for the international customs community to jointly stop those offences that are prejudicial to the legitimate trade. Based on the evolvement of its recommendations on mutual assistance between customs administrations since 1953, the Customs Cooperation Council, at its meeting in 1977 in Nairobi, Kenya, adopted the International Convention on Mutual Administrative Assistance for the Prevention, Investigation and Repression of Customs Offences (also known as the 'Nairobi Convention').

The Nairobi Convention consists of a Body and 11 Annexes. The Body prescribes these items: the purpose and scope of customs mutual assistance; procedures of requesting and providing the assistance; conditions for using the intelligence, documents or any other information; the role of the WCO (Customs Cooperation Council) and its bodies in administering the Convention, etc. The Annexes classify the patterns where customs mutual assistance will be requested and provided, and thus enable the contracting parties to choose the patterns that are compatible with their national legislations. A contracting party may accept any of the Annexes that are independent of each other (in a sense, like the case of Specific Annexes in the Revised Kyoto Convention) but has to accept at least one Annex.

Based on the perception that 'customs administrations shall afford each other mutual assistance with a view to preventing, investigating and repressing customs offences',[38] the Nairobi Convention underlines the principle of reciprocity: a contracting party has the obligation to render assistance to another one, only when both parties have accepted the same Annex.

The TFA Article 12 is also about customs cooperation. In comparison to the Nairobi Convention, Article 12 of the TFA narrows down the scope (and ambition) of customs cooperation, and overstresses the conditionality for a Member in making a request, the discretions that the requested Member has in providing information or refusing a request, and the protection and confidentiality of the requested information. On the other hand, when it comes to maneuvering in the 164 WTO Members that are nearly three times the 52 contracting parties[39] of the Nairobi Convention, the TFA Article 12 ought to be more modest. In terms of multilaterally regulating the customs mutual assistance, a more comprehensive set of rules than the TFA Article 12 are, nevertheless, desirable.

In 2003, the WCO tabled the International Convention on Mutual Administrative Assistance in Customs Matters (also known as the 'Johannesburg Convention') that would rejigger the Nairobi Convention. However, the Johannesburg Convention has not entered into force, because the numbers of contracting parties so far are not as sufficient as the Convention per se requires.[40]

Box 7.2   Other WCO conventions relating to trade facilitation

- Customs Convention on ECS Carnets for Commercial Samples (1957)
- Customs Convention on the Temporary Importation of Packings (1962)
- Customs Convention on the Temporary Importation of Professional Equipment (1962)
- Customs Convention concerning Facilities for the Importation of Goods for Display or Use at Exhibitions, Fairs, Meetings or Similar Events (1962)
- Customs Convention on the ATA Carnet for the Temporary Admission of Goods (ATA Convention) (1963)
- Customs Convention concerning Welfare Material for Seafarers (1965)
- Customs Convention on the Temporary Importation of Scientific Equipment (1969)
- Customs Convention on the Temporary Importation of Pedagogic Material (1971)
- Customs Convention on Containers (1975)
- Convention on Temporary Admission (Istanbul Convention) (1993)

Note: in the parentheses are the years of entry into force

Source: the WCO

Support to the WTO negotiations

Since the very beginning of the WTO trade facilitation negotiations, the WCO had dynamically provided support to the negotiations. Shortly after the launch of Doha Round, the WCO, in 2002 and 2003, communicated its reviews respectively of GATT Article V, VIII and X [41] and its capacity building strategies[42] and tools[43] to the WTO Council for Trade in Goods. The WCO's communications (i) highlighted the role of international customs community in trade facilitation; (ii) demonstrated that the WCO's instruments were compatible with and complementary to GATT Article V, VIII and X; and (iii) stated that the customs capacity building would be supportive of the developing countries and least-developed countries.

At the dawn of the WTO Cancún Ministerial Conference, when negotiations on trade facilitation were supposed to be decided to take place, the WCO issued a Message from the International Customs Community on Partnership for Economic Development through Trade Facilitation. The Message declared the continued contributions of customs to the WTO trade facilitation process and envisaged enhanced cooperation with the WTO. The WCO urged that 'the views of customs be taken account of in the formulation of national policy with respect to the upcoming Ministerial Conference in Cancún and any ensuing negotiations'.[44] The Message called on customs administrations to brief the trade ministries of their home countries on the sound customs' readiness for the run-up to Cancún.[45]

In 2005, the WCO presented its self-assessment checklists (TN/TF/W/16) to the WTO with a view to supporting the trade facilitation negotiations. The checklists took the form of a questionnaire that could survey the status quo of customs administrations against the GATT Article V, VIII and X in respect of strategic management, resources, legal framework, systems and procedures, information and communication technology, external cooperation and communication and partnership, and integrity. The checklists could help Members take a simple snapshot of their customs performance and identify the problems that needed to be addressed.

World Bank

According to Articles of Agreement of International Bank for Reconstruction and Development (IBRD), one of the missions of the World Bank is 'to promote the long-range balanced growth of international trade'.[46] The World Bank's involvement in trade facilitation started from its work on transport facilitation in Latin America in 1976. In the mid-1980s, isolated trade facilitation components, particularly focusing on governance reform, were increasingly included in the World Bank's structural adjustment loans. Since 1990, the World Bank has explored ways of addressing the wide range of policy and administrative issues concerning trade facilitation, which led to useful conditionalities of adjustment loans and new types of programmes.[47]

The World Bank has published its Trade Strategy 2011–2021,[48] which is propped up by its Four Priority Themes for Trade Support Activities. 'Trade facilitation, transport logistics and trade finance', which aims to 'reduce the costs of trade-related transport and logistics and increase their timeliness and reliability',[49] is one of the priority themes.[50] The Strategy recognizes that the priorities for trade facilitation have been evolving in the last few years and vary across countries. Therefore, a range of new issues (e.g., broader border management reform extending beyond customs modernization, making transit systems work, improving the quality of services, facilitating the cross-border movement of service suppliers) shall be included in the priorities for trade facilitation.[51] The Strategy will be implemented by means of three major instruments: (i) lending, (ii) technical assistance and knowledge to support strategic priorities, and (iii) external partnerships.[52]

Trade Facilitation Support Program (TFSP)[53]

In 2014, the World Bank, together with other donors, initiated the Trade Facilitation Support Program (TFSP), which 'will focus on the effective implementation of trade facilitation reforms in developing countries to enhance private sector competitiveness, thus leading to increased trade, investments and job creation'.[54] The Program has two main components:

(i) The Program provides technical assistance to help developing countries reform their trade facilitation-related laws, procedures, processes and systems in a manner consistent with the TFA. The Program will provide support in the design and implementation of policy, regulatory, legal and institutional aspects, taking into account countries' schedules of commitments, identified gaps and implementation capacity.

(ii) The Program 'complements and underpins project interventions with the development of knowledge, learning and measurement tools'.[55] Such interventions may include benchmarking progress in the TFA implementation, conducting impact assessments and evaluations, piloting best practices in trade facilitation and border management and developing project-level monitoring and result measurement indicators. Peer-to-peer learning and experience-sharing events within and across regions may also be organized to help encourage dissemination of best practices between developing countries.[56]

Selection criteria of the Program prioritize the International Development Association (IDA)-eligible, low-income, or conflict-affected and fragile countries, as well as middle-income countries that act as gateways to least-developed countries or whose performance significantly impacts on the regional least-developed countries. Nevertheless, countries are expected to have demonstrated a strong commitment to implementing reforms in the areas covered by the TFA, when they receive support under the Program.[57]

Trade Facilitation Facility (TFF)

In April 2009, the World Bank launched a 40 million USD multi-donor trust fund – Trade Facilitation Facility (TFF), aiming to assist developing countries in improving their competitiveness through improvements in their trade facilitation systems. Responding to the requests of governments or regional organizations – e.g., Common Market for Eastern and Southern Africa (COMESA), Southern African Development Community (SADC), East African Community (EAC), West African Economic and Monetary Union (WAEMU), Association of Southeast Asian Nations (ASEAN), the TFF assistance will be delivered through (i) technical advisory services and capacity-building activities to support implementation of regulatory and policy reforms; (ii) design and improvement of regional trade facilitation and transit regimes; (iii) improvement of border management, clearance, technical controls and standards systems; and (iv) better design, investment and management of critical trade-supporting infrastructure.[58]

The TFF focuses initially on low-income countries, sub-Saharan African countries and lower-middle-income countries that have trade facilitation impacts on the neighboring low-income countries. Meanwhile, eligibility is expected to extend to other developing countries.

A programme management team monitors and markets the TFF projects. A programme committee comprised of managers and senior experts advises and oversees the TFF activities. On the upper level, a steering committee, which includes one representative from each donor and some management staff from the World Bank and the International Financial Corporation (IFC), makes decisions regarding strategic direction and operation of the TFF. The TFF and another programme – the Multi-donor Trust Fund for Trade and Development (MDTF-TD) – are both managed by the World Bank International Trade Department. However, the Aid for Trade Coordination Council, made up of members of the TFF and MDTF-TD steering committees, reinforces the coherence of these two programmes that are supported by different sets of donors and follow different procedures.[59]

Support to the WTO negotiations

Since 2005, the World Bank started a programme to support the achievement of an ambitious and development-friendly WTO trade facilitation agreement.[60] The World Bank's support initially focused on encouraging developing countries to participate actively in the negotiations. As a part of this effort, the World Bank developed the WTO Trade Facilitation Negotiations Support Guide (TN/TF/W/51), which was intended to 'assist developing and least-developed WTO Members to establish practical and cost-effective mechanisms' and to 'provide WTO Members with a range of options for establishing effective communication and coordination mechanisms to support the trade facilitation negotiation process'.[61]

In 2007, in response to increasing demands for national assessments, the World Bank, working with the WTO and other Annex D organizations, prepared the WTO Negotiations on Trade Facilitation Self Assessment Guide (TN/TF/W/143) to assist the WTO Members in accurately assessing their own needs and priorities for technical assistance and capacity building support. The Guide was produced in the view that 'it would make good sense for any long-term assistance and capacity building support provided to achieve compliance with a basic legal standard to be effectively integrated into wider and more comprehensive reform and modernization efforts'.[62] The Guide (TN/TF/W/143/Rev.8 as the last version) was continuously renewed in step with the updated draft consolidated negotiating text till the formation of the TFA (WT/L/931) in 2014. The WTO Members used the Guide to determine their positions in the negotiations and their commitments to the TFA.

Logistics Performance Index (LPI)

The World Bank periodically publishes *Connecting to Compete: Trade Logistics in the Global Economy*, which is characterized by the Logistics Performance Index (LPI). The LPI is an interactive benchmarking tool that measures how well countries/economies connect to international logistics networks and helps them 'understand the challenges that they and their trading partners face in making their national logistics perform strongly'.[63]

Based on a worldwide survey of logistics professionals on the ground, such as freight forwarders and express carriers, the LPI ranks logistics 'friendliness' of the countries/economies from the international and domestic perspectives. International LPI provides evaluations of a country/economy by its trading partners, who are logistics professionals working outside the country/economy, on the basis of their scoring on six core components of logistics performance (namely, the efficiency of customs and border management clearance, the quality of trade and transport infrastructure, the ease of arranging competitively priced shipments, the competence and quality of logistics services, the ability to track and trace consignments, and the frequency with which shipments reach consignees within scheduled or expected delivery times). Domestic LPI reflects both qualitative and quantitative assessments of the logistics environment of a country/economy according to the feedbacks from the logistics professionals working inside it.[64]

In the wake of the 2007, 2010, 2012, 2014 editions, the World Bank has presented the updated LPI 2016, which allows for comparisons across 160 countries/economies. LPI 2016 indicates that 'trade facilitation tools and principles have taken hold in many countries thanks to growing awareness and international initiatives to support trade facilitation reforms in developing countries'.[65]

Trade and Transport Facilitation Audit (TTFA)

In 2001, the World Bank developed the Trade and Transport Facilitation Audit (TTFA) toolkit with the aim 'to examine and evaluate difficulties and obstacles presented to the cross-frontier movement of a routine consignment and means of associated payment'.[66] This toolkit benefited many countries (from least-developed countries to emerging economies), as part of their preparation for trade or transport projects.

By semantically revising the toolkit to the current edition of Trade and Transport Facilitation Assessment (2010), the World Bank has expanded its scope to reflect 'the practical evolution of the operational concept of trade facilitation in the context of developing countries' and to meet 'growing demand for facilitation reforms in an environment of increasing global competition, expanded trade in intermediate goods and greater synchronicity in the supply of inputs to production and the delivery of products to point of sale'.[67]

The new TTFA is designed to be implemented in two phases. Phase 1 is intended to identify general bottlenecks in infrastructure, regulations, transport and logistics services, and border procedures that affect trade competitiveness in the countries or region. The expected output of this phase would be a preliminary report and a concept note for the Phase 2 assessment. Then Phase 2 examines the relative importance of the problems found in Phase 1, defines a plan of action that includes a series of project components and permits an in-depth assessment of how services within a supply chain can add value to traded goods.

The TTFA is founded on facts and data collected through meetings and interviews with the main public and private participants in the international supply chains, including customs and other border agencies, transport regulators, port authorities, exporters, freight forwarders, transport operators, bankers, etc. Based on the comprehensive diagnosis of operational and procedural constraints to trade and transport, the TTFA can help the countries develop implementable plans of action to improve their logistics performance in three main dimensions: (i) infrastructure, (ii) services, and (iii) procedures and processes.[68]

Table 7.1 Other international organizations' work on trade facilitation*

Organization	Work	Purpose/Effect
UN/ECE	Customs Convention on the International Transport of Goods under Cover of TIR Carnets (TIR Convention, 1975)	Allowing goods to transit in sealed load compartments with customs control recognition along the supply chain, thus minimizing administrative and financial burdens and customs duties and taxes that may become due are covered by an international guarantee.
UN/CEFACT (under UN/ECE)	United Nations Layout Key for Trade Documents	Serving as a basis for designing aligned series of forms employing a master document in a reprographic one-run method of document preparation.
	Recommendation and Guideline on Establishing a Single Window (Recommendation No. 33)	Setting up guidelines for the establishment of single window.

(*Continued*)

Table 7.1 (Continued)

Organization	Work	Purpose/Effect
UNCITRAL	**UNCITRAL Model Law on Electronic Commerce (1996)**	Facilitating the use of modern means of communications and storage of information, such as electronic data interchange (EDI).
ITC	**Programme on Non-tariff Measures (NTMs)**	Helping countries identifying and defining national strategies and policies that overcome NTBs to trade by conducting surveys in countries and interviewing companies.
IMO	**Convention on Facilitation of International Maritime Traffic (1965)**	Preventing unnecessary delays to ships, passengers and cargoes in maritime traffic; aiding cooperation between governments; and securing the highest practicable degree of uniformity in formalities, documentary requirements and other procedures.
ICAO	**Facilitation (FAL) Program based on some articles and Annex 9 of the Convention on International Civil Aviation (Chicago Convention)**	Helping States achieve maximum efficiency in their border clearance operations and at the same time achieve and maintain high-quality security and effective law enforcement.

* Not exhaustive

A symphony of trade facilitation

According to the TFA Article 22:5, United Nations Regional Commissions and regional development banks shall be invited to pitch in with the activities related to trade facilitation. The quintuple Annex D organizations are therefore enlarged to the so-called 'Annex D plus organizations'. Indeed, each Annex D plus organization has its own fortes in terms of lending, TACB deliveries, programmes, international standards, or research methodologies. Those fortes are complementary to the TFA. For example, (i) the lending, TACB deliveries and programmes which an Annex D plus organization can provide to a WTO Member are essential for the Member's acquisition of capacities for implementing the TFA; (ii) an Annex D plus organization, out of its expertise, may have a say in interpreting a specific TFA article; and (iii) the international standards and research methodologies developed by the Annex D plus organizations are supportive of the WTO Members' understanding and implementation of their commitments under the TFA. However, an Annex D plus organization might also feel ambivalent towards the TFA: on the one hand, they might be afraid that the new WTO achievement will overshadow their work; on the other hand, they are willing to take advantage of the multilateral trading system to raise their profile. Under such circumstances, would the Annex D plus organizations play a symphony of the TFA?

Nevertheless, 'multilateralism is the future'.[69] The United Nations Millennium Declaration,[70] adopted by the 55th UN General Assembly, already played the overture of the Annex D plus organizations' symphony. The 55th UN General Assembly, held at the dawn of the new millennium, resolved to

> ensure greater policy coherence and better cooperation between the United Nations, its agencies, the Bretton Woods Institutions and the World Trade Organization, as well as other multilateral bodies, with a view to achieving a fully coordinated approach to the problems of peace and development.[71]

The 60th UN General Assembly adopted the 2005 World Summit Outcome, in which Heads of State and Government reaffirmed not only 'the vital importance of an effective multilateral system' but also the international community's commitment 'to the global partnership for development set out in the Millennium Declaration [. . .]' and 'to open, equitable, rule-based, predictable and non-discriminatory multilateral trading and financial systems'.[72] The Millennium Development Goals (MDGs), which sprang from the United Nations Millennium Declaration, specified a set of development and poverty eradication targets (e.g., halving extreme poverty and hunger, achieving universal primary education, promoting gender equality) by the year of 2015. Goal 8 of the MDGs (MDG 8) called for 'a global partnership for development', and defined 'develop further an open, rule-based, predictable, non-discriminatory trading and financial system' as its target A. The WTO system is most relevant to this target. The MDGs should be due for completion in 2015. What to do after 2015 then? 'The best way to prepare for the post-2015 era is to demonstrate that when the international community commits to a global partnership for development', stated Ban Ki-Moon, then UN Secretary General.[73] In 2015, the 70th UN General Assembly endorsed the 2030 Agenda for Sustainable Development, where the international community recognized that 'we will not be able to achieve our ambitious Goals and targets without a revitalized and enhanced Global Partnership and comparably ambitious means of implementation'.[74] Under the auspices of the United Nations' resolutions, the partnership among the Annex D plus organizations for the newest WTO agreement (namely, the TFA) as a result of the development-oriented multilateral trade negotiations (namely, the Doha Development Agenda) is well-founded.

'Despite the good relations and exchanges of information among [the international organizations], the planning of their work programs and projects [on trade facilitation] needs to be better integrated and coordinated. The establishment of a joint management approach should be considered'.[75] The early joint management approach took the form of Memorandum of Understanding (MOU). For example, the Global Facilitation Partnership for Transportation and Trade (GFP) was established in 1999 on the basis of a MOU signed by a group of partners – public and private, national and international – who 'desire to cooperate in executing activities conducive to the development and implementation of more efficient and effective international trade and transport procedures'.[76] The GFP is composed of three categories of partners (i.e., core partners, sponsoring partners, regular partners), who differ in their contributions and commitments. The ICC, WCO, UNCTAD, UNECE, UNIDO and the World Bank chair the steering committee. Full GFP meetings, comprising all GFP partners, take place twice a year in order to review progress and the results achieved, according to the MOU. The GFP partners had started playing a symphony of trade facilitation.

What marks the TFA off from other trade facilitation instruments is that this Agreement not only imposes legally binding commitments on most of the countries/ economies in the world but also advocates a *moral fiber* that empowers the international community to join hands in the field of trade facilitation. The Annex D plus organizations are keen to carry on with this moral fiber that secures 'long-term benefits from the TFA'.[77] On July 22, 2014, they[78] released a joint statement:

> We commit to assisting developing, transition and least-developed countries, drawing on our respective strengths and areas of expertise. This will take the form of immediate assistance, for example in determining the categorization (A, B, or C) of measures under the TFA, establishing National Trade Facilitation Committees, creating faster and more efficient cross border and regulatory procedures through effective collaboration among all relevant stakeholders, including the private sector, as well as longer term implementation planning and support in implementing comprehensive reform programs built on the TFA measures. We commit to continuing to make available, to all countries, the trade facilitation tools, recommendations and standards we produce.

The roles of the Annex D plus organizations as defined by the TFA, by and large, are: (i) providing TACB to help the developing country Members and LDC Members acquire the capacity to fully implement their commitments; (ii) giving advice for administering the Agreement; and (iii) taking part in discussions on relevant international standards.

At present, providing TACB, which is not limited to developing country and LDC Members' notifications under Category C (as there are also, for example, TFA awareness-raising TACB deliveries provided by relevant international organizations), remains the Annex D plus organizations' primary task on the suckling TFA. TACB in the WTO context normally falls under the roof of Aid for Trade (AfT), which is 'about assisting developing countries to increase exports of goods and services, to integrate into the multilateral trading system and to benefit from liberalized trade and increased market access'.[79] AfT covers projects and programmes that 'have been identified as trade-related development priorities in the recipient country's national development strategies'.[80]

The WTO Hong Kong Ministerial Declaration had mandated the WTO to provide recommendations 'on how to operationalize Aid for Trade' and 'on how Aid for Trade might contribute most effectively to the development dimension of the [Doha Development Agenda]'.[81] With regard to operationalizing AfT, the Paris Declaration on Aid Effectiveness and the Accra Agenda for Action contain the key principles that meaningfully guide AfT. The Paris Declaration on Aid Effectiveness was issued in March 2005 when ministers of developed and developing countries responsible for promoting development and heads of multilateral and bilateral development institutions held a meeting. The Ministers and Heads resolved to take far-reaching and monitorable actions to reform the ways aid would be delivered and managed.[82] In the Paris Declaration on Aid Effectiveness, donors and their partner countries (beneficiaries) make their partnership commitments in five dimensions: (i) ownership – partner countries exercise effective leadership in developing and implementing their national development strategies and in coordinating aid at all levels; (ii) alignment – donors base their overall support on partner countries' national development strategies, institutions and procedures; (iii) harmonization – donors' actions are more harmonized, transparent and collectively effective; (iv) managing for results – aid is managed and implemented with focus on the desired results and by use of information to improve decision-making; and (v) mutual accountability – donors and partners are accountable for development results. In Accra, Ghana, in September 2008, the Ministers and Heads endorsed the Accra Agenda for Action, which figured out more concrete actions (e.g., 'we will continue to change the nature of conditionality to support ownership')[83] to accelerate and deepen implementation of the Paris Declaration on Aid Effectiveness.

At the heart of AfT is the Enhanced Integrity Framework (EIF), which originates from the Integrated Framework for Trade-Related Technical Assistance to LDCs ('IF' for short) set up in 1997 as a programme 'to improve the capacity of the LDCs to formulate, negotiate and implement trade policy so as to be able to fully integrate into the multilateral trading system'.[84] Six multilateral organizations (WTO, IMF, ITC, UNCTAD, UNDP and the World Bank) at that time offered support and made up the IF core agencies. Since 2005, on the basis of diagnosing some weakness of IF (e.g., it had not provided adequate financial and human resources to the LDCs to deliver the intended outcomes; the national IF structures had generally not worked to integrate trade into the development process), the IF Steering Committee (IFSC) determined to enhance the IF by providing it with additional resources.[85] After a 4-year revamp, the Enhanced Integrity Framework (EIF) took form,[86] with 'a renewed focus on results, accountability, stronger donor coordination and governance with LDCs in the driving seat'.[87] The EIF projects are composed of two 'tiers' – Tier 1 and Tier 2. Under Tier 1, a country will go through the key trade-enabling building blocks, in particular the National Implementation Arrangements (NIAs) and a Diagnostic Trade Integration Study (DTIS), to prioritize actions needed to promote its economic growth and sustainable development. Under Tier 2, the EIF focuses on mainstreaming the country's trade into its national development plans, and supports priority small-scale projects to build up its trade-related and supply-side capacities.[88] Accredited as the 'flagship' trade-related TACB programme,[89] the EIF fills a distinctive role in the TFA:

> Members shall endeavor to apply the following principles for providing assistance and support for capacity building with regard to the implementation of this Agreement:
>
> (i) promote coordination between and among Members and other relevant institutions, including regional economic communities, to ensure maximum effectiveness of and results from this assistance. To this end:

(ii) for least-developed country Members, the Enhanced Integrated Framework for trade-related assistance for the least-developed countries should be a part of this coordination process.[90]

In the 2013 global review of AfT, trade facilitation was more conspicuous than other trade topics (e.g., global value chains, competitiveness). The partner countries broadly identified trade facilitation as one of their top priorities; the donors (e.g., the US, UK, Germany) laid particular stress on trade facilitation in their AfT strategies.[91] According to OECD and the WTO, in 2011, aid for trade facilitation commitments had increased substantially by 365 percent since the 2002–2005 baseline, and amounted to 381 million USD.[92]

TACB essentially depends on the availability of financial and human resources from donors. A donor country, however, is prone to target certain partner countries and projects in its political or commercial interests (e.g., a donor country might be interested in funding a TACB project on single window in a sub-Saharan country, because sub-Saharan Africa is the target market to sell its single window techniques). Other countries and projects, therefore, would be possibly neglected (e.g., a Latin American country that has weak trade links with the donor country may be ineligible for the project, or the sub-Saharan country is not able to apply for a project on authorized operators which corresponds to its needs more than single window does). The TFA also embraces non-Member donors.[93] It means that any Annex D plus organization can equally act as a donor. However, an Annex D plus organization often gets funds from the donor countries and needs to consider those donor countries' ideas when deciding which partner countries can obtain the TACB. Furthermore, those organizations usually have different counterpart government agencies in a partner country: for instance, the IMF speaks to the central bank; UNCTAD normally liaises with the trade administration; and the WCO contacts the customs administration. It would lead to the situation: government agencies, on behalf of the same partner country, are severally seeking approaches to different Annex D plus organizations for TACB, but some TACB requests through different approaches could be similar and even competing with each other. As a result, the TACB deliveries – no matter provided by the donor countries or by the Annex D plus organizations – might be lacking or uneven, if there is no synergy among the donors. It is reasonable for the developing country Members and LDC Members to fear that 'some might find it difficult to access the necessary support'.[94]

In response to this fear, the WTO launched the Trade Facilitation Agreement Facility (TFAF), which is funded by WTO donor Members on a voluntary basis, in July 2014. The TFAF will 'become operational when the protocol to insert the TFA into the existing regulatory framework is adopted by WTO Members'[95] and 'act as a focal point for implementation efforts'.[96] According to Roberto Azevêdo, 'to thrive and succeed, it will continue to need the buy-in of us all – from developing and least-developed countries, to donors at the bilateral, regional and multilateral levels'.[97] The TFAF, as the donors' synergistic effort, is meant for complementing and enhancing the existing TACB projects and programmes rather than replacing them. The TFAF carries out four functions: (i) supporting developing country Members and LDC Members to assess their specific needs and prepare their notifications and scheduling; (ii) ensuring the best possible conditions for the flow of information between donors and partner countries by creating an information-sharing platform for the demand and supply of TFA-related TACB; (iii) matching Members with donor funds to implement their projects; and (iv) providing funds for the exceptional cases where Members have made thorough attempts to find assistance but have failed to receive the support they need.[98]

The TFA, indeed, is not unprecedented in terms of creating a facility for a specific WTO agreement. The Standards and Trade Development Facility (STDF), specialized in sanitary and phytosanitary (SPS) measures, was already ahead. In 2001, Heads of the Food and Agriculture Organization of the United Nations (FAO), the Office International des Epizooties (OIE),[99] the World Health Organization (WHO), the World Bank and the WTO submitted to the Doha Ministerial Conference a joint communiqué where the five organizations were determined to undertake technical assistance activities and investment in infrastructure to assist developing countries in the establishment and implementation of appropriate food safety and animal and plant health measures, to explore jointly new technical and financial mechanisms for coordination and resource mobilization and to build alliances between standard-setting bodies and the implementing and financing agencies so as to ensure the most effective use of technical and financial resources. The STDF was established in 2002 and has become 'one rare successful community-building project currently in action'.[100] A 2014 review reported that 'the major success of the STDF has been as a funding mechanism for project grants (PGs) and project preparation grants (PPGs)'.[101] The STDF has set the pattern for the functioning of the TFAF.

Apart from TACB, the Annex D plus organizations will exert other influences on the implementation and administration of the TFA. In particular, future WTO disputes on trade facilitation will find that these organizations are indispensable for the WTO interpretation process, which 'elucidates the current and normal meaning of the interpreted term'.[102] The Annex D plus organizations have played a part in interpreting the WTO terms. For instance, (i) the Panel on *Mexico – Telecoms* referred to the OECD Council Recommendation Concerning Effective Action Against Hardcore Cartels, when it interpreted the term of 'anti-competitive practices';[103] (ii) in the case of *Thailand – Cigarettes*, both the complainant (the Philippines) and the respondent (Thailand) cited a letter from the WCO Secretariat to explain who was responsible for the burden of proof to demonstrate whether the buyer and seller were related;[104] (iii) the letter from the WCO Secretariat (2003) to the Panel on *EC – Chicken Cuts* explained the meaning of the term of 'salted' in tariff heading 02.10. Brazil (the complainant) referred to the WCO's letter, while the EC (the respondent) disagreed with the argument presented in the WCO's letter;[105] (iv) when the respondent (Argentina)[106] in the case of *Argentina – Import Measures* argued that its Advance Sworn Import Declaration (*Declaración Jurada Anticipada de Importación*, DJAI) procedure was a customs or import formality established in accordance with Article VIII of the GATT 1994 and the WCO SAFE Framework of Standards to Secure and

Facilitate Global Trade ('WCO SAFE Framework' for short), the Panel, in order to examine this issue, sought the assistance of the WCO Secretariat to clarify certain aspects related to the WCO SAFE Framework in November 2013.[107] The WCO Secretariat replied a few days later and suggested that some important elements of the DJAI procedure did not relate to the WCO SAFE Framework, so the Panel expressed the view that the DJAI procedure 'is not a mere formality imposed by Argentina in connection with the importation of goods'.[108]

The functions of the Annex D plus organizations will come into play under the WTO Committee on Trade Facilitation:

> The Committee shall maintain close contact with other international organizations in the field of trade facilitation, such as the WCO, with the objective of securing the best available advice for the implementation and administration of this Agreement and in order to ensure that unnecessary duplication of effort is avoided. To this end, the Committee may invite representatives of such organizations or their subsidiary bodies to:
>
> (a) attend meetings of the Committee; and
> (b) discuss specific matters related to the implementation of this Agreement.[109]

As noted, the interaction and coherence between the WTO and other international organizations as embedded in the TFA (also extensively in other WTO agreements) carry forward the partnership built ever since the negotiations on trade facilitation.

Besides the cooperation among the international organizations in the sense of *constructivism*, during the WTO Nairobi Ministerial (MC 10) in 2015, the Global Alliance for Trade Facilitation – 'a new public-private platform that seeks to use private sector expertise and resources to support trade facilitation reforms'[110] – was launched. This platform involves the World Economic Forum, the International Chamber of Commerce and the Center for International Private Enterprise, which extensively represent the private sector (including SMEs).[111] From the erstwhile recommendations of the International Chamber of Commerce (e.g., ICC Brochure 121 (1947), Brochure 130 (1949), Brochure 153 (1951)) to the Global Alliance for Trade Facilitation today, the course of public-private interdependence on trade facilitation has lasted for seven decades.

Now, a symphony of the TFA can be played together by all the institutions – public and private, national and international – related to trade facilitation. The symphony is evocative of the spirits enshrined not only in the Havana Charter for an International Trade Organization,[112] by which the beaten-up world after World War II aimed to design a multilateral trading system for 'attainment of the higher standards of living, full employment and conditions of economic and social progress and development',[113] but also in the Agreement Establishing the World Trade Organization,[114] by which 'an integrated, more viable and durable multilateral trading system'[115] has been created eventually and shall be consolidated further.

Notes

1 Articles of Agreement of the International Monetary Fund, Article I (ii).
2 WTO, G/C/W/80/Rev.1 (2000), paras. A 5.1–5.2.
3 IMF, 'The IMF's Trade Integration Mechanism (TIM)', September 19, 2016, www.imf.org/en/About/Factsheets/Sheets/2016/08/02/19/51/Trade-Integration-Mechanism.
4 Convention on the Organization for Economic Cooperation and Development, Paris, 1960, Article 1 and 2.
5 In 2000, OECD sated it was not engaged in trade facilitation yet. See WTO, G/C/W/80/Rev.1 (2000), para. 10.1.
6 OECD, TAD/TC/WP(2009)2.
7 OECD added a separate element of goods governance and impartiality of border administrations that did not exist in the consolidated draft of negotiating text, and put it as an indicator. In its first phase of work, 2011, there were 12 indicators. In the second phase, 2012, four transit-specific indicators were developed.
8 See UNCTAD, TAD/TC/WP(2012)24/FINAL.
9 See UNCTAD, TAD/TC/WP(2011)5/FINAL.
10 United Nations, Proceedings of the United Nations Conference on Trade and Development: Final Act and Report, E/CONF.46/141 Vol. I (1964), Annex A.II.4, p. 31.
11 The Interregional Advisory Services on Trade Facilitation was initiated under the UNECE Resolution 4(XXIV) which was endorsed by the United Nations Economic and Social Council, and financed by the United Nations Development Programme.
12 See UN Economic Commission for Latin America, 'Trade Procedures in the Caribbean', CARIB/INT/82/12 (1982), pp. 19–20.
13 UNCTAD, 'The Cartagena Commitment' (1992).
14 Ibid.
15 See UNCTAD, *The New Frontier of Competitiveness in Developing Countries: Implementing Trade Facilitation* (2014), p. 7.
16 See WTO, G/C/W/80/Rev.1 (2000), para. A 1.3.
17 See UNCTAD, www.asycuda.org.
18 See UNCTAD, 'UNCTAD's Technical Assistance Package on Trade Facilitation' (2014), http://unctad.org/en/PublicationsLibrary/domtcs2014d1_en.pdf.
19 See UNCTAD, *The New Frontier of Competitiveness in Developing Countries: Implementing Trade Facilitation* (2014), UNCTAD/DTL/TLB/2013/2, p. 47.
20 See UNCTAD, http://tft.unctad.org/?page_id=1232.
21 See *supra* note 18.
22 See UN Economic and Social Council, TRADE/CEFACT/1999/11.
23 See WTO, G/C/W/80/Rev.1 (2000), para. A 1.29.
24 UNCTAD, *Landlocked Developing Countries: Facts and Figures* (2014), UNCTAD/ALDC/2014/1, p. iii.
25 UN, A/RES/2971(XXVII) (1972).
26 UN, A/RES/52/183 (1997).
27 See WTO, G/C/W/427 (2002).
28 The International Ministerial Conference of Landlocked and Transit Developing Countries and Donor Countries and International Financial and Development Institutions on Transit Transport Cooperation was held in Almaty, Kazakhstan, August 25–29, 2003. The achievements of the Conference were the Almaty Declaration and the Almaty Program of Action. The Almaty Declaration and Program of Action reflects the strong commitment of the international community to addressing the special needs and problems of landlocked developing countries as called for in the United Nations Millennium Declaration.
29 See UN, A/RES/69/137 (2015).

30 This part mainly quotes the materials on the website of http://businessfacilitation.org.
31 Convention Establishing a Customs Cooperation Council.
32 It was adopted at the 83/84 Sessions of the Customs Cooperation Council on June20–22, 1994.
33 WCO's Mission Statement, www.wcoomd.org.
34 Resolution of the Policy Commission of the WCO on the Conclusion of an Agreement on Trade Facilitation by the WTO (WCO Dublin Resolution), December 11, 2013.
35 Kunio Mikuriya, 'Ready to Implement the Trade Facilitation Agreement', *WCO News*, June 2014, p. 10.
36 Ibid., p. 11.
37 WTO, G/C/W/80/Rev.1 (2000), para. 3.7.
38 The Nairobi Convention, Chapter II, Article 2 :1.
39 As of June 2012, see WCO, EG0019E1a (2012).
40 The Johannesburg Convention provides that the Convention shall only enter in to force when at least five entities have ratified their acceptance of the Convention. An entity may be any member of the Customs Cooperation Council and any member of the United Nations or its specialized agencies. However, there are so far only 3 contracting parties that have ratified the Convention.
41 See WTO, G/C/W/392 (2002); G/C/W/407 (2002); G/C/W/426 (2002).
42 See WTO, G/C/W/467 (2003).
43 See WTO, G/C/W/445 (2002).
44 WCO, Doc.SC0050 (2003), Annex III.
45 Ibid.
46 IBRD Articles of Agreement, Article I (iii), as amended.
47 WTO, G/C/W/80/Rev.1 (2000), para. A 4.1.
48 See World Bank, Leveraging Trade for Development and Inclusive Growth (2011).
49 Ibid., p. 14.
50 Other three priority themes are 'trade competitiveness and diversification', 'support for market access and international trade cooperation', 'managing shocks and promoting greater inclusion'.
51 World Bank, Leveraging Trade for Development and Inclusive Growth (2011), p. 14.
52 Ibid., pp. 23–33.
53 See e.g., World Bank, 'Trade Facilitation Support Program', https://gfptt.org/sites/default/files/refread/Trade%20Facilitation%20Support%20Program%20Fact%20Sheet.pdf.
54 World Bank, 'New Trade Facilitation Support Program to Provide Technical Assistance for Developing Countries', June 10, 2014, www.worldbank.org/en/news/feature/2014/06/12/new-trade-facilitation-support-program-to-provide-technical-assistance-for-developing-countries.
55 See www.wbginvestmentclimate.org/advisory-services/regulatory-simplification/trade-logistics/trade-facilitation-support-program/approach.cfm.
56 Ibid.
57 Ibid.
58 World Bank, Trade Facilitation Facility Brochure (2009).
59 World Bank, 'Trade Facilitation Facility Program Description', May 17, 2009, http://siteresources.worldbank.org/INTRANETTRADE/. . ./Program_Description.pdf.
60 World Bank, Leveraging Trade for Development and Inclusive Growth (2011), p. 35.
61 WTO, TN/TF/W/51 (2005), p. 1.

62 World Bank, Needs, Priorities and Costs Associated with Technical Assistance and Capacity Building for Implementation of a WTO Trade Facilitation
   Agreement: A Comparative Study Based on Six Developing Countries (2006),
   pp. 6–7.
63 Jean-François Arvis et al., *Connecting to Compete 2014: Trade Logistics in the
   Global Economy* (World Bank, 2014), p. iii.
64 Jean-François Arvis et al., *Connecting to Compete 2016: Trade Logistics in the
   Global Economy* (World Bank, 2016), pp. 55–58.
65 Ibid., p. 3.
66 John Rave, "Trade and Transport Facilitation: A Toolkit for Audit, Analysis, and
   Remedial Action", the World Bank Discussion Paper (2001), p. 2.
67 World Bank, *Trade and Transport Facilitation Assessment: A Practical Toolkit for
   Country Implementation* (World Bank, 2010), p. 2.
68 Ibid., p. vi.
69 UN, A/CONF.199/20 (2002), para. 31–33.
70 See UN, A/RES/55/2 (2000).
71 Ibid., para. 30.
72 UN, A/RES/60/1 (2005), paras. 6, 20, 36.
73 UN, *Millennium Development Goal 8 the Global Partnership for Development:
   The Challenge We Face* (United Nations, 2013), p. iii.
74 UN, A/RES/70/1 (2015), para. 60.
75 Tom Butterly, 'Trade Facilitation in a Global Trade Environment', in Carol Cosgrove-Sacks and Mario Apostolov (eds.), *Trade Facilitation: The Challenges for
   Growth and Development* (United Nations, 2003), pp. 29–62.
76 See GFP Memorandum of Understanding, www.gfptt.org/node/2783.
77 Joint Statement on Coordinated Assistance for Implementation of the WTO
   Trade Facilitation Agreement of July 22, 2014, www.wto.org/english/news_e/
   news14_e/tfjointstatment_e.pdf.
78 They include UNCTAD, World Bank, WCO, OECD, ITC, UNECE, UNE-
   CLAC, UNESCAP, UNESCWA.
79 WTO, WT/AFT/1 (2006), para. B.
80 Ibid., para. D.
81 WTO, WT/MIN(05)/DEC (2005), para. 57.
82 Paris Declaration on Aid Effectiveness, para. 1.
83 Accra Agenda for Action, para. 25.
84 WTO, WT/IFSC/W/15 (2006), para. 1.
85 Ibid.
86 See Pascal Lamy, opening statement at the WTO Ministerial Breakfast on LDCs
   issues on December 1, 2009, www.wto.org/english/thewto_e/minist_e/min09_
   e/ldc_lamy_opening_e.doc.
87 Enhanced Integrated Framework (EIF), 'EIF in Brief', http://enhancedif.org.
88 Ibid.
89 See Pascal Lamy, opening statement at the Ministerial Breakfast on the Enhanced
   Integrated Framework (EIF) on December 1, 2009, https://www.wto.org/
   english/thewto_e/minist_e/min09_e/ldc_breakfast_e.htm.
90 The TFA Article 21:3.
91 See OECD and WTO, *Aid for Trade at a Glance 2013: Connecting to Value
   Chains* (OECD and WTO, 2013), pp. 38–44.
92 Ibid., p. 69.
93 See the TFA Article 16: 1(d) and 16: 2(e).
94 Roberto Azevêdo, statement at the launch of TFAT on July 22, 2014, www.wto.
   org/english/news_e/news14_e/fac_22jul14_e.htm.
95 Ibid.
96 Ibid.
97 Ibid.

98   Ibid.
99   It has been called 'The World Organization for Animal Health' since May 2003.
100 Sungjoon Cho, *The Social Foundations of World Trade: Norms, Community and Constitution* (Cambridge University Press, 2015), p. 231.
101 SAANA Consulting, *STDF Mid-Term Review Final Report* (2014), p. iv, http://www.standardsfacility.org/sites/default/files/STDF_MTR_Jan-14.pdf.
102 Marina Foltea, *International Organizations in WTO Dispute Settlement: How Much Institutional Sensitivity?* (Cambridge University Press, 2014), p. 117.
103 WTO, WT/DS204/R (2004), para. 7. 236.
104 See WTO, WT/DS371/R (2010), para. 5.76.
105 See WTO, WT/DS269/AB/R (WT/DS286/AB/R) (2005).
106 The complainant was the European Union.
107 See WTO, WT/DS438/R (WT/DS444/R, WT/DS445/R) (2014), paras. 1.37–38, 6.427–6.445.
108 Ibid., para. 6.433.
109 The TFA Article 23: 1.5.
110 WTO, 'Azevêdo welcomes efforts to help implement Trade Facilitation Agreement', December 17, 2015, www.wto.org/english/news_e/news15_e/dgra_17dec15_e.htm.
111 See Roberto Azevêdo, speech at the launch of Global Alliance for Trade Facilitation on December 17, 2015, www.wto.org/english/news_e/spra_e/spra106_e.htm.
112 See *The Havana Charter*, Article 87.
113 Ibid., Article 1.
114 See the Agreement Establishing the World Trade Organization, Article V.
115 Ibid., Preamble.

Conclusion
The road ahead of the Agreement on Trade Facilitation

According to Article X:3 of the Agreement Establishing the WTO, the Agreement on Trade Facilitation (TFA) shall take effect only if two-thirds of the WTO membership (equally 110 Members) have formally ratified the Agreement.

Since the conclusion of the TFA, the international community has been dedicated to enabling the Agreement to enter into force. 'The focus in 2015 should in particular be on the entry into force of the WTO Trade Facilitation Agreement',[1] leaders of the main industrialized countries once urged. 'We will also need to increase our efforts to implement all the elements of the 'Bali package', including [. . .] the prompt ratification and implementation of the Trade Facilitation Agreement',[2] G20 leaders subsequently declared at the 2015 Antalya Summit. In 2016, G20 leaders reaffirmed that 'we commit to ratify the Trade Facilitation Agreement by the end of 2016 and call on other WTO Members to do the same'.[3]

The prospect of the TFA did not fall into a mirage after all. On February 22, 2017, the number of Members that presented their instruments of ratification to the WTO exceeded 'the required threshold of 110'.[4] At last, the TFA entered into force.

The first priority in the post-Bali era is to implement what was agreed in Bali.[5] Upon entry into force of the TFA, the onus of implementing the Agreement will accordingly fall on the government of each Member and be further assigned to the corresponding government agencies for trade, customs, quarantine, transport, international development, etc. The customs administration is responsible for over 90 percent of the TFA Section I; the quarantine authority deals with some provisions such as 'notifications for enhanced controls or inspections' and 'test procedure'; the transport department plays an important role in implementing the article on transit; providing technical assistance and capacity building (TACB) as required in the TFA Section II would be the job of a developed country Member's international development agency. Needless to say, organizing the overall implementation of the TFA basically counts on the trade department, which normally acts as the Member's national focal point for the WTO affairs. In implementing the TFA, all the relevant government agencies should be kept in the loop, preferably under the roof of the National Committee on Trade Facilitation (NCTF).

To fulfill the schedule of tariff concessions, a Member only needs to lower the tariff rates of certain Harmonized System (HS)[6] codes. Implementation of the TFA, however, would be largely different: it entails a holistic reform in a wide range of respects (e.g., policy/legal framework, procedures, institutional framework, human resources and training, communication and information technology, equipment and infrastructure). The WTO self-assessment tool (TN/TF/W/143), which was designed to assist Members in diagnosing the gaps between their status quo and the draft consolidated negotiating text of the TFA, already made reference to these respects when the negotiations were going on. This tool is still useful for Members' preparation for their TFA obligations in the post-Bali era.

We can take 'advance rulings' and 'border agency cooperation' as examples to demonstrate how a Member shall gear up for implementing its obligations under the TFA. In order to implement the article on advance rulings, a Member needs to reform in respect of:[7]

Policy/Legal Framework: The government shall start with lawmaking work on advance rulings at the national level, specifying the matters applicable to advance rulings (e.g., tariff classification, origin of the goods), scope of applicants, validity of the rulings (e.g., whether they are binding to both the decision maker and applicant), time limit, the protection of commercial confidentialities, the circumstances of revocation or modification of an advance ruling, etc. In particular, a designated government agency (mostly customs administration) shall be legitimately authorized to issue advance rulings.

Procedures: The responsible government agency shall set forth the procedural requirement and workflow for submitting the advance ruling applications, issuing the ruling decisions, dealing with disputes on the rulings, etc. The procedural requirement and workflow shall of course be as simple as possible and easily available to the public.

Institutional Framework: The responsible government agency shall establish or designate (if there already exists a relevantly functional unit) an internal unit (at headquarter or at local branches) to administer its advance ruling programme. The build of this unit depends on the volume of regular applications, which largely differ between countries.

Human Resources and Training: The responsible government agency shall be staffed by competent officials commensurate with the workloads on advance rulings. The officials shall be adept in tariff classification, origin and other relevant customs matters. Since most of the Members will start from scratch even when they are implementing advance rulings, an orientation training (under the auspices of TACB) to the officials will be desirable.

Communication and Information Technology: In administering advance rulings, special information technology infrastructure, for the most part, is not indispensable, but a Member would better build its advance ruling programme into its existing customs automation system. The module for advance rulings will have the functions of online application, record-keeping, question and answer (Q&A), publishing the rulings, etc.

Equipment and Infrastructure: Unlike single window, no special equipment and infrastructure are needed for operating advance ruling. However, at least, office facilities are necessary.

As Section I of the TFA are composed of disparate articles (see Chapter 6), the implementation of each individual article will be relatively independent. Therefore, preparation for border agency cooperation, different from advance rulings, entails another set of reforms:

Policy/Legal Framework: It would be preferable if Memoranda of Understanding (MOUs) are signed between relevant border agencies of a Member or between neighboring countries. The MOUs will provide a legal basis for border cooperation, either domestically or internationally.

Procedures: All the relevant border agencies need to re-engineer their formalities and streamline their data and documentation requirements with a view to avoiding overlapping or redundant controls. They can also hopefully provide a 'one-stop shop' service.

Institutional Framework: It would be the National Committee on Trade Facilitation that most appropriately coordinates the border agencies. However, there is always a question about what border agencies should participate in the cooperation mechanism. Generally, the government agencies for trade, customs, transportation and quarantine should be participants. The private sector should also be encouraged to take a place.

Human Resources and Training: There shall be, at least, full-time officials in place. These officials shall be in charge of organizing cooperation and coordination activities on a day-to-day basis.

Obviously, any of the aforementioned reforms will not come cheap. According to the argument of Ronald Coarse, '[t]he governmental administrative machine is not itself costless; [i]t can, in fact, on occasion be extremely costly'.[8] Trade facilitation is brought forth for the purpose of cutting trade costs, but implementation of the TFA is costly: (i) a Member's government has to appropriate a certain amount of budget for activities related to trade facilitation (e.g., establishing the websites to publish trade regulations, building infrastructures for single window); and (ii) the government needs to mobilize the relevant agencies (through institutional restructuring, personnel reallocation, training, etc.), which might be deeply entrenched in the way they usually process trade, to go ahead with their new tasks under the TFA. In the case of the developing country Members and LDC Members, the 'one-size-fits-all' disciplines in the TFA Section I would probably force them to punch above their weight.[9] This evokes the debate between the trade facilitation proponents (i.e., the Colorado Group) and those (i.e., the Core Group) who were reluctant to put trade facilitation on the negotiating agenda (see Chapter 5). TACB, nevertheless, would serve as a springboard for the developing country Members and LDC Members to enhance their capacities of implementing the TFA, if appropriately provided through bilateral channels or multilateral mechanisms where the donors play a 'symphony' (see Chapter 7). Indeed, TACB is still all about money. Albeit implementation of the TFA in any event cannot go without money, it remains a rewarding trade policy. As Peter Mandelson, former European Commissioner for Trade, said, 'in trade negotiations, you get what you pay for'.[10] A Member – no matter if it is a developed country Member, a developing country Member, or a LDC Member – shall get its money's worth for implementing the TFA, in light of the generous dividends that trade facilitation brings to both the business community and the government itself (see Chapter 2).

At present, the thorough implementation of the Agreement on Trade Facilitation (given that there are transitional periods of time for some Members) is on the road far ahead. In the context of free trade, implementation of the Agreement has gone beyond carrying out a WTO trade deal – it is more about the morality of the world trading system. Against this morality, when we view the future of the Agreement (either optimistically or pessimistically), we can pose these questions to ourselves:

Shall we respect the hard-earned outcome of the 18-year multilateral negotiations (see Chapter 4)?
Shall we value the international community's all-out efforts on trade facilitation for nearly one century (see Chapter 3)?
Shall we persist in ameliorating our business environment for the diminution of externality of trade costs (see Chapter 1)?
Shall we, at last, still believe the principles of free trade?

Notes

1 G7 Leaders' Declaration, Schloss Elmau, Germany, June 8, 2015.
2 G20 Leaders' Communiqué at Antalya Summit, Turkey, November 15–16, 2015, para. 12.
3 G20 Leaders' Communiqué at Hangzhou Summit, China, September 4–5, 2016, para. 27.
4 WTO, 'WTO's Trade Facilitation Agreement Enters into Force', February 22, 2017, www.wto.org/english/news_e/news17_e/fac_31jan17_e.htm.
5 Roberto Azevêdo, 'Bali Can Herald a New Era in the WTO', speech at the Crawford School of Public Policy, Australian National University in Canberra on July 17, 2014, www.wto.org/english/news_e/spra_e/spra28_e.htm.
6 The Harmonized Commodity Description and Coding System, administered by the WCO.
7 See WTO, TN/TF/W/143/Rev.7 (2014).
8 Ronald Coase, 'The Problem of Social Cost', (1960) 3 *The Journal of Law and Economics* 1, pp. 1–44.
9 If a Member designates a TFA Section I article in its Category C commitments, it means it punches above its weight in terms of implementing this article.
10 Peter Mandelson, 'Conclusions of the Sixth WTO Ministerial Conference in Hong Kong', speech at the Plenary Session of the European Parliament on January 16, 2006, http://trade.ec.europa.eu/doclib/docs/2006/january/tradoc_127019.pdf.

Index

Note: Page numbers in **bold** indicate a table on the corresponding page, and page numbers in *italics* indicate a figure on the corresponding page.

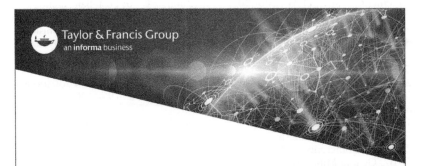